Strategic Management

Strategic Management

B. Hiriyappa
M.Com., M.Phil., Ph.D.

Associate Professor
KKECS Institute of Management, Bangalore
Sap Consultant
Visiting faculty of MBA and MHA
for
Padamshree Group of Institutions
Raja Rajeswari Group of Institutions
Bangalore, Karnataka

PUBLISHING FOR ONE WORLD

NEW AGE INTERNATIONAL (P) LIMITED, PUBLISHERS

New Delhi • Bangalore • Chennai • Cochin • Guwahati • Hyderabad
Jalandhar • Kolkata • Lucknow • Mumbai • Ranchi
Visit us at www.newagepublishers.com

Published by New Age International (P) Ltd., Publishers
First Edition: 2008

ISBN (10): 81-224-2283-7

ISBN (13): 978-81-224-2283-2

Rs. 195.00

C-07-11-2136

Printed in India at Chaman Offset, Delhi.
Typeset at Shubham Computers, Delhi.

PUBLISHING FOR ONE WORLD

NEW AGE INTERNATIONAL (P) LIMITED, PUBLISHERS
4835/24, Ansari Road, Daryaganj, New Delhi - 110002
Visit us at **www.newagepublishers.com**

Dedicated to

My Teacher

Dr. D.M. Basavaraja

Foreword

"Strategic management is not a box of tricks or a bundle of techniques. It is analytical thinking and commitment of resources to action"
Peter Drucker

Without a strategy the organization is like a ship without a rudder"
Joel Ross and *Michael Kami*

Strategic Management is a core syllabi at **MBA, MCOM, PGDBM, PGDMM, PGDHRM, ICWAI, and ICFAI programme because of its characteristics and contemporary relevance to business students for formulation of policy, implementation of policy and controlling of policy at national, international level.** This book presents an indepth and comprehensive coverage of strategic management concept like strategic and business policy, strategic management, strategic management process, types of strategy, define the organization mission and social responsibility, internal environment of the organization, external environment, competitive advantage, value chain concept and analysis, business and investment level strategy, industrial environment, vertical integration, diversification and strategic alliances, acquisitions and joint ventures, strategies for competing in globalising markets, strategy framework and restructuring the corporation, strategic change management, tailoring strategy to fit specific company and industry situations, corporate culture and leadership, designing organization structure, strategic control systems, matching structure and control, and current issues of strategic management.

Strategic Management is perspective, position, plan, and pattern. Strategy is the bridge between policy and high-order goals on the one hand and tactics or concrete actions on the other. Strategy and tactics together straddle the gap between ends and means. In short, strategy is a term that refers to a complex web of thoughts, ideas, insights, experiences, goals, expertise, memories, perceptions, and expectations that provides general guidance for specific actions in pursuit of particular ends. Strategy is at once the course we chart, the journey we imagine, and, at the same time, it is the course we steer, the trip we actually make. Even when we are embarking on a voyage of discovery of facts, with no particular destination in mind, the voyage has a purpose, an outcome, and an end to be kept in view.

This book has been designed with the latest developments in business and industry scenario have been included. Latest strategy concepts have been discussed in detail with all the respects of strategic management. Each chapter contains the contents and learning objectives which provides the direction to the students, managers, directors, teachers, strategic consultants and CEO. Boxes present the latest

industrial incidents and developments. Exhibits tables, and charts illustrate the concepts in a simple and lucid manner. Numerous examples and case studies make the concept easy to understand.

I heartly congratulate B. Hiriyappa for his instant efforts to meet the needs of the students, faculty, planner, director, CEOs of the companies.

K.R. Narendra Kumar
Director
RK and KKECS Institue of Management
and Computer Sciences
Bangalore.

Preface

Strategic Management is a stream of decisions and actions with view to develop effective long term and short term planning and policies with technological business forecasting that would help the organization achieve its superior goal. Strategic Management includes strategic analysis, strategy formulation, strategic choice, and strategy implementation and control strategic decisions for an organization might be to deploy resources into new opportunities. Such strategy decisions may result in need for strategies for environment analysis, value chain concept and analysis, integration, diversification, mergers and acquisitions, new product development, product redesigning, upgradation, strategies for marketing, technology, new customers, finance, geographic areas and entry into new markets. Strategic Management may have to be decided to survive, grow, and develop.

It is sincerely hoped that the book will be useful to the CEO, Directors, Managing Directors, Strategy Planner, Students and Faculty Members of MBA, MCOM, PGDM, PGDBM, PGDHRM, ICFAI and competitive examinations in India and abroad. I invite suggestions from one and all for improvements in next edition of this book.

Strategic Management has been introduced as a subject in MBA, MCOM, PGDM, PGDBM, PGDHRM, and ICFAI. I have made humble effort to fulfill the needs of the strategy planner, CEO, Directors of MNCs, Students and teachers of the subject by covering necessary topics, explaining, analysising and assessing the various aspects and subjects.

In writing this book I have drawn on a vast amount of literature in strategic management. Naturally, I owe an intellectual debt to numerous authors who have enriched the stream of literature in strategic management by their contributions. My profounded debt is to American scholars to George Stenier, Ansoff, Newman, Warren, Peter Drucker, Akcoff, Christenson, Kenneth, Bower and Vacil, Acherman, Robinson, Piere, Wheeler and Hunger, Charles W.L. Hill and Gareth R.Jones. In the UK I owe a great debt to Argeni, Hussey, and Barnard Taylor, Thomson and other scholars.

Many individuals have rendered their helping hand to me. I take this opportunity to thank all of them. I thank Dr. D.M. Basvaraja, my teacher and professor from Kuvempu University for his constant inspiration and support. Prof. C.M. Thyagaraj, Dr. G.T. Govindappa, Dr. J. Madegowda my teachers and professors of Kuvempu University. I am immensely indebted to them. I also thank A.C. Shanmugam, Chairman, ACS and RajaRajeswari Group of Institutions in Chennai and Bangalore.

1. Dr. N. Naganna, Director, Dept, of MBA, DR.AIT, Bangalore
2. K. Narendra Kumar, Director of KKECS, and RK Institutions, Bangalore
3. T.N. Suresh, Director of Padmashree Group of Institutions, Bangalore
4. C.N. AswathNarayan, Chairman of Padmashree Group of Institutions. Bangalore
5. Dr. A. Venkta Raju, Professor, ATNCC, Shimoga
6. Dr. P.V. Surbramanya , Principal of RR MBA College, Bangalore
7. Dr. Bakkappa, Coordinator, PG Centre, Davanagere, Kuvempu University
8. Ruplia Naik, Faculty of MBA of RR College, Bangalore
9. Dr. P.N. Readdy, Director, KKECS Institue Bangalore.
10. Appannaiah, Director, Surana PG Centre, Bangalore.
11. Dr. Nagaraja, Faculty of MBA of RR College, Bangalore
12. George Thomas, Faculty of MBA of RR College, Bangalore
13. Dr. Rajashekar, Department of Commerce, Kuvempu University
14. Dr. Anitha, Reader, Department of Commerce, Kuvempu University
15. Dr. Murgaih, Professor, Department of Business Administration, Kuvempu University
16. Dr. Ashoka. M.N. Department of Commerce, Mysore University.
17. Eswar, Faculty of Department of Commerce, Kuvempu University
18. Dr. Laxman, Faculty of Department of Commerce, Kuvempu University
19. B.M. Basavaraj, DIS, Thomson, Bangalore
20. Avinash K., Business Analyst, Reuters, Bangalore
21. Sateesha Sindhe, Faculty, M.S. Ramiah College, Bangalore
22. Sheshchalla, Faculty, KKECS, Bangalore
23. Prof. Sathyanarayana, Faculty of MBA, KKECS, Bangalore
24. Prof. Shiva Murthy, Faculty of MBA, KKECS, Bangalore
25. Shekar, Faculty, KKECS, Bangalore
26. Rajesh Vaidya Chief Editor, New Age International Publishers
27. Anil, Faculty, Bangalore City College, Bangalore
28. Dayananada, Faculty, Padamashree Group of Institutions, Bangalore
29. Chandru, Software Engineer IBM, Bangalore
30. Manjunatha Yogieshwara, Senior Software Engineer, Bangalore.
31. Jayarama, faculty of Reva Institute of Management.
32. Mallukurjana, Business Analyst, Thomson Financials, Bangalore
33. Shivanna, Faculty of MBA Programme, KKECS, Bangalore
34. Dr. Hirimani Naik, Department of Commerce, Belegum PG Centre, Karnataka University

Shri Soumya Gupta, MD, and Shri V.R. Babu, Marketing Manager, New Age International Publisher, both persons are the main initiators and monitors of this project. I express my sincere gratitude to both of them.

It is my prime responsibility to thank my parents, brother, sisters and friends.

Bangalore **B. HIRIYAPPA**

Contents

Chapter – 1

Strategy and Business Policy

CONTENTS

- Introduction
- Definition of strategy
- What is strategy?
- Concept of strategy
- Characteristics of business
- Components of business
- Industry
- Types of industry
- Commerce
- Trade
- Policies
- Importance of business policy
- Classification of business policy

LEARNING OBJECTIVES

In this chapter, we shall look at the strategy, characteristics, business and its components, industry and its types, commerce and trade. In addition, this chapter has focused on policies, importance and different types of business policies.

INTRODUCTION

The concept of strategy has been borrowed from the military and adapted for use in business. This book has reviews of strategy formulation, implementation, controlling and monitoring strategic events, which have to suggest that adopting the concept is easy to business and industry. In business, as in the military, strategy bridges the gap between policy and tactics. Together, strategy and tactics bridge the gap between ends and means. Also this book reviews various issues like strategic and business policy, strategic management, strategic management process, types of strategy, define the organization mission and social responsibility, internal environment of the organization, external environment, competitive advantage, value-chain concept and analysis, business and investment level strategy analysis, industrial environment analysis, vertical integration, diversification and strategic alliances, acquisitions and joint ventures, strategies for competing in globalizing markets, strategy framework and restructuring the organization, strategic change management analysis, tailoring strategy to fit specific company and industry analysis, corporate culture and leadership, designing organization structure, strategic control systems analysis, matching global structure and control for the purpose of clarifying the concept and placing it in this context. Strategy is a course of action to achieve targets.

DEFINITIONS OF STRATEGY

The term strategy is derived from the Greek word 'strategia' which means "generalship". In the military, strategy often refers to the branch of military science dealing with military command and the planning and conduct of a war. According to this strategy refers to the deployment of troops. Once the enemy has been engaged, attention shifts to tactics. Here, the employment of troops is central. Substitute "resources" for troops and the transfer of the concept to the business world begins to take form. It is concerned with deciding what business an organisation should be in, where it wants to be, and how it is going to get there.

Strategy According to B. H. Liddell Hart

In his book, *Strategy*, Liddell Hart examines wars and battles from the time of the ancient Greeks through World War II. He concludes that Clausewitz' definition of strategy as "the art of the employment of battles as a means to gain the object of war" is seriously flawed in that this view of strategy intrudes upon policy and makes battle the only means of achieving strategic ends. Liddell Hart has observed that Clausewitz later acknowledged these flaws and then points to what he views as a wiser definition of strategy set forth by Moltke: "the practical adaptation of the means placed at a general's disposal to the attainment of the object in view." In Moltke's formulation, military strategy is clearly a means to political ends.

Concluding his review of wars, policy, strategy, and tactics, Liddell Hart arrives at this short definition of strategy: "the art of distributing and applying military means to fulfil the ends of policy." Deleting the word "military" from Liddell Hart's definition makes it easy to export the concept of strategy to the business world.

Strategy According to George Steiner

George Steiner is the father of strategic planning in the business world. George Steiner, a professor of management and one of the founders of *The California Management Review* which generally considers a key figure in the origins and development of strategic planning. His book, *Strategic Planning* closes to being a bible on the discipline. Yet, Steiner does not bother to define strategy except in the notes at the end of his book, *Strategic Planning*. There, he notes that strategy enters the management literature as a way of referring to what one did to counter a competitor's actual or predicted moves. Steiner also notices that there is very little agreement as to the meaning of strategy in the business world. Some of the definitions in use to which Steiner pointed have outlined:

- Strategy of the top management which is the greatest importance to the organization.
- Strategy refers to basic directional instructions and set of decisions which relates to purposes and missions.
- Strategy consists of the important actions and moves which necessary to realize these directions.
- Strategy always answers to the question: What should the organization be doing?
- Strategy answers the problem: What are the ends we seek and how should we achieve them?

Strategy According to Henry Mintzberg

Henry Mintzberg wrote a book, *The Rise and Fall of Strategic Planning*, in 1994. It has pointed out that people use "strategy" in several different ways, the most common being these four as outlined:

- Strategy is like a plan, a "how", a means of getting from here to there.
- Strategy represents a pattern in actions over time; for example, a company regularly markets very expensive products is using a "high end" strategy.
- Strategy represents position; it reflects decisions to offer particular products or services in particular markets.
- Strategy represents perspective like vision and direction of the company.

Mintzberg has argues that strategy emerges over time as intentions collide with and accommodate a changing reality. Therefore, one might start with a perspective and conclude that it calls for a certain position, which is to be achieved by way of a carefully-crafted plan, with the eventual outcome and strategy reflected in a pattern evident in decisions and actions over time. This pattern in decisions and actions defines what Mintzberg called "realized" or emergent strategy.

Strategy According to Kenneth Andrews

Kenneth Andrews is a professor of Harvard Business School and for many years editor of the Harvard Business Review. Kenneth Andrews wrote a book, *The Concept of Corporate Strategy.* It has presented this lengthy definition of strategy as

> *"Corporate strategy is the pattern of decisions in a company that determines and reveals its objectives, purposes, or goals, produces the principal policies and plans for achieving those goals, and defines the range of business the company is to pursue, the kind of economic and human organization it is or intends to be, and the nature of the economic and non-economic contribution it intends to make to its shareholders, employees, customers, and communities."*

Andrew's definition obviously anticipates Mintzberg's attention to pattern, plan, and perspective. Andrews also draws a distinction between "corporate strategy", which determines the businesses in which a company will compete, and "business strategy", which defines the basis of competition for a given business. Thus, he also anticipated "position" as a form of strategy. Strategy as the basis for competition brings us to another Harvard Business School professor, Michael Porter, the undisputed guru of competitive strategy.

Strategy According to Michael Porter

Another Harvard Business School professor, Michael Porter is the undisputed guru of *Competitive Strategy*. Michael Porter argue that competitive strategy is "about being different". He adds, "It means deliberately choosing a different set of activities to deliver a unique mix of value." In short, Porter argues that strategy is about competitive position, about differentiating yourself in the eyes of the customer, about adding value through a mix of activities different from those used by competitors. In his earlier book Competitive Strategy, Porter defines competitive strategy as "a combination of the ends (goals) for which the firm is striving and the means (policies) by which it is seeking to get there." Thus, Porter seems to embrace strategy as both plan and position. (It should be noted that Porter writes about competitive strategy, not about strategy in general).

Strategy According to Kepner-Tregoe

In *Top Management Strategy*, Benjamin Tregoe and John Zimmerman, of Kepner-Tregoe, Inc., define strategy as "the framework, which guides those choices that determine the nature and direction of an organization." Ultimately, this boils down to selecting products (or services) to offer and the markets in which to offer them. Tregoe and Zimmerman urge executives to base these decisions on a single "driving force" of the business. Although there are nine possible driving forces, only one can serve as the basis for strategy for a given business. The nine possibilities are listed below:

- Products offered
- Market needs
- Technology
- Production capability
- Method of sale
- Method of distribution
- Natural resources
- Size/growth
- Return/profit

It seems Tregoe and Zimmerman takes the position that strategy is essentially a matter of perspective.

Strategy According to Michel Robert

Michel Robert takes a similar view of strategy in, *Strategy Pure & Simple*, where he argues that the real issues are "strategic management" and "thinking strategically." For Robert, this boils down to decisions pertaining to four factors listed below:

- Products and services
- Customers
- Market segments
- Geographic areas

Like Tregoe and Zimmerman, Robert claims that decisions about which products and services to offer, the customers to be served, the market segments in which to operate, and the geographic areas of operations should be made on the basis of a single "driving force." Again, like Tregoe and Zimmerman, Robert claims that several possible driving forces exist but only one can be the basis for strategy. The 10 driving forces cited by Robert are listed below:

- Product-service
- User-customer
- Market type
- Sales-marketing method
- Distribution method
- Natural resources

- Production-capacity capability
- Technology
- Size/growth
- Return/profit

Strategy According to Treacy and Wiersema

The notion of restricting the basis on which strategy might be formulated has been carried one step farther by Michael Treacy and Fred Wiersema, authors of *The Discipline of Market Leaders*, Treacy and Wiersema assert that companies achieve leadership positions by narrowing, not broadening their business focus. Treacy and Wiersema identify three "value-disciplines" that can serve as the basis for strategy: operational excellence, customer intimacy, and product leadership. As with driving forces, only one of these value disciplines can serve as the basis for strategy. Treacy and Wiersema's three value disciplines are briefly defined below:

- Operational Excellence
  - Strategy is predicated on the production and delivery of products and services. The objective is to lead the industry in terms of price and convenience.
- Customer Intimacy
  - Strategy is predicated on tailoring and shaping products and services to fit an increasingly fine definition of the customer. The objective is long-term customer loyalty and long-term customer profitability.
- Product Leadership
  - Strategy is predicated on producing a continuous stream of state-of-the-art products and services. The objective is the quick commercialization of new ideas.

Each of the three value disciplines suggests different requirements. Operational excellence implies world-class marketing, manufacturing, and distribution processes. Customer intimacy suggests staying close to the customer and entails long-term relationships. Product Leadership clearly hinges on market-focused R&D as well as organizational nimbleness and agility.

WHAT IS STRATEGY?

A strategy is a long-term plan of action designed to achieve a particular goal. Strategy applies to many disparate fields, such as: *Military strategy *Marketing strategies *Strategic management *Football strategy *Game theoretical strategy *Economic strategy *Neuro-linguistic programming strategy. According to Fred Nickoles, What, then, is strategy? Is it a plan? Does it refer to how we will obtain the ends we seek? Is it a position taken? Just as military forces might take the high ground prior to engaging the enemy; might a business take the position of low-cost provider? A plan or method including options and priorities towards the achievement of a defined goal or objective is a strategy. A startegy is a long-term plan for success, to achieve an advantage. In force terms, this is the key milestones and targets for the coming year. On the other hand, does strategy refer to perspective, to the view one takes of matters, and to the purposes, directions, decisions, and actions stemming from this view? Lastly, does strategy refer to a pattern in our decisions and actions? For example, does repeatedly copying a competitor's new product offerings signal a "me too" strategy? Just what is strategy?

It is an elaborated and systematic plan of action. Strategy is all these—it is perspective, position, plan, and pattern. Strategy is the bridge between policy and high-order goals on the one hand and tactics or concrete actions on the other. Strategy and tactics together straddle the gap between ends and means. In short, strategy is a term that refers to a complex web of thoughts, ideas, insights, experiences, goals, expertise, memories, perceptions, and expectations that provides general guidance for specific actions in pursuit of particular ends. Strategy is at once the course we chart, the journey we imagine, and, at the same time, it is the course we steer, the trip we actually make. Even when we are embarking on a voyage of discovery, with no particular destination in mind, the voyage has a purpose, an outcome, and an end to be kept in view.

A strategy is a planned, deliberate goal-oriented procedure (has an identifiable outcome) achieved with a sequence of steps subject to monitoring and modification. Strategy, then, has no existence apart from the ends sought. A general framework provides guidance for actions to be taken and, at the same time, is shaped by the actions taken. This means that the necessary precondition for formulating strategy is a clear and widespread understanding of the ends to be obtained. Without these ends in view, action is purely tactical and can quickly degenerate into nothing more than a flailing about.

It is concerned with deciding what business an organisation should be in, where it wants to be, and how it is going to get there. When there are no "ends in view" for the organization writ large, strategies still exist and they are still operational, even highly effective, but for an individual or unit, not for the organization as a whole. A company's overall plan of development. Corporate strategy can be more formally defined as a comprehensive plan or action orientation that identifies the critical direction and guides the allocation of resources of an entire organization. The strategy is typically a statement about what should be done to ensure prosperity based on the company's vision, values and mission. Besides a corporate strategy, each business unit of a large corporation may have its own strategic plan. It is absence of a clear and widespread understanding of the ends sought.

CONCEPT OF STRATEGY

A strategy is a long-term plan of action designed to achieve a particular goal. Strategy applies to many disparate fields such as: Military strategy, economic strategy, environmental strategy, corporate strategy, business strategy, industry strategy, commerce, science, grand, stability, expansion, retrenchment, combination, modernization, diversification, integration, turnaround, divestment, hybrid, alliance, merger and acquisition strategy etc.

Strategy is essentially linked with military science. It implies facing the enemy under war conditions that are to one's advantage. A policy when given a particular meaning under a prevailing situation and in view of the enemy or competitor policy becomes strategy. So, strategy can be defined as interpretative planning. Strategy includes the determination and evaluation of alternative paths to an already established mission or objectives, and eventually choosing the right alternatives. In common sense, a strategy outlines how management decides and plans to achieve its goal and objectives. Management formulates strategy to shed out the effect of other policie of it's overall plan and programs of the competitors, policy to avail competitive advantage.

Characteristics of Strategy

As listed below are the important strategy characteristics. They are:

- Strategies are specific actions suggested to achieve the objectives.
- Strategies are action oriented.
- Everyone is empowered to implement the strategy.
- Strategies are means to an end.
- Strategies are concerned with uncertainties with competitive situations like risk etc., which are likely to take place at a future date.
- Strategy is deployed to mobilize the available resources in the best interest of the company.

Business

The term 'typically' refers to the development and processing of economic values in society. Normally, the term is applied to portion of economic activities whose primary purpose is to provide goods and services for society in an effective manner. It is also applied to economics and commercial activities of institutions which having other purposes.

Business principally comprises an all profit seeking activities of the organization which provide goods and services that are necessary to economic system. It is the major economic pulse of a nation, striving to increase society's standard of living. Finally, profits are a primary mechanism for motivating these activities.

Business is in any organization which makes distribution or provides any article or service to the customers, who are belonging to members of the society. Business may be satisfied customers needs for this purpose customers are able and willing to pay for it.

Business may be defined as "the organized effort by individuals to produce goods and services to sell these goods and services in a market place and to reap some reward for this effort."

Functionally, we may define business as "those human activities which involves production or purchase of goods with the object of selling them at a profit margin".

CHARACTERISTICS OF BUSINESS

- Business is to provide goods and service to the people. It provides the public with the things it needs and wants in order to survive, enjoy life and improve in a material sense. From the point of view of consumer, business is the satisfier of needs and desire of the customer demands which should be provided by business.
- Goods that have been produced or procured for sale in retail for price enter the realm of business. This activity of selling results is the creation of the wealth for the society. In satisfying demand, business uses the resources of land, labor and capital. These resources when taken separately have little value; but business combines structures and refines the resources to produce to the value of the society. Further, business employees' people who exchange their talents for wages and salaries. Therefore, these people exchange their compensation for the desired goods and service.
- Business is profit–seeking activity. It supplies goods and services to customers who are satisfying their demand and desire. It adds to society's value by earning a profit. Profit is the biggest stimulus for maintaining the survival of the business and its future development. Society permits business to earn profit as a reward for assuming the risks of operating a business.

- Business is also an essential participant in society. For satisfying society demand which supplying goods and services and earning profits. Business involves the most fundamental activities of the society. As a result, society looks to business for something more than products, services and profits. It looks to business for leadership and direction in helping to achieve society's objectives. It expects business to assist in the establishment of a better service to the society.

COMPONENTS OF BUSINESS

Business includes the total enterprise of the country. Business activity has two branches. They are as follows:

- Industry
- Commerce

INDUSTRY

In broad sense, industry is the branch of business activity which concerned with raising production, fabrication or possessing of goods and services. In other words, industry is an activity concerned with conversion of raw materials or semi-finished goods into finished goods. Industry provides two types of goods namely Consumer goods and Industrial goods. Consumer goods are those goods manufactured by industry for ultimate use of a customer. For instance brush, paste, cloth and food products etc. Industrial\Capital goods are those goods produced and used for further production. For instance machineries, tools and raw material etc.

TYPES OF INDUSTRY

Industry is further classified into five broad types. They are as listed below:

1. Extractive industries
2. Genetic industries
3. Manufacturing industries
4. Construction industries
5. Territory\Service industries

Extractive Industries

Extractive industries are those industries concerned with extraction of wealth from surface of the earth, soil, forest, water, air etc., for instance agriculture, mining etc.

Genetic Industries

Genetic industries are those industries concerned with reproduction and multiplication of plants animals for making profit on their sale. For example, nurseries, cattle building and poultry farming.

Manufacturing Industries

Manufacturing industries are engaged in the conversation and process of raw material through separation, combination, and transformation into finished goods. Such as machinery and plants of all types, iron and steel, sugar, paper, cotton clothes, electrical appliances, zinc ore, paper pulp water power, etc.

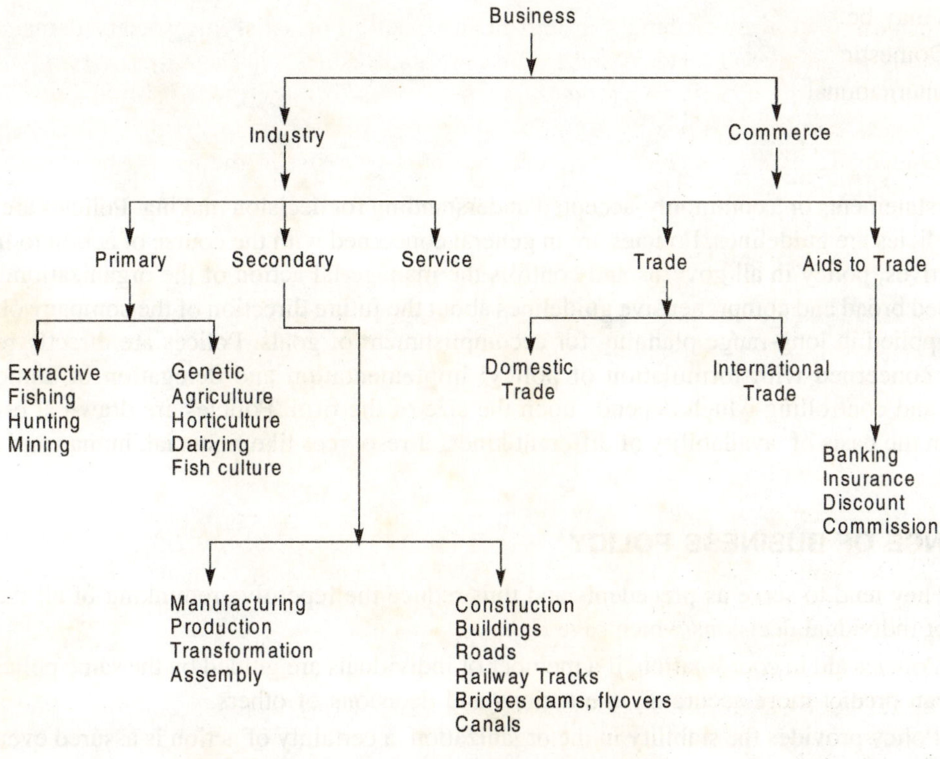

Figure 1.1 Components of Business

Construction Industries

Construction industries are concerned with the construction of roads, railway tracks, dams, canals, buildings, bridges etc., there are mainly concerned with the manufacture of non-movable items.

Territory or Service Industries

Service industry which produce intangible goods those which cannot be seen or touched included in this category are banking, transport, insurance, communication and services of a professional nature such as lawyers, doctors, dentists, management consultants, advertisers, chartered accountants and engineers, etc.

COMMERCE

Commerce has been defined as "the sum total of those processes which are engaged in the removal of the hindrance of persons (trade), place (transport and insurance), and time (warehousing) in the exchange (banking) of commodities".

TRADE

Trade means sale, transfer, or exchange of goods and services, through certain ancillary functions like packing, warehousing, banking, transportation, insurance, and advertising.

Trade may be

- Domestic
- International

POLICIES

Policies are statements or a commonly-accepted understanding for decision making. Policies are thought oriented. Policies are guidelines. Policies are in general concerned with the course of action to fulfill the set of objectives, policy in all governs and controls the managerial action of the organization. Policies have provided broad and comprehensive guidelines about the future direction of the company objectives which are applied in long-range planning for accomplishment of goals. Polices are directly related to goals. It is concerned with formulation of policy; implementation and delegation of authority for monitoring and controlling which depends upon the size of the firm. Policies are drawn at estimating the future on the basis of availability of different kinds of resources like financial, human and material etc.

IMPORTANCE OF BUSINESS POLICY

- They tend to serve as precedents and thus reduce the repetitive rethinking of all the factors of individual decisions which save time.
- Policies aid in coordination, if a member of individuals are guided by the same policies, they can predict more accurately the actions and decisions of others.
- Policy provides the stability in the organization, a certainty of action is assured even though the top management may change. The policies continue and this continuity promotes stability in the organization and thus reduces frustrations of members.
- Clear policies encourage definite individual decisions. Each functional manager has clear understanding of the range of policy within the organization which is helpful to make decision and thus feel less uncertain as to whether he\she can give answers to subordinates without "getting into trouble."
- Policies clearly specify routes towards the related goals of the organization. Policies serve as a standard or measuring yard for evaluation performance in the organization. The actual results can be compared with the policies of the organization which is to determine how well the members of an organization have lived into their professed and intentioned to what extent goals have been achieved.
- Sound policies help to build up employee's enthusiasm and loyalty for the organization. This is specifically true when they reflect established principles of fair play and justice and when they help people to know that within an organization.
- They setup the pattern of behavior and permit to participants to plan with a greater degree of confidence and lead to better co-operation in the organization.
- Policies are monitored and controlling of the organization which guides for delegated decision-making. They seek to ensure consistency and uniformity in decisions relating to problems that recur frequently and under similar but not identical circumstances.
- Policies always with clarity, relevance and reasonableness and enable a firm to make the optimum utilization of scarce available resources and thereby bring about an efficient level of operations because wastage must be avoided.

- Corporate policies always build up an image of the business in the eyes of the public and this brings in more reputation, goodwill; sale and profits so that more and more acts of social responsibilities may be undertaken by organization.
- Proper administration and implementation of policies that encourage initiative in the employees so that they act with full responsibility with in the framework of the policies of the organization. This naturally improves the working environment like very good labor management relations within the organization.

CLASSIFICATION OF BUSINESS POLICY

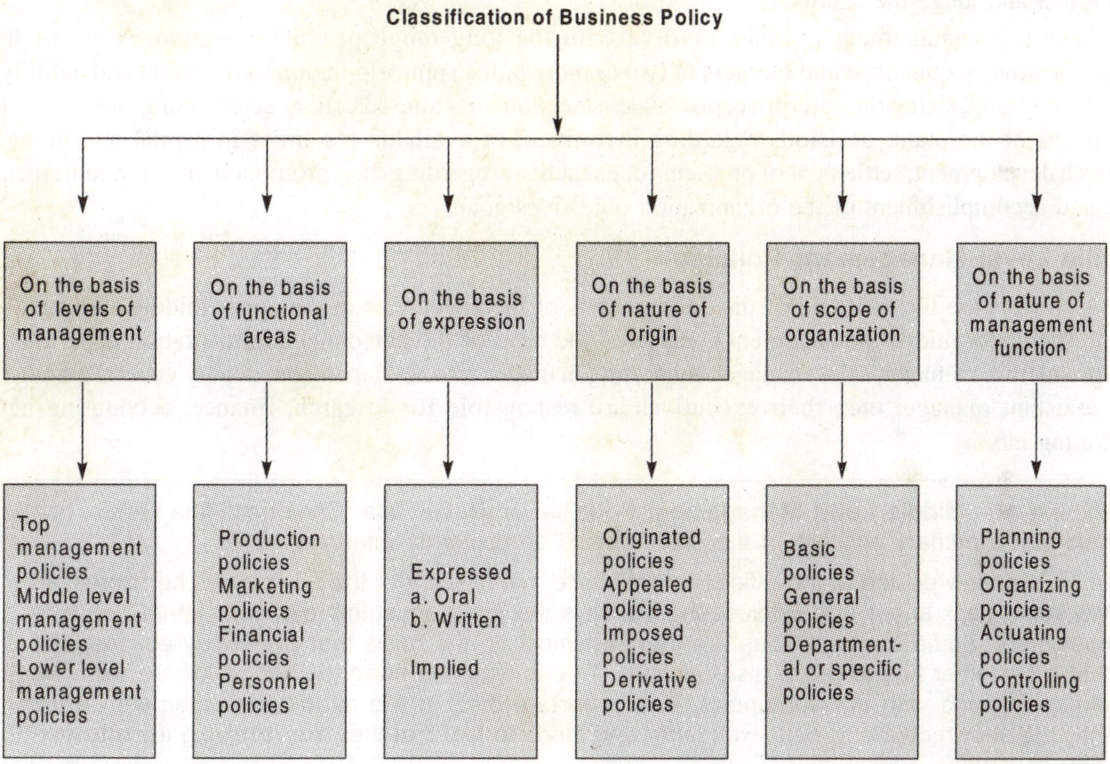

Figure 1.2 Classification of Business Policy

Figure 1.2 indicates the classification of business policy. Different types of business policy are as follows:

- On the basis of level of management
- On the basis of functional areas
- On the basis of expression
- On the basis of nature of origin
- On the basis of scope of organization
- On the basis of nature of management function

On the Basis of Level of Management

Business policies are framed at different levels of the management, and accordingly these may be classified as:

Top Management Policies

These policies are derived from the top management planning. The top management principally comprises the board of directors, chairman/president, vice-president/vice-chairman, managing director, general manager etc., and the top management frames the policies by themselves and it is, therefore, responsible for these. These people are the ultimate level of authority in the operation of the enterprise. The policy makers plan to set the objectives, define the goals, establish the policies, see that these policies are put into effect and judge the results.

The top management policies involve with the long-range product selection extent of its diversification, acquisitions and mergers of two or more units, spin-offs-their nature, extent and liability, sales forecasting, sizing the enterprise, process of selection, machine selection, determining site, location and needs of the plant, decisions regarding investment of available resources in capital and human research development, settlement of problems of executives regarding their promotion, transfer, retirement etc., and accomplishment of the organization objectives/goals.

Middle Level Management Policies

These policies are the outcome of the deliberations of the executives at the upper middle and middle level. The upper middle management consists of the head of the personnel administration department like production manager, sales manager, marketing manager, financial manager, deputy general manager and assistant manager etc., their executives are responsible for research, finance, accounting and marketing etc.

Exhibit 1.1: Middle Level Management Policies Mr. Ratan Tata, Chairman, Tata Group, has said that a primary concern of the Tatas should be customer interface.

In an interview posted at the official Tata Website, reminiscent of the frank views he expressed few years back about Tata Engineering, he says the group must improve in its interaction with customers. Some of our policies are framed almost on the basis that everybody abuses, and that a customer has to prove his bonafides. That is what we need to change. Where we have direct dealings with our customers, it is important that, at the middle management levels, they are shown courtesy, dealt with fairly, and made to feel that they are receiving the attention they deserve.

"The interface with the customer should be a seamless one. Judging from the number of letters I get complaining about the manner in which people are treated by some of our companies, I would say that we as a group have a lot to change in terms of how we deal with our customers," he said. It covers channel partners too, as love lost between them and a company, eventually results in customer dissatisfaction.

Asked about the challenges companies faced with respect to customer acquisition and retention, he says, "If you introduce a new vehicle, for example, and the management cannot adequately determine what the market wants, the company is in trouble.

Theoretically, the top managers of a company should take up the role of that ideal customer.

(*Contd...*)

They should be driving their competitors' vehicles, they should be driving the best-of-breed vehicles, and they should be making cost comparisons. "While a top manager should be the ideal customer, he should also be the greatest critic of his company's products. If the CEO compromises, or is only looking at the margins, then even if he is successful, the company's success will be shortlived."

Further, "Market feedback is very important, but it has to be stripped of its colour. You have to be able to strip away the vested interest or the bias that sometimes comes in. You have to view it objectively, not defensively."

On how to enthuse CEOs and employees to create value for shareholders and customers, he says, "We need to make it our responsibility to expose employees to the company holistically.

"I often tell some of my colleagues, 'You don't have to face the shareholders when you make a loss. I do. May be you should stand up one day and face the shareholders for what you've deprived them of.' Selectively involving people in shareholder meets, investor conferences, and dealer meets will help in exposing them to different situations that they may face. We have been doing that at Tata Engineering."

What would the Tata differentiator be in a market with so many competing brands and products?

He says, "I would like the customer to say that the next product he buys will also be a Tata product because of everything that he experienced. That is really what customer retention is all about."

Source: Business Line, Dated March19, 2003

They lay down the policies regarding the establishment of organization, selection of the best-suited executives staff and employees to carry out the plans, installation of proper departments, designing of operating policies and operating routines, deciding processes, methods and techniques of production with exploration of new markets and decisions about channels of distribution for assignment of duties to each department and to each individual, who are deciding about source of manpower, resources and their selection, deciding about wage, salary and incentive plans for them, obtain necessary finances, controlling costs and solving problems of actual sales activities etc.

Middle management consists of the deputy heads of the various sections under different functional departments—employment and training, industrial relations, labor welfare and social security. Junior executive, superintendents of departments divisions etc., these executives are the deputy head of the functional department like sales, production, research, finance and accounting divisions of the organization. They frame policies which are known as *middle management polices.*

Lower-level Management Policies

The lower-level management people are men and women who have direct supervision over the working force in office, factory, sales field, and other areas of activity of the organization. They are directly related to the accomplishment of the task for the small sub-divisions of the whole enterprise. They chalk out policies or the assignment of the jobs to the best-suited persons in the organization. The lower level management policies guidelines of the provision of adequate tools, raw materials, training of the workers, issuing of orders, maintenance of quality, improving working conditions, morale, maintaining discipline and controlling absenteeism etc.

Operating Force Policies

These are the rules or a code for doing the job which enriched to a particular worker performance. These are usually written down in the notebooks of the organization. Operating policies notice to the worker how long each job work should take a time, what tricks of the trade are required, and what quality feature are emphasized.

On the Basis of Functional Areas

On the basis of functional areas business policies may be classified as production policies, marketing and sales policies, financial policies and human resource development policies.

Production Policies

Production policies are framed and concerned with the following issues:

- The product to be produced (product line, type of product).
- The type of technology, processes, equipment and tools, to be used.
- The selection of factory\office\plant site, location and layout.
- The decisions regarding scale of production.
- Making of production budgets, manufacturing costs and deciding about total cost and cost of installation and its maintenance.
- The selection of junior executives.
- Inventory control.
- Collective bargaining and labor relations.
- Organization and co-ordination of their activities.
- Selection of systems of quality, cost production control.
- Production policies are the basic determinants of the total policy-making procedure.

Marketing and Sales Policies

These policies relate to policies in market analysis, business law, display, salesmanship and advertising etc, *i.e.*, they are concerned with total process of marketing which covers both 'product mix' and 'market mix'. The product mix includes decisions regarding the type, quantity and quality of product design, contents shape, methods and techniques of production etc. Market mix covers the issues like price, place, promotion, channels of distribution, advertising policies, packaging and branding decisions, consumer psychology and behavior and pricing of the product etc.

- Since the modern concept of market has treated as 'consumer as a king', every product is brought to satisfy customer needs. Hence, its gamut is very fast. The policies in this field, therefore, deal with the following issues:
- Spotting out of the present and potential markets, the size and nature of consumers.
- The degree of competition in the market and how best could it be met.
- The location of prospects and persuading them to purchase.
- Fixing price of product, offering rebated, discounts and other concessions.
- Compensating salesman adequately; and providing them with training and developmental opportunities.
- Selecting channels of distribution or employing representatives and agents.

- Dividing the total market into branch or dealer areas.
- Establishing advertising policies like:
  - (*i*) Setting up sales control policies.
  - (*ii*) Establishing sales volume and expense budgets.

Financial Policies

Financial policies may be regarded as the most important business policies of the organization. It depends on the entire success and failure of a business unit of the organization. Properly and careful framed financial policies help to effective utilization of the resource like men, machine, market, method, materials and long-term survival of the business while improper framed financial policies ruin the business activities of the organization.

Financial policies are essential to organization. They are as listed below:

- To know the capital requirement of the organization in terms of short, medium and long-term and know-how to procure and effectively utilize finance in the organization.
- The method of raising funds and the ratio between the various types of sources of funds, particularly the proportion of owned funds to borrowed funds.
- Utilizations of the funds and the ratio between different types of asset.
- The credit policy, declaration and distribution of dividend to the shareholder.
- Profit policy, provisions for taxes, renovations and modernization of plants and machinery.

Costing policy includes the policy for selecting the method of costing, the method of allocating, apportioning, reapportioning and absorbing overheads.

Accounting policy includes the following areas:

- The basis of valuation of stock in trade at the year end; whether at total cost, or at direct cost or at works costs.
- The issue price of the raw material; whether to follow first in first out method or last in first out method or average cost or any other methods of issue of raw materials.
- Depreciation policy; whether straight-line method or reducing balance method or mileage method or any other method.
- The treatment of deferred revenue expenditure, intangible asset, fictitious assets and preliminary expenses.
- Capitalization of expenditure during construction period.
- The policy for provision of bad and doubtful debt, investment losses, etc.

Human Resource Development Policy

Personal policy are concerned with human resource utilization, its recruitments and selection, source of supply, training of employment, training of the employees at whole cost; the promotion and transfer policy, the issues regarding compensation to the employees, wage incentive and other perks, benefits and services etc.

On the Basis of Expression

On the basis of expression, policy may be classified into express policies, oral policies and written policies.

Express Policy

Express policies are those policies, which are expressed in terms of clear words either orally or in writing.

Oral Policies

Oral policies are those, which are issued or stated by the management in terms of speech to their subordinates. Such policies are generally adopted when an organization is small and face-to-face communications is desired. Since they are direct, they are more effective and, hence can be better understood and implemented. They are more flexible and can be adjusted to the different organizational conditions.

Limitation

The main drawback of such policies is that they are not written as such.

Second is they are interpreted in any way by the persons receiving them.

Thirdly they are often not remembered for long time and easily forgotten, especially when there are number of policies and where their frequency of issues is great. Therefore, usually oral policies are not in popular use.

Written Policy

Written policies are those, which are normally, put in black and white and stated in clear terms so that persons whom they are addressed to easily understand them. For putting the policies in written, much care has to be taken, for instance;

- Policy is always written in terms of words which are neither vag nor unnecessarily academic, nor in any way offensive to those for whom it is meant.
- Words, sentence and paragraphs should be short and statement of policy should be complete and precise.
- It should not contain irritating words or expression which are antagonistic or cast as persons on others.
- The tone should be warm, without use of any legalistic phraseology.
- The frame should be convenient and handy for management reference and application.

Written policies are desirable in the following situations:

- The subject matter on which a policy is to be formulated, is of a very controversial nature.
- The distance between the top and lower levels of management is so wide as to make personnel/ informal contact and communications rather difficult.
- Consistent treatment is needed and certainty of action desired.
- Preciseness and complete understanding is needed to convoy to the employees at the different levels.

Advantages

There are distinct advantages of written policies as follows:

- The writing of policies makes commitments on the part of an organization.
- Writing ensures uniformity of application and assures continuity of action even when the management is changed.

- Its limits freedom of action on the part of the management, for it is work with in the boundary of policies.
- The written policies provide something concrete on which to base an appeal if there is any disagreement about what is the organization's policy.
- Writing helps to ensure that the professed policies are right for organization tries to put its best foot forward.
- The likelihood of wrong interpretation or misunderstanding is very much lessened.
- Written policies facilitate easy and smooth compliance.
- The results in greater convenience both to the policy frame worse and implementers.

However, written policies cannot be easily changed and perfect secrecy, when desired cannot be maintained and writing of good policies need fluency in English that every person does not possess.

Even then, in all large organizations, written policies are a rule rather than exception.

Implied Policies

These are the policies, which are implied from the code of conduct or from mode of behavior of business executives; but they are not stated orally. They generally flow from the philosophy of the business, it is social values and even traditions, for instance, smoking and drinking may be prohibited not in writing but is implied by the conduct of superior executives who refrain from these habits while on the duty.

Originated Policies

Originated policies emanate from the company objectives which are determined by the top management, who are primarily responsible for shaping business policies to guide and direct them and the subordinate in the attainment of organization's objectives these are framed by the board of directors, the president and general manager etc., and passed on to the executives in hierarchy for implementation.

The subordinates usually readily accept such policies because they have been framed by higher ups in power that entrusted with the shaping of business policy for concern.

Appealed Policies

Appealed policies are often known as "suggested policies." Because they are framed on the suggestions of the subordinates or those who implement the policies. The idea is to make a policy more effective so that particular problems could find solutions under it. Such policies also have general acceptance as that of the originated policy because, they have already got the approval of the top management.

QUESTIONS FOR DISCUSSIONS

1. What is strategy?
2. Define strategy.
3. Define concept of strategy.
4. Write a note on the business policy.
5. Describe the types of industry.
6. Discuss the components of the business.
7. What is the manufacturing industry?

8. Write a short note on the following:
   (*a*) Extractive industry
   (*b*) Genetic industry
   (*c*) Construction industry
   (*d*) Service/Territory industry
9. Define strategy. What are the characteristics of strategy?
10. Define business. What are the characteristics of business?
11. What is policy? What are the principles to be considered while framing the policies?
12. Examine different types of policies and how they evolve.
13. Discuss
    (*a*) Original policies
    (*b*) Appealed policies
14. Highlight the important needs of the business policy.

REFERENCES

1. *Strategy* (1967). B.H. Liddell Hart. Basic Books.
2. *Strategic Planning* (1979). George Steiner. Free Press.
3. *The Rise and Fall of Strategic Planning* (1994). Henry Mintzberg. Basic Books.
4. *The Concept of Corporate Strategy*, 2nd Edition (1980). Kenneth Andrews. Dow-Jones Irwin.
5. *What is Strategy*? Michael Porter. Harvard Business Review (Nov-Dec 1996).
6. *Competitive Strategy* (1986). Michael Porter. Harvard Business School Press.
7. *Top Management Strategy* (1980). Benjamin Tregoe and John Zimmerman, Simon and Schuster.
8. *Strategy: Pure and Simple* (1993). Michel Robert. McGraw-Hill.
9. *The Discipline of Market Leaders* (1994). Michael Treacy and Fred Wiersema. Addison-Wesley.
10. *Customer Intimacy and Other Value Disciplines*. Michael Treacy and Fred Wiersema. Harvard Business Review (Jan-Feb 1993).
11. *The Span of Control*. Lionel Urwick. Harvard Business Review (May-Jun 1956).
12. Fred Nickolas, *Stratetgy: Definitions and Meaning,* Distance Consulting.
13. William F. Glueck, *Business Policy and Strategic Management* (Auckland: McGraw-Hill International Book Co., 1972).
14. Arthur Sharplin, *Strategic Management*, (Newyork: McGraw-Hill Book Co. 1985).
15. Allred Chandler, *Strategic Management,* Cambridge, MIT Pres, 1962.
16. Fred R. Davied, *Strategic Management*, Newyork MacMillan Publishing Co. 1993.
17. Leslie and Phyllis G. Holland, *Strategic Management*, Newyork, McGraw-Hill Book Co. 1989.

Chapter – 2

Strategic Management

CONTENTS

- Introduction
- Meaning of strategic management
- Characteristic/nature of strategic planning
- Scope of strategic management
- Evolution of strategic management concept
- Dimensions of strategic decision
- Levels of strategic management
- Role of managers at various levels
- Characteristic of strategic management decisions at different levels
- Benefits of strategic management
- Risks of strategic management

LEARNING OBJECTIVES

This chapter aims to provide: Meaning of strategic management, characteristic/nature of strategic planning, scope of strategic management, evolution of strategic management, levels of strategic management, role of managers at various levels, characteristic of strategic management decisions at different levels, benefits of strategic management and risks of strategic management.

INTRODUCTION

"Strategic management is not a box of tricks or a bundle of techniques. It is analytical thinking and commitment of resources to action"

—Peter Drucker

"Without a strategy the organization is like a ship without a rudder"

—Joel Ross and Michael Kami

MEANING OF STRATEGIC MANAGEMENT

Strategic management is a stream of instructions, guidance, directions for decisions and actions with view to develop effective long-term and short-term planning of the organization. Strategic management decisions help organization for accomplishment of goals and objectives of the business. Forecasting the strategic decisions would help the organization to achieve its superior goal. Strategic management includes strategic analysis, strategy formulation, strategy implementation and strategic controlling and monitoring of all events of the organization. Strategic decisions might be to deploy resources in the organization into new business opportunities. Strategy decisions normally are representation of the environment analysis, value chain concept and analysis, integration, diversification, mergers and acquisitions, new product development, product redesigning, upgradation, strategies for marketing, technology, new customers, finance, geographic areas and entry into new markets. Strategic management decisions help to survival, growth and development of organization.

Strategic management is defined as "The set of decisions and actions resulting in formulation, implementation of strategies designed to achieve the objectives and goals of an organization". This definition reveals the following factors:

- Determining the mission of the organization which consists of broad statements about its purpose, philosophy and goals.
- Developing a company profile which reflects internal environment conditions and capabilities of the organization.
- Assessment and appraisal of the external environments of the organization in terms of growth, competitive and general contextual factors.
- Analysis of strength, weakness, opportunity and threatens of the organization.
- Identifying the desired options of the organization like uncovered possibilities are considered in the light of the company mission.
- Set of strategic choice for the achievement of long-term objectives and grand strategies.
- Development of annual/short term objectives without affecting of long-term objectives and grand objectives of the organization.
- Implementing strategic choice decisions which are based on budget resource allocations and emphasizing the matching of tasks, people, structure, technologies and reward system of the organization.
- Strategic control, monitoring, review and evaluation represent the accomplishment of the strategic objectives and goals of the organization.

As these factors indicate that strategic management involves the planning, directing, actuating, leading, communication, staffing, coordination, motivation, budgeting and controlling of the strategy-related decisions and actions of business.

CHARACTERISTIC/NATURE OF STRATEGIC PLANNING

It is an Entrepreneurial Function

This function is related to overall business activities like management and administration of the organization. It is an implication of the strategic management which is felt by the results is positive or negative of the organization.

Changing Orientations

According to Anthong Pats "strategic management is a process having the formulation of long-range strategy and grand strategic policy type plans that change the character direction of the organization."

Long Term Nature

Generally a strategic management involves long-term prospective. Strategic management requires considerable commitment and expertise gained out of the experiences of several experts in the field within and outside the organization for long-term without affecting the short-term planning goal with sensible future business proficiency.

It is an Intellectual Process

Intellectual process involves analytical thinking, formations of the set of decisions, selection of long term strategy for effective utilization of scarce available resource without affecting the internal and external environment of the organization. Strategy implementation and strategy monitoring and controlling is an intellectual process. The executives are utilized well efficient skills for judgment of the project. And they study about all areas of the project like policies, strategic decisions, programme resource, business environment etc., to integrate them into suitable planning for achieving the objectives of the company/organization/firm.

Continuous Process

Strategic management is not a one-time exercise and it is a dynamic process in the organization. It requires special skills for implementation of strategies and to know the different policies of the organization for analysis, interpretation of strength, weakness, opportunity, and threat from the internal and external environment. One cannot be expected at any time to set a time table. Strategic management should always ensure to proper changes in the organization.

SCOPE OF STRATEGIC MANAGEMENT

- Strategic management as a process is concerned with directing the efforts of human activities at all levels and all types of establishment—whether they are profit making or service rendering organization, whether they are big or small, whether government or private sectors. The scope of strategic management is quite broad and includes within its fold almost all aspects of business operations. However the following are included in it:
- **Subject Matter of Management**
  - Strategic management includes strategy analysis, its choice, its formulation, its implementation, and control.
- **Functional Areas of Strategic Management**

  Functional areas of strategic management issues are listed below:

- *Strategic and business policy*– it includes strategy, concepts, characteristic, functions, business policy and types of business policy.
- *Strategic management overview*–it includes strategic management nature and scope, characteristics, process, components and limitations.
- *Strategic environment*–it includes micro, macro, internal and external environment political, social, cultural, technological, legal, demography, and demand and competitive environment.
- *Types of strategy*–it includes grand strategy, stability strategy, expansion strategy, retrenchment strategy, and combination strategy.
- *Value chain concept and analysis*–it includes organizational analysis, process of organizational analysis, company profile analysis, industry analysis, strategic analysis and choice.
- *Integration, diversification, mergers and acquisitions*–it includes horizontal integration, vertical integration, factors influence to diversification, horizontal and vertical merger strategy.
- *Strategic change management*–it includes strategic change, power and conflict.
- *Training strategy*–it includes strategic use of marketing variables, product development strategy, marketing mix strategy, customer and channel strategy.
- *Implementation and control*–it includes corporate culture, leadership, culture guiding and evaluating strategy.
- *Current issue of strategic management*–it includes strategic audit and managing technology.

Strategic Management is an Interdisciplinary Approach

For the correct application of the strategic management to study of commerce, science, economics, statistics, psychology, and mathematics is very essential.

EVOLUTION OF STRATEGIC MANAGEMENT CONCEPT

The word 'strategy' is derived from the Greek word 'strategia' which implies the science, art, tact, and quality of being an efficient and effective army general. The word strategia was first time quoted around B.C. 400 among the Greeks. A Greek army general had to define and explain the purpose; the objectives and tactical procedures to be followed in leading an army against the enemies to win the battle, hold territory, defend and protect the country from invasion, or to conquer new territory.

According to Greek general, strategy was more than fighting a battle. Since that period the concept of strategy has been followed as a matter of principle in any firm of war throughout the history. The concept was gradually gaining coinage in other countries too, even in the battle of Plassay. The East India Company could prevail by adopting strategies against Siraj-ud-Daullah and conquer Bengal, Bihar, Mysore and Orissa to establish English rule in India. Indian history dating back to the 17th century shows marked similarities in the case of the British strategy to win and conquer state after state in Asia, Europe and African countries.

> **Exhibit 2.1: Tata Strategic Management Group** is one of the fastest-growing Management Consulting firms in the sphere of Strategy Formulation, Strategy Deployment and Competitiveness Enhancement. Our ability to provide unmatched value through innovative strategic advice and implementation support has earned us an enviable reputation in the business fraternity. We deliver practical, implement able solutions that have a lasting impact on improving your business performance.

(Contd...)

The Evolution of TSMG

TSMG was founded with just five people in the year 1991. From a small organization operating out of 'Bombay House'— the corporate headquarters of the Tata Group, we have since grown exponentially into a 50 member strong consulting powerhouse.

Our initial clientele included a fair share of Tata Group entities and its holding companies. From here, TSMG has successfully expanded its client base to include several non-Tata Group companies, both from India and overseas. Today we work with a healthy mix of multi-national companies, Indian corporates and public sector undertakings.

A feather in the TSMG cap came in the late nineties when we worked for the Prime Minister's Council to prepare a blue print to kick-start "Infrastructure Development in India." This was followed by a study for "Revival of India's Traditional Industries." Both of these have had significant impact on policymaking, heralding TSMG's contribution to nation building through influencing government thinking.

Today, TSMG is a name to reckon with in the consulting fraternity. Competition from multinational consulting firms not withstanding, TSMG has passed the test of time. We are poised for greater growth and glory. We seek to further grow our services across business areas, functional expertise and geographic boundaries and most of all in quality and impact.

Source: Tata Strategic Group Management (website)

In 1750, with the advent of industrial revolution, products and markets in Europe started developing a similar trend was also noticed in other parts of the world. By 1850 industrial advancement was significant with accomplishments in strategic management. The process of gradual accomplishment through strategic management gained some momentum during the first World War. During the second world war, the world was divided into camps. Trading of commodities between one territory and other was suspended because of the division of process. To meet the requirement of the war every nation had to develop a new strategy, industrial firms were asked to develop new under-substitute of products and the war footing in order to meet the defence requirements. Thus significant changes took place in the environment in which business operated when war was over; competition for business became major issues throughout the world since there had been rapid growth both in size and complexities of business organization. Thus, competition for business and market share change in line with the strategy of war.

Management components opened: "Business is also like war in one respect. In war a nation is to fight with enemy to win. In business every organization has to win with competitors in competitive market to capture and expand the market share. The objectives in both the issues remained same to win for survival, growth and development." In 1962 business historian, Afraid D. Chandler defined strategy as "the determination of the basic long term goals and objectives of an enterprise and the adoption of course of action necessary for carrying out these goals."

In the decade between 1965 and 1975, the term strategy became more popular in the business world as opposed to policy only and was inducted in management studies for wider use of concept in business management. The changes in the industrial scenario were significant in the early 1970s. The commercial climate and international business environment was beginning to change and become more and more complex with rapid development of technology, global competition was starting to make on impact and markets were expanding and maturing.

The concept of strategic management is much broader today. It includes various activities such as determination, formulation, implementation and evolution of strategy. Thus, strategic management has assumed and attained the most important task of management which includes a set of decisions and actions resulting in the formulation and implementation of strategies designed to accomplish the ultimate objectives of an organization.

DIMENSIONS OF STRATEGIC DECISIONS

Strategic decisions dimensions are listed below:

Top Management Decisions are Based on the Strategic Issues

Strategic decisions consist of several areas of organization like marketing, production, finance, accounting, human resource management and research and development operations. Top management involves in decision making is an obvious factor for business activities of the organization. Only at this level is for understanding and anticipating broad analysis, implication and ramification and power to authorize the resource allocations necessary for implementation of strategic issues.

Strategic Issues Involve the Allocation of Huge Amount of Organization Resource

Strategic decisions involved substantial resource allocation for functional department of the organization. Money, material, men, machine, method and markets are essential resource of the business. These are secured internally and externally from the organization's environment.

Strategic Issues are Likely to Make a Significant Role on the Long-term Prosperity, Survival and Growth of the Organization

The strategic decisions are committed the organization for a long period of time typically for five years or more. Once an organization has been committed itself to particular strategic options. It has developed competitive image and advantages are usually tied to committed strategy, therefore, organization become known in certain markets, for certain products with certain characteristic. Therefore, strategic decisions have enduring effects on organization for positive or negative results performance oriented.

Strategic Issues are Future Oriented

Strategic decisions are based on future forecast made by the strategic manager of the organization. Special importance is on developing projections which will enable the organization to select the most promising options. In the complex and competition free environment has build up a successful organization in most proactive stance toward changes.

Strategic Decisions Usually have Major Multi-functional or Multi-business Consequence

A strategy decision is coordinative decisions like customer mix, competitive emphasis or organizational structure which necessarily involve a number of organization's business unit, functions, divisions, programme units. These areas will be affected by allocation and reallocation of responsibilities and resource related to the functional department decisions.

Strategic Decisions Consider External Environmental Factors of the Organizations

All business organizations exist in an open market system. Strategic manager has beyond their control of the external environmental factors like legal, economic, cultural and competitive force. Therefore, the strategic manager is to accomplish the organizations objectives and goal in its future competitive situations. The strategic manager looks beyond the limits of organization's own operations and considers the competitors, customers, suppliers, creditors, government and labor.

LEVELS OF STRATEGIC MANAGEMENT

There are three levels in strategic management. They are as outlined:

- Corporate-level Strategic Management
- Business-level Strategic Management
- Functional-level Strategic Management

Alternative 1: Single business firm

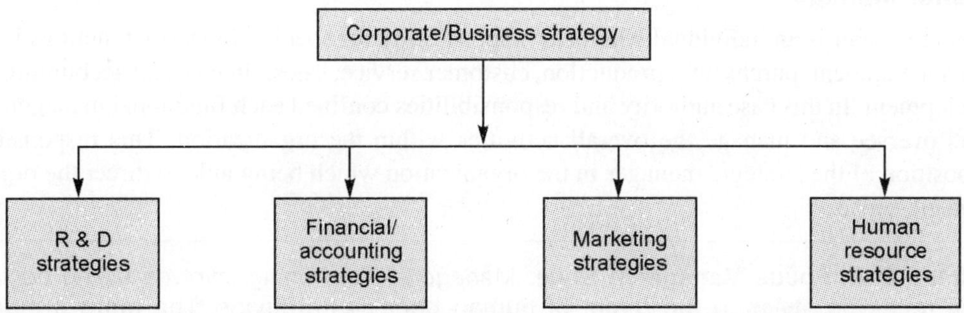

Alternative 2: Multiple-business firms

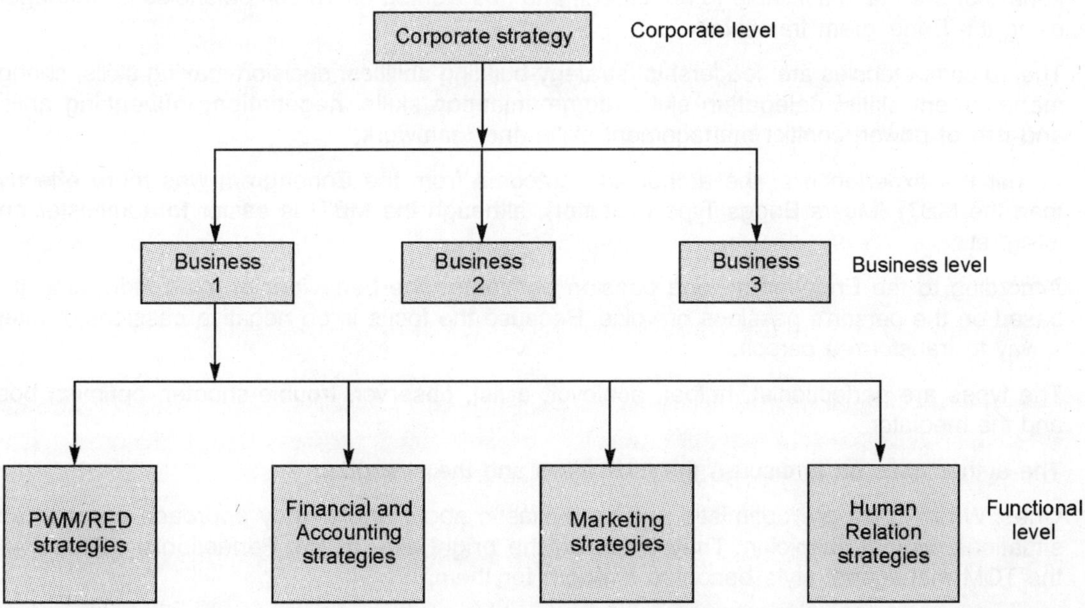

Figure 2.1. Strategic Management Structure

ROLE OF MANAGERS AT VARIOUS LEVELS

In most sophisticated organizations, one can find two types of managers:

- General Manager
- Functional Manager

General Manager

General manager is individual who bears the responsibility for the overall performance of the organization. He has the responsibility of the survival, growth and development of the organization. He has to guide and monitor the performance of the organization with effective utilization of scarce and available resource.

Functional Manager

Functional manager is an individual who bear responsibility for specific business functions like human resource development, purchasing, production, customer service, sales, finance and accounting, research and development. In this case authority and responsibilities confined each functional manager. Strategic managers oversee and manage the overall activities within the organization. This responsibility has unique position of the strategic manager in the organization which being able to direct the organization in a strategic sense.

Exhibit 2.2: In Focus Managerial Style. Managerial functioning involves taking decisions, which reflect in styles in the realm of human behavioural styles. The more a manager understands these behavioural styles, higher is the facilitation in the exercise of decision-making.

According to the author, managerial competence is increased when other possibilities for behaviour are made available to managers, and has worked on 10 competencies for managers using the Enneagram framework.

The 10 competencies are: leadership, strategy-building abilities, decision-making skills, change management skills, delegation skills, communication skills, negotiation, influencing ability and use of power, conflict management skills and teamwork.

As per the experience of the author, the outcome from the Enneagram was more effective than the MBTI (Myers Briggs Type Indicator), although the MBTI is easier to administer and interpret.

According to the Enneagram, one passion dominates the behaviour of each individual. It is based on the person's passions or voice. Because the focus is on negative passions, it offers a way to transform a person.

The types are perfectionist, helper, achiever, artist, observer, trouble-shooter, optimist, boss and the mediator.

The author goes on to discuss the nine flaws and the strengths:

Ones: When Ones are optimistic and enthusiastic about future, they approach persons and situations without suspicion. They focus on the bright side of life. Perfectionist attitude and the TQM managerial style becomes strength for them.

Twos: When Twos strive to express themselves as very empathetic persons, they become altruistic and their customer service style becomes strength.

(Contd...)

Threes: When Threes take on a greater loyalty to their whole group then their achievement orientation and MBO style becomes their strength.

Fours: When Fours make an effort to counteract disorder and error in the pursuit of perfection they become hard working and are able to overcome their moodiness, and their innovative style becomes strength for them.

Fives: When Fives take pride in being strong persons, they gravitate naturally to power and when they become involved with other persons, their strategic management becomes strength.

Sixes: When Sixes are seldom upset by inner conflicts, they make excellent reconcilers. When they overcome their worries, their bureaucratic style is an advantage and they are participative managers.

Sevens: When Sevens become more observant and empathetic, and accept pain, failures and hard work, their optimistic style becomes an asset for them.

Eights: When Eights seek out people who need their help, their autocratic style becomes strength.

Nines: When Nines set objectives for themselves and others take on the image of being efficient persons, then their participative style becomes an asset for them.

The author states that an understanding of Enneagram type helps one to understand managerial style and other managers' styles. This identification is also a source of comfort because it shows that one is not alone in this particular managerial style.

The book is full of analytical descriptions and illustrations of managerial styles and is written in an understandable and formal style.

However, according to the reviewer, whether it is MBTI or Enneagram, the questionnaire administering method of determining managerial styles has a iot of limitations.

On the contrary, an ideal way to develop managers should be to make them understand the various styles (analytically), appreciate them in their own merits and finally, try to develop in them skills/ability of adopting the appropriate style, depending on the particular or contextual need, rather than prescribing ideal percentile patterns, which may result as products of immaturity.

Source: The Hindu, Dated 2002/07/08

A typical multi-business company has three levels of management as listed below:

- The corporate level
- The business level
- Functional level

General managers are found at the first two of these levels, but their strategic roles are different which depending on their sphere of responsibility. Functional managers too have a strategic role, though of a different kind, now we shall look at each of the three levels and strategic roles assigned to managers within them.

Corporate Level

The corporate level of strategic management consists of the chief executive officers/president/chairman, the board of directors, senior executives, corporate staff and administrative officers. They are the responsible for the apex for decision making within the organization. The CEO is the main general manager at this level. His or her strategic role is to overlook the development of the strategic issues for decisions in the organization. Typically, this role involves defining the mission and goals of the organization, in determining organization business it should be in allocating resource among the different organization functions and providing leadership for the rest of the organization.

Business Level

In multi-business organization, the business level consists of the business and corporate managers and their support staff. In a single industry company, the business and corporate levels are very important and equal. Business level is self-contained and has its own functional departments like as finance, production, purchase, marketing and human resource departments.

The main strategic managers at the business level are the heads of the functional departments. Their strategic role is to translate general statements, mission and vision of the business decision strategies for organization. Business level managers are concerned with strategies which are specific to a particular business.

Functional Level

Functional managers bear responsibility for the specific business functions like human resource development, manufacturing, production, marketing, accounting and finance, research, and development departments' functions. Functional level strategies are playing significant role in strategic decisions and buildup their own responsibility to develop functional strategies in manufacturing, marketing, R&D, and so on. This help to fulfill the strategic objectives that set by business and corporate level general managers. It is important for general managers to listen and develop to strategies at competitive environment of business. An equal responsibility of the managers at the functional level involves strategy implementation in terms of the execution of corporate and business level decisions.

Characteristic of Strategic Management Decisions at Different Levels

Characteristic of strategic management decisions at corporate level

- Corporate level decisions tend to be value oriented, conceptual, and less concrete than those at the business or function level of strategy formulation and implementation.
- Corporate level decisions are also characterized by greater risk, cost and profit potential, as well as by longer time planning and greater needs for flexibility.
- These characteristics are logical consequences of the more far-reaching futuristic, innovative and pervasive nature of corporate–level activity.
- Instance of corporate level decisions include the level of choice of business, dividend policies, source of long-term financing and priorities for growth.

Characteristic of Strategic Management Decisions at Functional Level

- Functional level decisions principally involve action–oriented operational issues.

- These decisions are made periodically and lead direct implementation of some part of the overall strategy formulated at the corporate and business levels.
- Functional level decisions are relating short range and involve low risk and modest costs because they are dependent an available resources.
- Functional decisions usually determined actions requiring minimal organization wide co-operations.
- Functional level decisions are usually concrete and quantifiable; they receive critical attention even though their comparative profit potential is low.
- Functional level decisions include generic versus brand name labeling, basic versus applied R&D, high versus low inventory levels, general versus specific purpose production equipment, and close versus loose supervision.

Characteristic of Strategic Management Decisions at Business Level

- Bridging corporate and functional level decisions are those made at the business level.
- Business level decisions are less costly risky, and potentially profitable than corporate level decisions, but they are more costly, risky, and potentially profitable than functional level decisions.
- Business level decisions involve plant location, marketing segmentation and geographic coverage and distribution channels.

BENEFITS OF STRATEGIC MANAGEMENT

- The strategic management approach emphasizes interaction by managers at all levels of the organization at hierarchy in planning and implementation.
- Strategies formulation activities should enhance the problem prevention capabilities of the organization. As a result of encouraging and rewarding subordinates attention to planning considerations, executives are aided in monitoring and forecasting responsibilities by workers who are made alert about the needs of strategic planning.
- All strategic plans are attached the employee motivation and morale should improve in terms of employees better productivity and reward relationship.
- Gaps and overlaps in activities among diverse individuals and groups should be reduced as participation in strategy formulation.
- Resistance to change should be reduced. The required participation helps eliminate the uncertainty associated with the change, which is at the root of most resistance.

RISKS OF STRATEGIC MANAGEMENT

- Strategic management is relatively recognized that the strategic management process is costly in terms of time invested by the chief executive of the organization.
- If the formulators of strategy are not intimately involved in implementation, individual responsibility for input to the decision process and subsequent conclusions can be avoided.
- Strategies must be trained to anticipate, minimize or constructively respond when participating subordinated become disappointed over unattained expectations.

QUESTIONS FOR DISCUSSIONS

1. Define strategic management.
2. Explain strategic management.
3. What are the characteristics of strategic planning?
4. Discuss the importance and limitations of the strategic management.
5. Write short notes on
   - Corporate level strategy
   - Functional level strategy
   - Business level strategy.
1. Discuss the dimensions of strategic decisions.
2. Briefly describe the evolution of the strategic management.
3. Discuss the strategic management characteristics at various levels.
4. What are the benefits of the strategic management?
5. Discuss the risks of the strategic management.
6. Describe the scope of the strategic management.

REFERENCES

1. A.A. Thomson and A.J. Strickland 111, *Strategy Formulation and Implementation Tasks of the General Manager*, Plano, TX: Business Publications,1983.
2. A.A. Thomson and A.J. Strickland, *Strategic Management Concepts and Cases*, Tata McGraw –Hill Publishing Company Limited, New Delhi, 2003.
3. Collins, James C., and Jerry I. Porras, *Building your Company's Vision*, Harvard Business Review 74, no. 5 (September–October 1996), pp. 65-77.
4. Porter, Michael E. *What is Strategy*? Harvard Business Review 74, no. 6 (November–December 1996), pp. 61-78.
5. Shaw, Gordon; Robert Brown; and Philip Bromiley. *Strategic Stories*: *How 3M is Rewriting Business Planning*. Harvard Business Review 76. no. 3 (May–June 1998), pp. 41-50.
6. Mintzberg, Henry, Bruce Ahlstrand ; and Joseph Lampel, *Strategy Safari: A Guided Tour through the Wilds of Strategic Management*. New York: Free Press, 1998.
7. Caves, R.E., and M.E. Porter, *From Entry Barriers: Conjectural Decisions and Contrived Deterrence to New Competition*. Quarterly Journal of Economics 91 (1976), pp. 421-34.
8. Porter, M.E., *Industrial Market Structures and Economic Performance*. Review of Economics and Statistics 61 (1979), pp. 214–27.
9. John, A. Pearce II, Richard B. Robinson, JR. *Strategic Management Strategy Formulation and Implementation*. A.I.T.B.S. Publishers & Distributors (Regd), New Delhi, 2002.
10. Hofer, C.W., and D. Schendel. *Strategy Formulation: Analytical Concepts*. St.Paul, Minn.: West Publishing, 1978.

17. Karger, D.W., and Z. A. Malik. *Long–Range Planning and Organizational Performance.* Long–Range Planning, December 1975, pp. 60–64.
18. Kudla, R.J. *Elements of Effective Corporate Planning*. Long-Range Planning, August 1976, pp. 82–93.
19. Pearce, J.A., II, and W.A. Randolph. *Improving Strategy Formulation Pedagogies by Recognizing Behavioral Aspects*, Exchange, December 1980, pp. 7–10.
20. Robinson, R.B., Jr. *The Importance of 'Outsiders' in Small Firm Strategic Planning*. Academy of Management Journal, March 1982, pp. 80-93.

Chapter – 3

Strategic Management Process

CONTENTS

- Introduction
- Strategic management process
- Strategic management model
- Components of the strategic management
- Limitations of the strategic management model
- Tasks in strategic management
- Five force model
- Strategic groups
- Limitations on the five forces and strategic group models

LEARNING OBJECTIVES

We shall discuss the following issues:

- Discuss the strategic management process.
- Briefly, explain the components and limitations of the strategic management.
- Describe the Porter's five-force model and its limitations.
- Discuss the strategic groups and its implications.

INTRODUCTION

Strategic management process includes a set of managerial decisions and actions which determined the long-term planning and effective performance of superior objectives and goals of the organization. It involves important aspects like setting the organization mission, company or organization profile, external environment, operating industry, multinational analysis, developing objectives, development of strategic analysis and choice and implementing the strategies, to accomplishment of the long-term objectives and short-term objectives and finally control, monitor, guide and evaluate the organization, objectives.

STRATEGIC MANAGEMENT PROCESS/STEPS

Strategic management process/steps as listed below:

- Define organization or company mission
- Analysis of business environment
- Identifying the present strategies and objectives
- Evaluating the present strategy
- Analysis strategic choice
- Development of strategy
- Formulation strategy
- Implementation of the strategy
- Control, monitor, guide and evaluate the strategy

STRATEGIC MANAGEMENT MODEL

Strategic management model provides three major functions listed below:

- It provides a visual representation of the major components of the entire strategic management process. This model also shows how the components are related and how they are related throughout the process.
- This model provides the general overview of the strategic management process of the organization.
- This model recommends the strategy formulation, implementation and control, monitor, guide and evaluation of the organization objectives.

COMPONENTS OF STRATEGIC MANAGEMENT

Strategic management components are listed below:

- Company mission
- Company profile
- Environment analysis
- Strategic analysis and choice
- Long-term objectives
- Grand strategies
- Annual objectives
- Functional strategies
- Policies
- Institutionalizing strategy
- Control and evaluation strategy

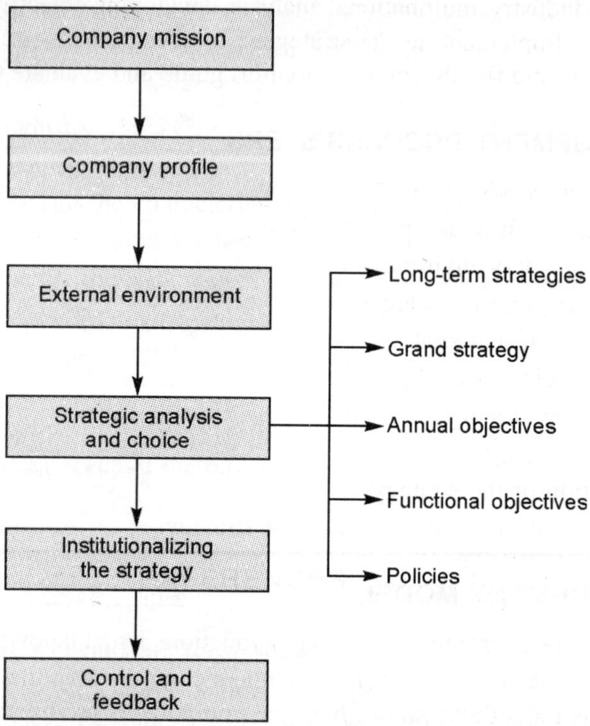

Figure 3.1 Strategic Management Model

Above are the important components of strategic management. Components of strategic management provide process of the strategic management. We shall discuss the strategic management components as below:

Organization/Company Mission

Organization/company mission statement is the basic issue point of the strategic management. Organization/company mission will guide future execution policies and objectives. It sets the policies and objectives which are formulated for execution of policies and objectives of business organization. The mission statement contains the business philosophy of strategic decision makers, a definition of the organization/company's business, a statement of the major goals of the organization/company. The organization/company mission explains the product, market, and technological areas of the business.

Organization/Company Profile

Organization/company profile is to determine strength, weakness, opportunity, and threats of the business. It involves to the internal environment of the organization and its functions like marketing, production, accounting, finance, research and development, human resource management and customer relations. These functions are identifying the quantity, research and development, method, materials and production which are normally available to the organization. An organization/company profile has depicted own strengths and weakness of the business.

External Environment

It is the third component of the strategic management process. It is the analysis of the organization external environment. External environment consists of all conditions and forces are typically beyond the control of organization. The strategic management component shows the external environment which consists of the operating/micro and remote/macro environment.

The operating /micro-environment consist of force and conditions within a specific industry and specific competitive operating advantages. It is external to organization which influence to selection and attainment of alternative goals of strategy combination. A change in the operating environment brings results from the strategic action taken by the organization or its competitors, consumers, users, suppliers and creditors.

The remote/macro environment consists of economic, social, government, legal, cultural, international, competitive, demand, demography and technological factors that may affect the organization.

Strategic Analysis and Choice

Simultaneous assessment of strategic environment enables an organization to identify strength, weakness, opportunity and threats. The comparison of the strength, weakness, opportunity, and threats are normally referred to SWOT analysis. This process results in the selection of strategic choice. It is meant for the combination of the long-term objectives and grand strategy that will optimally position the organization in encompass functional level, business level and corporate level and global strategies. The process of strategic management choice requires the organization to identify the set of functional level, business level, corporate level and global strategies that would best enable it to survival and prosper in the fast changing and globally competitive environment analysis which characterizes most modern industries in the world.

Strategic analysis involves matching each of the possible and desirable interactive opportunities with reasonable long-term objectives and targets. In turn, these are matched with the most promising i.e., as grand strategies for achieving desired results. Each of the sets of alternatives is than individually and comparatively to determine the single set or group of sets that expected to best achieve the company mission. The chosen set is known as the *strategic choice*.

Critical assessment of strategic alternatives initially involves developing criteria for comparing one set of alternatives with all others as if in making choice; organization strategic involves evaluating alternatives that are rarely wholly acceptable or wholly unacceptable.

Among the factors used in assessing strategic choice alternatives are strategic executives' attitudes towards risks, flexibility, stability, growth, profitability and diversification.

Long-Term Objectives

Long-term objectives typically seek five year or more period of time. Long-term objectives are typically involved the following areas of the organization:

- Profitability
- Return on investment
- Competitive position
- Technological leadership
- Productivity

- Employee relations
- Public responsibility
- Employee development
- To be greatest value, each objective must be specific, measurable, achievable, and consistent with other objectives of the organization.

Exhibit 3.1: Objectives of IOCL

Objectives to serve the national interests in the oil and related sectors in accordance and consistent with government policies.

To ensure and maintain continuous and smooth supplies of petroleum products by way of crude refining, transportation and marketing activities and to provide appropriate assistance to the consumer to conserve and use petroleum products efficiently.

To earn a reasonable rate of interest on investment.

To work towards the achievement of self-sufficiency in the field of oil refining by setting up adequate capacity and to build up expertise in laying of crude and petroleum product pipelines.

To create a strong research and development base in the field of oil refining and stimulate the development of new product formulations with a view to minimise/eliminate their imports and to have next generation products.

To maximise utilisation of the existing facilities in order to improve efficiency and increase productivity.

To optimise utilisation of its refining capacity and maximise distillate yield from refining of crude to minimise foreign exchange outgo.

To minimise fuel consumption in refineries and stock losses in marketing operations to effect energy conservation.

To further enhance distribution network for providing assured service to customers throughout the country through expansion of reseller network as per Marketing Plan/Government approval.

To avail of all viable opportunities, both national and global, arising out of the liberalisation policies being pursued by the Government of India.

To achieve higher growth through integration, mergers, acquisitions and diversification by harnessing new business opportunities like petrochemicals, power, lube business, consultancy abroad and exploration and production.

Obligations

Towards customers and dealers

To provide prompt, courteous and efficient service and quality products at fair and reasonable prices.

Towards suppliers

To ensure prompt dealings with integrity, impartiality and courtesy and promote ancillary industries.

(Contd...)

Towards employees
Develop their capability and advancement through appropriate training and career planning.

Expeditious redressal of grievances
Fair dealings with recognised representatives of employees in pursuance of healthy trade union practice and sound personnel policies.

Towards community
To develop techno-economically viable and environment-friendly products for the benefit of the people.

To encourage progressive indigenous manufacture of products and materials so as to substitute imports.

To ensure safety in operations and highest standards of environment protection in its manufacturing plants and townships by taking suitable and effective measures.

Towards defence services
To maintain adequate supplies to Defence Services during normal and emergency situations as per their requirement at different locations.

Financial objectives
To ensure adequate return on the capital employed and maintain a reasonable annual dividend on its equity capital.

To ensure maximum economy in expenditure
To manage and operate the facilities in an efficient manner so as to generate adequate internal resources to meet revenue cost and requirements for project investment, without budgetary support.

To develop long-term corporate plans to provide for adequate growth of the activities of the Corporation.

To endeavour to reduce the cost of production of petroleum products by means of systematic cost control measures.

To endeavour to complete all planned projects within the stipulated time and cost estimates.

Source: IOCL

Grand Strategy/Generic Strategy

Grand strategies is the combination of the stability, expansion, retrenchment, concentration, market development, product development, innovation, horizontal integration, vertical integration, joint venture, concentric diversification, and conglomerate diversification, divestitute and liquidation strategy. All these strategic alternatives are considered as grand strategies. These are also termed as generic strategy.

Annual/Short-term Objectives

Annual/short-term objectives typically seek results of the organization within a year period are annual/short-term objectives. Strategic management involves the long-term planning and also co-operate with short-term/annual objectives of the organization without creating constraint for the long-term objectives.

Functional Strategies

Business functions strategies are marketing, finance, accounting, production, R&D and human resource strategy. These strategies are specific and integrative plan of action. Most strategic managers attempt to develop an operating strategy for each related to set of annual/short-term objectives.

Policies

Policies are directives which are designed to broad guidelines of the organization. It concerned with thinking, decisions, actions and responsibilities of managers and their subordinates for implementing the organization's strategy. Policies are providing guidelines for establishing and controlling the ongoing operating process.

Institutionalizing the Strategy

Institutionalizing strategy is the combination of the structure, leadership and culture of the organization. Above three organizational elements provide the fundamental long-term objectives of the organization. Institutionalizing the organization's strategy influence to the following factors:

- Structure
- Leadership
- Culture

Control and Evaluation

An implementation of strategy must be monitored and controlled to determine the extent to which objectives, mission, vision, philosophy and goals are to be achieved. The process of formulating strategy is largely subjective despite often-extensive efforts at objectivity. In the final analysis, an organization is to accomplish the designated objectives and goals.

LIMITATION OF THE STRATEGIC COMPONENTS MODEL

Limitations are important to understand the strategic management components model. Major limitations are as follows:

- The model is holistic
- The model is analytical
- The model is nonpolitical

Holistic

- The strategic management process involves strategy formulation, implementation and control. It is unrealistic because of potential tendency to minimize difficulties of the implementation of the strategy. In the following cases:
- Manager face greater risk, if planning may be inflexible.
- Holistic approach is too difficult to the development of strategies. It appears in superior of the organization.

Analytic

Strategic management model generally explains the logical or analytical process in many businesses actually use in their strategic activities. However, it does not describe the procedure and practice or routines necessary to carry out each process.

Non-Political

It is the third limitation of the strategic management model. The strategic management largely devoid of subjective assessments, biased interpretations, human errors, self-serving voting by individual managers, intuitive decision making, favoritism and other forms of political activities.

TASKS IN STRATEGIC MANAGEMENT

Hofer and Schendel have proposed six basic tasks in the strategic management process:

- A set of organization goals must be established.
- Environment-external influence —forecasting of environment conditions that the organization may expect to face in future.
- Strategy formulation task—a model of strategy formulation that must take into account the organizational goals and objectives.
- To evaluate past strategy and estimate the degree of success of future strategy.
- Strategy implementation—basically administrative tasks setting aside administrative goals in favour of larger organizational goals.
- Strategic control—the process of checking the strategy implementation against the strategies plan at period or critical intervals to determine of the corporation/organization is moving towards its strategic objectives.

FIVE FORCE MODEL

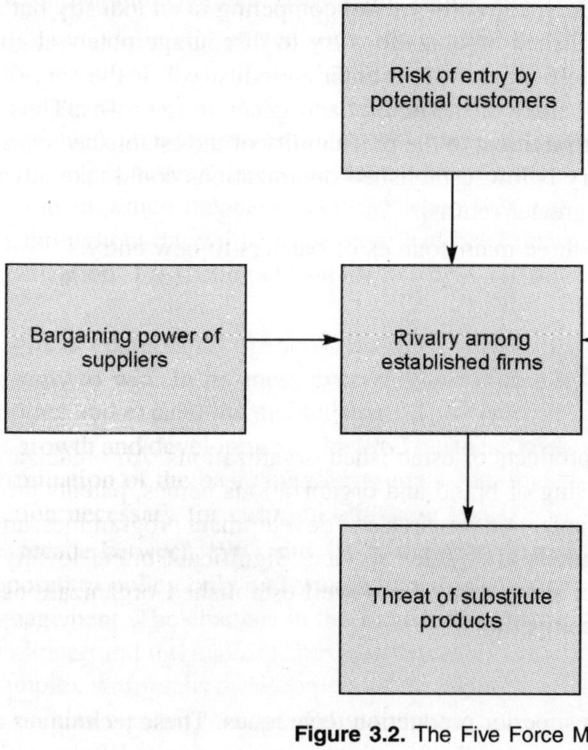

Figure 3.2. The Five Force Model

Organization offering products and services which are close substitute for each other. Close substitute are products and service. They are satisfied the essential consumer needs and desire. The task facing strategic managers is to analyze competitive force in an industry environment in order to identify the strengths, weakneses, opportunities and threats confronting an organization. Michael E. Porter, professor of the Harvard School of Business Administration has developed a framework, which is known as Five Forces Model. It appears in Fig. 3.2 helps to managers in their analysis of competitive force of the organization. This model focuses on five forces which shape to create competition within an industry. Five forces are as below:

- The risk of new entry by potential competitors
- Risk of entry by potential customers
- The degree of rivalry among established companies within an industries
- The bargaining power of supplier
- The closeness of substitute to the industry's product

Porter argues that the stronger each of these forces, the more limited is the ability of established organization to raise prices and earn greater profits. Within Porter's Framework, a strong competitive force regards as a threat since it depresses profits. A weak competitive force views as on opportunity for an organization to earn greater profits. Because of these forces beyond an organization's direct control like industry evaluation, the strength of five forces may change through time. In such circumstances, the task facing strategic managers is to recognize opportunities and threats in order to develop and to formulate appropriate strategic opportunities.

Potential Competitors

Potential competitors are organizations which currently are not competing in an industry but they have the capability to do if they choose. Established organizations try to discourage potential competitors from entering to the industry. Since the more organizations enter an industry, it is the very difficult for the established organizations to hold their share of the market and generate to profits. Thus, high risk of entry by potential competitors represents a threat to the profitability of the established organsiations. On the other hand, if the risk of new entry is low, established organizations could take advantages of this opportunity to raise prices and earn greater returns.

Economist Joe Bain who identified three main sources of barriers to new entry:

- Brand loyalty
- Absolute cost advantage
- Economies of scale

Brand Loyalty

Brand loyalty is buyer's priority for the products of established organizations. An organization create brand loyalty through continuous advertising of brand and organizations names, patents protection of products, products innovation through organization research and development programmes, an emphasis on high product quality and providing goods after sales service. Significant brand loyalty makes it difficult for new entrants to take market share away from well-established organizations. Thus, it reduces the threat of entry by potential competitors.

Absolute Cost Advantages

Absolute cost advantages can arises from superior production techniques. These techniques arises due to past experience, patents, hidden process; control of particular inputs required for production like labor, materials, equipment or management skills. These access to cheaper funds because exiting organization represent low risks than established organizations. If established organizations have an absolute cost advantages, then again the threat of entry decreases.

Exhibit 3.2: Cement companies adopt innovative cost-cutting measures FOR cement companies innovation may be the key to cost competitiveness. Hence, larger cement companies such as Grasim and Gujarat Ambuja are seen to be shifting to a number of innovative cost-cutting measures to enhance bottomlines.

These include bypassing the dealers to sell cement directly to the customer, shifting from the traditional rail-road option to cheaper sea transportation to target distant markets and even using crushed sugarcane for meeting fuel requirements.

According to an ICRA analysis, over 80 per cent of the cement is sold currently in India is through the dealer route. "The bigger cement companies are now shifting towards a dealer-free route to supply to bulk consumers, including builders and infrastructure companies to save on the dealer margin," an industry source said. Customers are encouraged to contact the cement companies directly with their requirements, following which the manufacturer delivers the requisite quantity of cement to their doorsteps. The move also gives the companies better price competitiveness as compared to those servicing customers through the dealer route, industry players said.

Bigger players are also saving on logistics expenses, which is one of the major operating costs faced by the industry. Companies such as Gujarat Ambuja are extensively relying on the coastal transportation route to service the southern market, rather than on rail or road, according to industry analysts. Several cement companies are also using high capacity Volvo trucks for road transportation to cut down on costs, industry sources said. In order to bring down energy costs, most of the cement companies have already shifted entirely to captive power stations and are using a variety of fuels, including pet coke and lignite. Gujarat Ambuja, in fact, has partially replaced coal with crushed sugarcane as a fuel for its Gujarat plant, according to analysts.

Cement companies are also tracking the international polypropylene prices to strike deals with manufacturers of polypropylene bags, used as packaging material in the country, according to ICRA. The scope for saving through this route is enormous, since in India cement is almost entirely sold in 50 kg bags, as opposed to it being sold in bulk in most other countries. Some of the domestic cement companies are also reportedly considering the bulk-sale route to optimise costs, industry sources said.

Source: Business Line, Dated June 29, 2004

Economies of Scale

Economies of scale are the cost advantages associated with large organization size. Sources of scale economies include cost reductions gained through mass producing a standardized output, discount on bulk purchase of raw material inputs and components parts, the spreading of fixed costs over a large volume. A new entrant faces the dilemma of either entering on a small scale and its result suffering a significant cost advantages or taking a very large risk by entering on a large scale and bearing significant capital costs. A further risk of large-scale entry results to increase the supply of the product will reduce the prices.

Rivalry Among Established Companies

It is the second of Porter's five competitive forces, it is the extent of rivalry among established organization within the industry. When this competitive force is weak, business organization have an opportunity to raise prices to earn greater profits. But if it is strong, business organization have an opportunity to reduce prices to earn fewer profits. It is significant due to price competition, including price wars, may result from the intense rivalry. Price competition limits reduce the profitability on sales. Thus intense rivalry among established organizations within industry is largely a function of three factors are listed below:

- Industry competitive structure
- Demand conditions
- The height of exist barriers in the industry

Competitive Structure

Competitive structure refers to the numbers, size, and distribution of products and service in the organization in an industry. Different competitive structures have different implications for rivalry. Fragmented industries consist of a large number of small or medium sized organizations, none of which is in a position to dominate the industry. A consolidated industry dominates by small number of large organization or, in extreme cases, a monopoly (by just in one organization). Fragmented industries included agriculture, video-rental, health clubs, real estate and pharmaceuticals etc.

Low entry barriers and commodity-type products are hard to differentiate characterize many fragmented industries. The combinations of these characteristics tend to result in boom and bust cycles of the industry. Low entry barrier indicates whenever demand is strong and their impacts on profits are high. In this circumstance, there will be a flood of new entrants to cash in the boom.

In the case consolidated industry, the competitive action of the organization directly affects the market share of its rivals, forcing to response from them. The result of the competitive interdependence can be dangerous to competitive spiral with rival companies. They are trying to undercut each other's prices of the products and service is pushing to industry and their profit down in this process. More typically, when price wars are threat, organization competes on nonprime factors like product quality and design characteristics. This type of competition constitutes an attempt to build brand loyalty and minimize the likelihood of a price war.

Demand Conditions

Industry demand conditions are another important determinant of the intensity of rivalry among the established organizations. Growing demand trends provide expansion and greater expansion of the production activity. When demand is growing, ultimate result is a searching of entrants of customers or if existing customers are purchasing more of an industry products. When demand is growing, organization can increases revenues without taking a market share away from other companies.

Therefore, declining demand result in more competition from rivalry organization. It is very difficult to maintaining revenue and market share of the organization. Consumers are leaving market place or when individual consumer buying less. Therefore, declines the demand, declining demand constitutes a major threat to organization.

Exit Barriers

When industry demand is declining because of exit barriers are serious competitive threat for organization. Economic, strategic and emotional factors are treated as exit barriers. It keeps organization competing in an industry even when returns are very low. Organization can become locked into an unfavorable industry when exit barriers are high. Excess productive capacity tends to lead to intensified price competition, with companies cutting prices in an attempt to obtain the orders needed to utilize their idle capacity.

Exit barriers include the following:

- Investment in plant, machinery and equipment that have no alternative uses and cannot be sold off if the organization wishes to leave the industry; it has to write-off the book value of the assets.
- High fixed cost exists like severance pay to workers who are being made redundant.
- Emotional attachments to an industry, as when a company is unwilling to exist from its original industry for sentimental reasons.
- Strategic relationships between business units. For instance, within multi-industry organization, a low return business unit may provide vital inputs for a high return business based in another industry. Thus, the company may be unwilling to exist from the low return business.
- Economic dependence on the industry, as when company is not diversified and so relies on the industry for its income.

The Bargaining Power of Buyers

It is third of Porter's five competitive forces; it is the bargaining power of buyer. Buyers can be influenced as competitive threat when they force down prices of the products and service. It means that when buyer demand is higher quality and better service which increase operating costs of the products and service of the organization.

According to Porter's buyers are more powerful in the following situations:

The supply industry which consists of many small organizations and the buyers are few in number and large. These situations allow the buyers to dominate supply organizations.

- The buyer purchase in bulk in such situations, buyers can be bargain for price reductions of the products and service organization.
- The supply industry depends on the buyers orders, buyers can bargained for price reductions of the products and service of the organization.
- The buyer can switch orders between supply organizations at a low cost, thereby playing off organizations against each other to force down prices.
- It is economically feasible for the buyers to purchase the products and service from the several organizations at once.
- The buyer causes threat to supply their own needs through vertical integration, its impact on the price reducing of the products and service organization.

The Bargaining Power of Suppliers

The bargaining power of suppliers is the fourth of Porter's competitive force. Supplier influenced as a threat when they are capable to force up the price that organization must pay for products and service or reduced the quality of goods supplied thereby, reducing the organizational profitability.

In other words, weak supplier gives opportunity to organization to force down the prices and demand higher quality. As with the buyer, the capability of supplier to make demands on an organization depends on power relative to organization. According to Porter's suppliers are most powerful in the following cases:

- The product suppliers have sell substitutes and are important to organization.
- The organization industry is not an important to customer to the suppliers have does not depend on the organization's industry, and supplier have little incentive to reduce prices or improve quality of the products and service.
- The suppliers of the respective products are differentiated which is to more expensive for organization to switch from one supplier to another. In such circumstance, the organizations depend on its supplier and cannot play them off against each other.
- To raise prices, suppliers use can threat of vertically integrating forward into the industry and competing directly with the organization products and service.
- Buying organization cannot use the threat of vertically directly with the organization product and service.
- The buying organization can not use the threat of vertically integrating backward supplying their own needs as a means to reduce the product and service.

The Threat of Substitute Products

The fifth and final force in the Porter's model is the threat of substitute products—the product of industries that serve identical consumer needs as those of the industry being analysis.

For instance, organizations in the coffee industry compete directly with those in the tea and soft drink industries. In the case of substitute products, if the price of the coffee rises too much relative to that of tea or soft drinks, then coffee drinkers will switch from coffee to those substitutes. The existence of close substitutes creates a strong competitive threat, limiting the price an organization.

STRATEGIC GROUPS

The Concept of Strategic Groups

Generally, an industry often differ from each other with respect to several factors like distributions channels used, market segment served, product quality, technological leadership, customer service, pricing policy, advertising policy, and promotions, within most industries. It is possible to observe groups of organization in which each member follows the same basic strategy as other organizations in the group but strategy is different from one followed by companies in other groups. These groups of organizations are known as strategic groups.

Normally, a limited number of groups capture the essence of the strategic difference between companies with an industry.

Implications of Strategic Groups

The concept of strategic groups has a number of implications for industry analysis and the identification of opportunities and threats are as outlined:

- Organization immediate competitors are those in its strategic groups. Since all the organizations in a strategic groups are pursuing similar strategies, consumer tend to view the products of such organization as being direct substitute for each other thus major threat to a company is profitability can come from within its own strategic groups.
- Different strategic groups can have a different standing with respect to each of Porter's five competitive forces. It means, that, the risk of new entry by potential competitors, the degree

of rivalry among organizations within a group, the bargaining power of suppliers, and the competitive force of substitute products can all vary in intensity among different strategic groups within the same industry.

LIMITATIONS ON THE FIVE FORCES AND STRATGIC GROUP MODEL

The major limitation of the five-force model and strategic groups' models:

- Present a static picture of competition which highlights the role of innovation and
- De–emphasize the significance of individual company differences while overemphasizing the importance of industry and strategic group structure as ascertainments of company profit rates.

Static Models in a Dynamic World

Over any reasonable length of time, in many industries competition process are driven by innovation. An organization is to pioneer new products, processes, or strategies can often earn huge profits. This prospect gives organizations strongly incentive to seek innovative products, processes and strategies.

Successful innovation can revolutionize industry structure. In a recent decades, one of the most common feature is innovation has been to lower and fixed costs of production, there by reducing barriers to entry and allowing new, and smaller organization to compete with large established organizations.

Michael Porter, the propagator of the five forces and strategic group concepts has explicitly described role of innovation in revolution industry structure. Porter's now talks of innovations as "unfreezing" and "reshaping" industry structure. His view seems to be that after a period of turbulence triggered off by innovation the structure of an industry one more settles down into a fairly stable pattern. The five forces and strategies be applied.

The five forces and strategic group models are static they cannot adequately capture what occurs during such periods of rapid change, but they are certainly useful tools for analyzing industry structure during periods of stability. The five force and strategic group models are limited since they represent no more snapshots of moving picture.

Industry Structure and Company Differences

The second criticism of the five forces and strategic group models is that they overemphasize the importance of the industry structure as a determinant of company performance underemphasis the important difference companies within industry or strategic group.

> **Exhibit 3.3: Satyam Corporate Profile**
>
> Satyam: An end-to-end IT services provider Satyam Computer Services Ltd. (NYSE: "SAY"), is an end-to-end IT solutions provider.
>
> It operates in *45 countries, with a customer base of over *300 global companies, including over *101 Fortune 500 corporations.
>
> Satyam's highly skilled, dedicated IT professionals, its subsidiaries and Joint Ventures provide customized IT solutions for several industries using our range of technical expertise and experience.

(Contd...)

Satyam's range of expertise

- Software development services
- Engineering services
- Systems integration
- ERP solutions
- Customer relationship management
- Supply chain management
- Product development
- Electronic commerce
- Consulting
- IT Outsourcing

Industry Verticals

- Banking & finance services
- Energy & utility
- Government
- Healthcare & insurance
- Manufacturing
- Retail
- Telecom

Satyam's subsidiary Satyam Infoway provides Internet Access & Hosting services and Network & Network-enabled services.

Satyam's BPO subsidiary Nipuna provides a host of Business Process Outsourcing services.

Satyam's range of consulting and IT skills have helped businesses re-engineer and re-invent their products, services and processes to compete successfully in an ever-changing marketplace.

Satyam's state-of-the-art software development centers in India, the United States, the UK, the UAE, Singapore, Malaysia, China, Japan and Australia work with a variety of business and technology partners to design and implement projects onsite, offshore and offsite.

The organization emphasizes on acquiring an in-depth knowledge of the customer's context and needs, and designs solutions fine-tuned to these needs. Satyam's ideas and products have resulted in technology-intensive transformations that have met the most stringent international quality standards.

Simultaneously, Satyam teams proactively work on turning new ideas into products that answer global market needs. One such product is Vision Compass, a web-enabled collaborative enterprise management software.

Satyam has developed strategic alliances with leaders in several technical areas. Through a web of over *75 technology and business partnerships, Satyam offers clients comprehensive, cutting-edge solutions.

Satyam's SEI CMM® Level 5 assessment reflects its commitment to Quality processes and products.

(Contd...)

Core Values

- Belief in people
- Pursuit of excellence
- Entrepreneurship
- Customer orientation

These values have led to the creation of a unique organizational structure, with every functional unit designated as an independent business enterprise, each responsible for its own resource management and its profits and losses.

Source: Satyam

QUESTIONS FOR DISCUSSIONS

1. Write short notes on:
   (*i*) Company mission
   (*ii*) Company profile
   (*iii*) Environment analysis
   (*iv*) Long-term objectives
   (*v*) Grand strategies
   (*vi*) Annual objectives
   (*vii*) Operating strategies
   (*viii*) Institutionalizing of strategy
2. Discuss the process/steps of strategic management.
3. Briefly explain the components of the strategic management
4. Discuss the five-force model of strategic management.
5. What are the limitation of the strategic management.
6. Discuss strategic groups and its concepts.
7. What are implications of the strategic groups?
8. Discuss the limitation of the five force and strategic group models.

REFERENCES

1. Burgelman, Robert A., *Strategy is Destiny*. New York: The Free Press, 2000.
2. Collins, James C., and Jerry I. Porras, *Building your Company's Vision,* Harvard Business Review 74, no. 5 (September October 1996), pp. 65–77.
3. Hamel, Gay. *Strategy as Revolution*. Harvard Business Review 74, no. 4 (July–August 1996), pp. 69–82.
4. Lipton, Mark. *Demystifying the Development of an Organizational Vision*. Sloan Management Review, summer 1996, pp. 83–92.

5. Mintzberg, Henry, Bruce Ahlstrand and Joseph Lampel, *Strategy Safari: A Guided Tour through the Wilds of Strategic Management*. New York: Free Press, 1998.
6. Caves, R.E., and M.E. Porter. *From Entry Barriers: Conjectural Decisions and Contrived Deterrence to New Competition*. Quarterly Journal of Economics 91 (1976), pp. 421–34.
7. John, A. Pearce II, Richard B. Robinson, JR. *Strategic Management Strategy Formulation and Implementation*. A.I.T.B.S. Publishers & Distributors (Regd), New Delhi, 2002.
8. Karger, D.W. and Z.A. Malik. *Long–Range Planning and Organizational Performance*. Long Range Planning, December 1975, pp. 60–64.
9. Kudla, R.J. *Elements of Effective Corporate Planning*. Long-Range Planning, August 1976, pp. 82–93.
10. Pearce, J.A., II, and W.A. Randolph. *Improving Strategy Formulation Pedagogies by Recognizing Behavioral Aspects*, Exchange, December 1980, pp. 7–10.
11. Robinson, R.B., Jr. *The Importance of 'Outsiders' in Small Firm Strategic Planning*. Academy of Management Journal, March 1982, pp. 80–93.
12. Brown , Shona L., and Kathleen M. Eisenhardt. *Competing on the Edge: Strategy as Structured Chaos*. Boston, MA: Harvard Business School Press, 1998.
13. Drucker, Peter. *The Theory of Business*. Harvard Business Review 72, no. 5 (September-October) , pp. 95-104.
14. Hamel, Gary, and C.K. Prahalad. *Strategic Intent*. Harvard Business Review 71. no. 4 (July–August) , pp. 69–82.
15. Kahaner, Larry. *What you can Learn from your Competitors Mission Statements*. Competitive Intelligence Review 6, no 4 (Winter 1995), pp. 35-40.
16. Lipton, Mark. *Demystifying the Development of an Organizational Vision*. Sloan Management Review, summer 1996, pp. 83-92.
17. Porter, M.E. *Industrial Market Structures and Economic Performance*. Review of Economics and Statistics 61 (1979), pp. 214–27.
18. Caves, R.E., and M.E. Porter. *From Entry Barriers: Conjectural Decisions and Contrived Deterrence to New Competition*. Quarterly Journal of Economics 91 (1976), pp. 421–34.
19. A.A. Thomson and A.J. Strickland 111, *Strategy Formulation and Implementation Tasks of the General Manager*, Plano, TX: Business Publications,1983.
20. A.A.Thomson and A.J. Strickland, *Strategic Management Concepts and Cases*, Tata McGraw –Hill Publishing Company Limited, New Delhi, 2003.
21. Gilmore, Frank. *Formulating Strategy in Smaller Companies*. Harvard Business Review, May–June 1971, pp. 75-85.
22. Glueck, William F. *Business Policy and Strategic Management*. 3rd. ed. New York: McGraw Hill, 1980.
23. Herold, David. *Long Range Planning and Organizational Performance: A Cross Validation Study*. Academy of Management Review, March 1972, pp. 91–102.
24. Karger, Delmar Karger. *Does Long Range Planning Improve Company Performance*? Management Review, September 1975, pp. 27-31.
25. Schoeffler, Sidney; Robert D. Buzzell; and Donald F. Heany. *Impact of Strategic Planning on Profit Performance*. Harvard Business Review, March–April 1974, pp. 137-45.

Chapter – 4

Types of Strategy

CONTENTS

LEARNING OBJECTIVES

In this chapter, we shall discuss about the different types of strategies like stability, expansion, retrenchment, combination, modernization, diversification, and vertical integration, turnaround strategies, and vertical forward, backward, horizontal concentric strategies.

INTRODUCTION

An organization may have to find the best possible strategy from different types of strategic alternatives. The major types of strategies are normally related to industrial business organization. They are as follows:

STABILITY STRATEGY

Stability strategy refers to the maintaining status quo of the existing business operation. Stability strategy aims at slow growth rate. It is followed as a matter of principle when an organization attempts incremental growth of its functional performance in terms of its customer groups, customer functions, and alternative technologies, whether in combination or individually. Thus, when organization decides to serve the same target customer groups with same products service and follows the same objective to maintain the stable business status, it can be termed as stability strategy.

EXPANSION STRATEGY

When an organization desired to expand extents its business network widening the scope of its customer groups, customer functions and state of the art technologies, we have the making of an expansion strategy. Expansion or growth strategy is principally adopted when an organization enhance its level of objectives with high target. Intensive expansion is a fundamental approach to safeguard and develop the organizations product market and thereby increased the volume of sales, profit, market share and total business network very rapidly.

RETRENCHMENT STRATEGY

When an organization decides to reduce its business operation by reducing the scope of customer groups or customer functions or alternative technologies with view to have better control for better performance, retrenchment strategies are accepted. In retrenchment strategy, unattractive and unwanted areas of business are sequenced gradually. It is not a matter of failure of business planning, rather well planned exercise to get rid of unprofitable parts of business which will help the organization concentrate its total attention to the most profitable and promising areas of business only.

COMBINATION STRATEGY

In changing business environment, an organization may also find it beneficial to adopt a unique combination of stability, expansion and retrenchment indifferent levels related areas of business which depending on the business environment. In other words, combination strategy refers to the combination of the stability, expansion and retrenchment strategy in different levels of the organization.

MODERNIZATION STRATEGY

Modernization strategy refers to innovation of the new technology which adopted in organization by removing the outdated old plant and machinery and equipment, product process and technologies. It copes with very fast technology advancement, modernization of machinery and plant seems to be more important for best productivity at minimum time, cost and energy. Modernization, renovation and revamping of the manufacturing units are very essential to keep pace with the changes in technological aspects of business environment. Modernization strategy may be adopted by an organization to gain competitive advantages and strategic strengths outdate the product, process and technology to establish commend in business world.

DIVERSIFICATION STRATEGY

Exhibit 4.1: Examples of Diversification Strategy of Wipro. Founded in 1945, Wipro has diversified into Information Technology, Consumer Care and Lighting, Engineering and Healthcare. Our diversification into IT happened in 1980 and since then there has been no looking back. Wipro had revenues of USD 902Mn in March 2003.

Milestones

1980: Diversification into Information Technology

1990: Incorporation of Wipro-GE medical systems

1992: Going global with global IT services division

1993: Business innovation award for offshore development

1995: Wipro gets ISO 9001 quality certification, re-certified twice for mature processes

1997: Wipro gets SEI CMM level 3 certification, enterprise wide processes defined

1998: Wipro first software services company in the world to get SEI CMM level 5

1999: Wipro's market capitalization is the highest in India

2000: Start of the Six Sigma initiative, defects prevention practices initiated at project level

2001: First Indian company to achieve the "TL9000 certification" for industry specific quality standards

2001: World's first PCMM Level 5 company

2001: Ranked 87 among 100 best performing technology companies globally (Business Week, June 2001)

2002: World's first CMMi ver 1.1 Level 5 company

2002: Ranked the 7th software services company in the world by Business Week (Infotech 100, November 2002)

Source. www.wipro technologies

Diversification strategy refers to diverting the business focus from the existing traditional areas to new promising areas. Since technology is changing day by day, it based on the customers expectations and to draw their attention to organization. Organizations focus to produce or manufactured new and substitute products and services for attract and draw attention of customers. These changing attitudes have been opening more and more new areas of promising business. Diversifications can be changed business focus may be either in terms of customer function, customer group and or new alternative technologies.

VERTICAL INTEGRATION STRATGEY

Exhibit 4.2: Reliance Industries Limited. This Group's principal activity is to produce and distribute plastic and intermediates, polyester filament yarn, fibre intermediates, polymer intermediates, crackers, chemicals, textiles, oil and gas. The group has its manufacturing facilities at Patalganga in Maharashtra, Ahmedabad, Surat and Manager in Gujarat. The brands include Recron, Relpet, Relene, Reclair, Repol, Reon, Relab, Vimal, Harmony, SlumbeRel, Ruerel and Reance. Refining accounted for 53% of fiscal 2003 gross revenues; petrochemicals, 45% and others, 2%.

Source: http://www.ril.com/

Vertical integration refers to diversification into new production line to produce items required as inputs for other main products of the same company. This may be undertaken by an organization with the purpose of either maintaining continuous flow or serving as a customer for outputs for marketing and selling the organization products by opening its own sales and marketing division and showroom instead of selling through agents or distributors. Producing input items may be necessary in case of unreliable suppliers letting down the company production with erratic and irregular supply of inferior inputs; or to have total control over the input supply and output distribution also. Vertical integration is of two types –

- Backward integration strategy
- Forward integration strategy

Backward Integration Strategy

- Backward integration strategy refers to diversifying the business operations towards some of the raw material or inputs supply.

Forward Integration Strategy

- Forward integration strategy refers to diversifying business operations for marketing, sales and distribution of products and services and taking up those activities to bring the organization closer to the ultimate customer.

TURNAROUND STRATEGY

Turnaround strategy refers to during recessionary conditions in any industry, or in the business or economic totality. When there is substantial and sustained downtrend in the business due to external factors, the turnaround strategy aims to check the declining position in performance of business and gradually improve long-run efficiency operations. It is an external retrenchment strategy and leads to divestment or liquidation. It is strategy of reversing negative trend. It focuses the main threats of organization as listed below:

- Cost reduction and wastage control with better inventory control and economic measures boycotting down redundant discretionary expenses, layoff and retrenchment of surplus manpower.
- Revenues increase with drive for sales promotion and revenue realization.
- Reduction of assets by selling off absolute plant facilities and disposal of surplus, scrap, and redundant materials along with reduction of unprofitable products and service.

  In the Indian situation, before a turnaround strategy is decided by any company officials, it has to be declared first as a sick company in accordance with the Sick Industrial Act 1985, which provides for a *quasi-judicial body* namely the Board for Industrial and Financial Reconstruction to investigate and diagnose the cause of sickness.

HORIZONTAL INTEGRATION STRATEGY

Horizontal integration strategy is undertaken in order to increase market share by expansion of same product lines with more varieties to serve customers in different areas of different types and affluence levels. Horizontal strategy may be taken up to expand business geographically in new territories by taking up a competitor in another area to benefit from economies scale and increased market share and improve business volume.

CONCENTRATION DIVERSIFICATION STRATEGY

Concentration diversification strategy refers to concentrate the direction of business for expansion and diversification in the same and attendant product lines. Concentric diversification may be taken the form of marketing related to technological-related diversification.

Again, the diversification strategy may be related or unrelated areas. Related diversification includes diversification of business in the related, existed product lines if same technology and manufacturing process while the diversification may be decided in unrelated i.e., new areas of business, with different technology and manufacturing process. All this depends upon the technological environment and market position.

DIVESTMENT/CUTBACK STRATEGY

It involves the sale and disposing off or shedding business units or product divisions or segments of business operations to reinvest the resources for other production and potential business purposes. Divestment is usually a part of revival, rehabilitation and restructuring plan attempted when a turnaround strategy becomes unsuccessful. The strategy in the case may be to sell off a part of business or products, or giving up the control over a subsidiary or a demerger so that the wholly owned subsidiaries may be floated off as independent organization. Organization may be choose to divest in two ways: a part of the organization may choose to divest by way of serving its financial and managerial control and separating it as independent organization for all purposes. Alternatively, an organization may sell a unit outright for which marketing strategy should be proven. The basic objective underlying organization unit may be hindrance on the total profitability and growth, particularly when opportunities of strategic alternative investment exist. So, divestment may be a sensible positive strategic decision and not due to helpless condition. Further there may be other types of strategies like business level strategy, functional level strategy, annual strategy, grand strategy, and corporate strategy.

Exhibit 4.3: MFL off the disinvestment list: CMD. Madras Fertilisers Ltd had been taken out from disinvestment list by the Centre, but its fortunes had taken a beating due to an anomaly in the Government's fertiliser pricing policy. Chairman and Managing Director Mr Sukumar N Oommen said today, "MFL was on the block for disinvestment. The new Government at the Centre has now decided to put disinvestment on hold. I do believe that MFL will be retained in the public sector", Mr Oommen said after announcing a tie-up with ING Vysya Life here. He said the fortunes of MFL were dictated by the fertiliser policy of the Government. If you look at our performance, we have achieved 102 per cent efficiency in urea production. The productivity of employees are at par with the private sector, Mr Oommen said. However, the Government had not been compensating the company for higher performance. Under the existing administered pricing mechanism in the fertiliser industry, MFL should be compensated in full for the cost of production, he said. During the year ended March 31, 2004, the company is expected to report a loss of Rs 60 crore. We would have made Rs 40 crore profit, if you remove the anomaly, he said. PTI

Source: Business Line, dated April 17, 2004

Marketing strategy, corporate strategy, merger strategy, takeover strategy and joint venture strategy, which are discussed in detail in separate chapters.

QUESTIONS FOR DISCUSSIONS

1. Write short note on
   - Stability strategy
   - Expansion strategy
   - Retrenchment strategy
   - Combination strategy
   - Modernization strategy
   - Diversification strategy
   - Vertical integration strategy
   - Backward integration strategy
   - Forward integration strategy
   - Turnaround strategy
   - Concentric diversification strategy
   - Divestment strategy
   - Discuss the types of strategies

REFERENCES

1. Business Line, dated April 17, 2004
2. http://www.ril.com/
3. www.wipro technologies
4. Samuel C. Cerko and J. Paul Peter. *Strategic Management*, (Chicago: Irwin, 1995).
5. John M. Harris, *Corporate Turnaround Strategy*, in Knneth J. Albert (Editor in Chief) The Strategic Management Handbook (Newyork: McGraw-Hill Book Co. 1983).
6. Pradeep N. Khandwalla, 10 *Elements in Turnaround*, Business World, June 7-20, 1989.
7. Donald F. Harvey, *Business Policy and Strategic Management*, Charles E. Merril Publishing Co., Columbus, Ohio, 1982.
8. T.A. Staudt, *Programme for Product Diverification*, Harvard Business Review, vol. 32, No. 6 Nov-Dec, 1954.

Chapter – 5

Defining the Organization Mission and Social Responsibility

CONTENTS

- Introduction
- The need for explicit mission of an organization
- Fundamental elements of a mission
- Components of mission statement
- Organizational goals
- Organization philosophy
- Organization public image
- Organization self concept
- Role of the Organization
- Claimant approach to organization responsibilities
- Defining organization mission
- Social responsibility of business
- The benefits of a strategic approach to managing
- Develop a strategic vision
- Elements of a strategy vision
- Swot analysis

LEARNING OBJECTIVES

Let us discuss mission, fundamental elements of mission, components of mission, organization goals, vision, social responsibility, the benefits of a strategic approach to managing, and how analyses the strength weakness, opportunity and threat of the organization/company.

INTRODUCTION

The basic objectives, goals, traits and philosophies are ascertained and shape organization strategic posture. These are developing a new business or reformulating direction for a going organization. Organization mission will guide future executive action. Therefore, the organization/company mission is defined as the fundamental, unique purpose which sets a business apart from other organizations its type and identifies the scope of its operations in product and market terms. In short, the organization mission describes the product, market, technological and innovation areas that emphasis for the business. Mission reflects the values and priorities of strategic decision makers in organization /company.

THE NEED FOR EXPLICIT MISSION OF ORGANIZATION

Defining organization mission is time consuming, tedious and not required by any external body like experts. The organization mission including few specific directives, which are broadly outlined or implied objectives and strategies traits, it is statement of attitude, outlook and orientation of the organization rather than of details and measurable targets in the business.

King and Cleland designed the organization mission as listed below:

- To ensure unanimity of purpose within the organization.
- To provide a basis for motivating the use of the organization's resource.
- To develop a basis for motivating the use of the organization's resources.
- To establish a general tome or organizational climate, for instance, to suggest, a business like operation.
- To serve as a focal point for those who can identify with the organizations purpose and direction, land to deter those who cannot from participating further in the organization's activities.
- To facilitate the transaction of objectives and goals into a work structure involving the assignment of tasks to responsible elements within the organizations.
- To specify organizational purposes and the translation of these purposes into goals in such a way that cost, time, and performance parameters can be assessed and controlled.

FUNDAMENTAL ELEMENTS OF MISSION

Fundamental elements are as follows:

- A general belief that the product or service which can provide benefits at least equal to its price.
- A general belief that the product or service which can satisfy a customer needs.
- Using of the technology for production which will provide a product or service at a quality and cost competitive.

- Hard work and the better interaction of the organization employees that help for survival, growth and are profitable of the organization.
- Business philosophy of the management will create in a favorable public image and will provide financial and psychological rewards from those willing to invest their labor, money and helping the organization for success.
- The organization's promoters self–concept of the business can be communicated and adopted by employees and stockholders.

COMPONENTS OF MISSION STATEMENT

There are three components of a mission statement, they are as listed below:

- Specification of the basic product or service of the organization.
- Primary market for the goods and service of the organization.
- Principal technology has adopted for production or distribution of goods and service of the organization.

ORGANIZATIONAL GOALS

Organization goals are depended on the three factors as listed below:

- Survival
- Growth
- Profitability

Survival

An organization mission statement reveals the organization's intention to secure its survival through development growth and profitability of the business. Strategic managers take more responsibility for survival of the organization business. Therefore, survival is an assumed goal of the business, if strategic managers often neglected survival, its impact on strategic decisions making for long term.

Profitability

Profitability is the vital goal of a business organization. Strategic managers are how to measure profitability or how to define profitability over the long term or short term of the organization. Profitability clearly indicates the organization's ability to satisfy the principal; claims and desires of employees and stakeholder of the organization.

Strategic managers are having analyses, interpretations of profit of the organization, and also how it creates an impact on survival of the organization.

Growth

An organizations growth is closely associated with its survival and profitability. Growth refers to overall development of the organization activities. Growth may be proactive change is a necessity for dynamic business environment. Growth refers to in terms of expansion, diversification and acquisition of business. Organization looks for survival, profitability and growth of the business activities.

ORGANIZATION PHILOSOPHY

Organization philosophy has ties with the principles, systems, belief, core values of the business. These are usually appeared as a part of the organization mission. It highlights the core basic beliefs, values, aspirations and philosophies priorities. Organization philosophies are different from one organization to another. Therefore, strategic executives and managers are implicitly accepted a general, unwritten, yet pervasive code of behavior. Organization's operating philosophy has further classified into several areas. They are as listed below:

- Marketing and customers service
- Management task
- Human resource
- Finance and control
- Research and development
- Technology

Exhibit 5.1: Satyam's CUSTOMER PHILOSOPHY. Satyam's organizational structure reflects our commitment to making the customer the driving force of all our initiatives. Satyam's processes are oriented to give the organization a sharp insight into customer needs. Satyam acts on these inputs and translates them into solutions for the customer. Satyam's Five Cs Approach

- Communication
- Collaboration
- Competency enhancement
- Customer intimacy
- Competitive edge

ORGANIZATION PUBLIC IMAGE

Public image refers to public to have identification of service and products of organization. Public image is very important particularly for the growing organization has involved in a redefinition of its mission. Public image attracts to present and potential customers attribute certain qualities to a particular business activities of the organization. Mission statements reflects public image which making the organization goals a more likely the results.

ORGANIZATION SELF CONCEPT

Exhibit 5.2: Wipro promise Our values are extremely important to us and form the bedrock of our vision and plans. Values are an integral part of our culture and present a common face to our customer. The four Wipro values: Human Values, Integrity, Innovative Solutions and Value for Money are encapsulated in our promise to the customer and in our identity. These values shape our thinking, our behaviour, our culture and how we come across to our customers, partners and to the world at large.

Source: Wipro

Organization self concept refers to continue success of the organization which is relating to external environment of the business. Self concept has to ascertain its place in competitive environment situation. Basically it requires and equates in terms of own strengths, opportunity, weakness and threat for competition.

ROLE OF THE ORGANIZATION

Organization' role based on the following factors:

- It is based on management perception relating to the society that responds the organization.
- The organization self-concept functions are direct and instructions of their employees.
- It clears the authority, responsibility and delegation of authority of top level, middle level and low level management of the organization that will in part to determine the corporate self concept.
- Modern organizations focus for communication to individuals who worked in organization and outside people who are customers, suppliers, media, competitors, investors, shareholders, general public and government official.

CLAIMANT APPROACH TO ORGANIZATION RESPONSIBILITY

Strategic executives and managers must recognise and acknowledge the legitimate claims of stakeholders and others of the organization. It may be defining or redefining the organization or company mission. Organization approach includes investors and employees as well as outsiders affected by the company actions which taken by the strategic executives and managers. Outsiders commonly include customers, competitors, local communities and the general public. Generally, shareholder claim appropriate return (dividend) their investments; employee seek broadly defined job satisfaction and salary, perks and promotions; customers want what they pay for products and service, supplier seek dependable buyers, government want tax and adherence to legislation; trade and employee unions seek benefits for members in proportion to contributions to organization or company success; competitors want fair competition in national and international market; local communities want organization or companies responsible citizens and the general public seeks some improvement in quality of product and service which are not harmful to environment and human being.

DEFINING ORGANIZATION MISSION

Defining organization mission as listed below:

- Identification
- Understanding
- Reconciliation and priorities
- Coordination with other elements

Identification

Identification refers to identification of core business environment functions like internal factors and external factors of the organization. Every business organization faces a slightly different set of claimants, who vary numbers, size, influence, and importance. These defining in organization mission, strategic executives and managers must identify all claimant groups and weight their realties to implement and get to success.

Understanding

Understanding refers to an organization has understanding of their employees and outsiders like suppliers, distributors, competitors, customers, general public for creation of good relationship to accomplishment of goals and objectives of the organization. Strategic decision makers should understand the core demands of each group. Then strategic managers will to make decisions for able to appreciate their concerns and initiates clearly defined in actions.

Reconciliation and Priorities

Reconciliation and priorities refers to the concerns of various claimants can be created conflict, for instance; the priorities for claims of government, creditors and stockholders. Therefore, these cases claims must be reconciled; to achieve unified approach by strategic managers have must define a mission that resolves the competing conflicting and contradictory claims. Objectives and strategies are clearly focused to be mission statements of the organization must display a single-minded approach to achieve though multidimensional approach to business aims.

Coordination with Other Elements

Coordination refers to core elements of the strategy makers, strategy makers can be coordinated among the people who are served their best service to the organization. Coordination helps to strategy makers for formulation of strategy, implementation, controlling, monitoring and evaluating of the organization superior goals. Organization strategy basic requirement is that the coordination among the functional department's human resource of the organization. Strategy makers must have concentration of interaction of external people of the organization.

Case 5.1:Cadbury's vision

Cadbury's world-wide vision is "Working together to create brands that people love." Cadbury has successfully done this for over 200 years. This success has been built upon understanding the needs of our consumers, customers and colleagues and by operating to a clearly defined set of values. But around us, the world changes. We want to recognise this as well as ensure the continuation of our own heritage.

Our strategy is to:

Create robust and sustainable regional positions in our core categories of confectionery and beverages through organic growth, acquisition and disposal. We will achieve this by Managing for Value. Our Managing for Value process incorporates:

- setting stretching financial objectives
- adopting value-based management for major strategic and operational decisions and business systems
- creating an outstanding leadership capability within our management
- sharpening our company culture to reflect accountability, aggressiveness and adaptability
- aligning our management rewards structure with the interests of our shareowners.

In India, Cadbury India has defined its vision as "Life full of Cadbury, Cadbury full of life"

This means:

- Broadening our consumer appeal and extending our reach to newer markets—Sustained growth of our market share through aggressive product development
- Striving for international quality in our products and processes

(Contd...)

- Focussing on cost competitiveness, productivity and innovative utilization of assets
- Energising and developing our people

Source: cadbaryindialimited

SOCIAL RESPONSIBILITY OF BUSINESS

According to Adolf Berie, social responsibility has been defined as "the manager `s responsiveness to public".

According to Eels and Walton it has been defined as the social responsibilities "when people talk about corporate responsibility, they think in terms of problems that arise when corporate enterprise casts its shadow on the social sense, and of the corporation ethical principle that ought to govern the relationship between the corporation and society. They are concerned with the impact of the corporation on the individual and the possibilities of reconciling big business, big labor, and big government with values deeply rooted in our form of government".

According to Steiner, "social responsibility is to understand public consensus, to recognize it, and to cooperate in achieving this. Each business has responsibilities in some way commensurate with its power".

According to Koontz and O'Donnell, "the personal obligation of the people as they act in their own interests to assure that the rights and legitimate interests of others are not infringed".

Concept of Social Responsibility

The organization social responsibility concept has influence to the society in terms of providing adequate facilities like engages cultural and social programs for development and create social awareness. Society has identification of organization social responsibility and impacts on business. Society has guide to organization for its business goals, performance, constructive social policies and comments about the mission and vision of the organization. The concept of social responsibility of organization is merely a first step towards social effectiveness of business. It is the underlying value that businessmen have sound based for social action. It is based on the philosophy of the organization which has justified business involvement in society. It must be followed by effective social action towards accomplishment of social strategy.

In the other words, philosophy without programme, it is a shadow without substance. Perhaps, one should take, therefore, less of corporate social responsibilities and more of corporate social responses. Organization opens, permits voluntary and creative undertakings by business on behalf of societies.

A Philosophy of Social Responsibility

The strategy makers consider the philosophy of social responsibility for obliged to actions which protect and improve the welfare of society as a whole along with their own interest. A philosophy has built a better quality of life, therefore, harmonies organizational actions with societies wants. The philosophy gives ideas to the businessman in terms of achievement social benefits along with the traditional economic gains which seeks by organization. His ideas has concerned with social responsibility as well as economic responsibility and the total effect of his economic and institutional actions on society.

A Social Responsible Strategy of the Organization

Strategist, strategic executives and managers in the organization has always been aware of the social responsibility to society, shareholders, financial institution, debenture holders, suppliers, customers, and employees of the organization while formulation, implementation and controlling strategy at the business, corporate and functional level. Organization or companies are committed to society to engage welfare activities thereby advertise their brand and products for market.

Case 5.2: Satyam's CORPORATE SOCIAL RESPONSIBILITY Satyam's Community Outreach Program. Satyam believes that wealth creation is incomplete unless it contributes to the well-being of society. It believes that creators of business value must constantly look for ways to use this value to fulfill a larger social responsibility. Thus, reaffirming its role as contributing members to the social and economic milieu. As a larger expression of its mission and core values, Satyam is actively involved in a variety of public service projects serving underprivileged groups in urban, semi-urban and rural areas. Satyam works through Alambana, an umbrella organization that brings together committed Satyam Associates, their spouses and other family members as volunteers. Alambana works in the areas of education, environment and healthcare. Alambana

Community Outreach/Social Responsibility

Satyam believes that wealth creation is incomplete unless it, in some measure, contributes to the betterment of society as a whole. Every society is judged by the opportunities that it provides its citizens to create wealth and obtain a continuously improved quality of life. Creators of business or market value must constantly look for ways in which this value can be used to fulfill the larger social responsibility. This is one way in which an organization reaffirms its role as a contributing member of the social and economic milieu it occupies. When all levels of a society gain from economic growth, the engines of that growth are further energized. As a larger expression of its mission and core values, Satyam is actively involved in a variety of public service projects serving underprivileged groups in urban, semi-urban and rural areas. Working through Alambana, an umbrella organization that brings together committed Satyam associates and their spouses, the Company contributes to social causes and organizes initiatives for social change, primarily in the areas of **education**, **environment** and **healthcare**, areas which we believe are inextricably tied to overall development and quality of life.

About Alambana

In Sanskrit, Alambana means "support". Formed in October 2000, Satyam Alambana is a volunteer-based charitable trust that identifies, plans, implements and supports projects that attempt to narrow the digital and economic-divide. Each of Alambana's activities makes use of Satyam's intellectual capital to create social equity and add value to society. The volunteers who run Alambana are committed Satyam Associates and their family members. Associates see Alambana as an opportunity to go beyond checkbook charity, so they spend a considerable amount of time and effort on planning and supervising projects. Alambana also draws upon Satyam's project management experience to turn each of its projects into economically sound business ventures that provide employment opportunities for the underprivileged and grow into self-sustaining entities. For this reason, all Alambana projects depend on the active and long-term participation of a committed group of people. And for the same reason, Alambana does not fund third party projects or one-time charitable activities.

(Contd...)

Alambana Projects

The Satyam Alambana Foundation identifies clearly demarcated projects within the broad areas of education, healthcare and environment, and works on turning these into sustainable ventures. On the one hand, underprivileged communities are given access to educational opportunities and access to healthcare, and on the other, these projects grow to provide employment opportunities for the same communities. Most of Alambana's work concentrates on pockets of disadvantage in Andhra Pradesh, both rural and urban. In the belief that development efforts should begin within and close to our own communities, we have chosen villages that are located in the vicinity of Satyam establishments.

THE BENEFITS OF A STRATEGIC APPROACH TO MANAGING

Today's business world executives are to think strategically about their organization or company's position and about the impact of changing conditions. They have to monitor the company's external business environment and internal environmental objectives that are closely enough to formulate, implement and controlling the changes. Strategist has to know the business well enough to determine what kinds of strategic changes to initiate for achievement of strategy.

Benefits

- Strategy provides better guidance to the entire organization on the crucial point of "what it is we are trying to do".
- Strategic executives and employees of the organization may be more alert to opportunities and threaten from environment development.
- Helping and interaction among the persons in the organization to unify the goal and objectives of the organization.
- Human resource creates good gesture to external and internal environment of the organization.
- Organization provides adequate resource for productivity and innovative of the organization performance.

DEVELOPMENT OF STRATEGIC VISION

Strategic management process is effective when strategy making begins with a vision of the organization or company that needs to head, vision is a noteworthy exercise in terms of thinking carefully about their objectives, goals and policies. It involves selecting the market areas in which to participate, putting the organization on strategic path and attempted to commit to follow that path i.e. strategic vision.

ELEMENTS OF A STRATEGY VISION

Important strategy vision elements are as outlined:

- The mission statement defines one of the roles the organization that special identify the business interest and path for growth and development.
- Strategy vision defines the organization's strategies path, technologies, customer groups and competitive scenario and the activities it performs in terms of well being.
- Nature of technology, productivity, innovativeness is an important to define an organization business.

- Mission and vision statements are crisply to be defined by organization.
- Organization should prepare future for its survival, growth and profitability.
- Vision and mission statement prepared and responsible by chief executive of the organization.
- Vision and mission statements are clearly the directions of the organization's future.

SWOT ANALYSIS

SWOT analysis is a tool for auditing an organization and its environment. It is the first stage of planning and helps marketers to focus on key issues. Once key issues have been identified, they feed into marketing objectives. It can be used in conjunction with other tools for audit and analysis, such as PEST analysis and Porter's Five Force analysis. It is a very popular tool with marketing students because it is quick and easy to learn. During the SWOT exercise, list factors in the relevant boxes. It's that simple.

SWOT stands for **strengths, weaknesses, opportunities, and threats.** Strengths and weaknesses are **internal** factors.

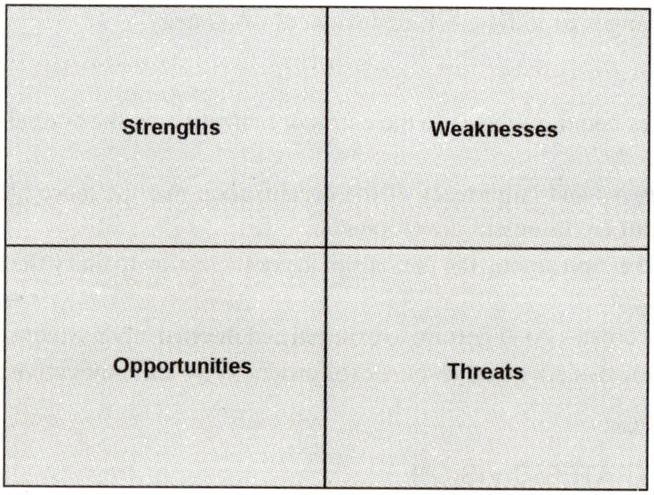

SWOT Analysis

Strength could be:

- Your specialist marketing expertise.
- A new, innovative product or service.
- Location of your business.
- Quality processes and procedures.
- Any other aspect of your business that adds value to your product or service.

A **weakness** could be:

- Lack of marketing expertise.
- Undifferentiated products and service (i.e., in relation to your competitors).
- Location of your business.

- Poor quality goods or services.
- Damaged reputation.

Opportunities and threats are **external** factors. For example:

An **opportunity** could be:

- A developing market such as the Internet.
- Mergers, joint ventures or strategic alliances.
- Moving into new market segments that offer improved profits.
- A new international market.
- A market vacated by an ineffective competitor.

A **threat** could be:

- A new competitor in your home market.
- Price wars with competitors.
- A competitor has a new, innovative product or service
- Competitors have superior access to channels of distribution.
- Taxation is introduced on your product or service.

A word of caution, SWOT analysis can be very subjective. Do not rely on it too much. Two people rarely come-up with the same final version of SWOT. TOWS analysis is extremely similar. It simply looks at the negative factors first in order to turn them into positive factors. So, use it as guide and not a prescription.

Simple Rules for Successful SWOT Analysis

- Be realistic about the strengths and weaknesses of your organization.
- Analysis should distinguish between where your organization is today, and where it could be in the future.
- Be specific. Avoid grey areas.
- Always analyze in context to your competition i.e., better than or worse than your competition.
- Keep your SWOT short and simple. Avoid complexity and over analysis.
- SWOT is subjective.

QUESTIONS FOR DISCUSSIONS

1. Discuss the need for explicit mission of organization.
2. What are the fundamental elements of a mission?
3. Briefly explain the components of mission statement.
4. What are the major organizational goals?
5. Write short notes on:
    - Organization public image
    - Survival
    - Profitability

    Growth

6. Explain the organization public image.
7. Describe the self-concept and its role in organization.
8. Define organization mission.
9. Discuss the social responsibility and its philosophy.
10. What are the elements of the strategic vision?
11. Discuss the SWOT analysis.

REFERENCES

1. Burgelman, Robert A. *Strategy Is Destiny*. New York: The Free Press, 2000.
2. Collins, James C., and Jerry I. Porras. *Building Your Company's Vision*. Harvard Business Review 74, no. 5 (September-October 1996), pp. 65–77.
3. Hamel, Gay. *Strategy as Revolution*. Harvard Business Review 74, no. 4 (July–August 1996), pp. 69–82.
4. Lipton, Mark. *Demystifying the Development of an Organizational Vision*. Sloan Management Review, summer 1996, pp. 83–92.
5. Mintzberg, Henry. Bruce Ahlstrand; and Joseph Lampel, *Strategy Safari: A Guided Tour Through the Wilds of Strategic Management*. New York: Free Press, 1998.
6. Caves, R.E., and M.E. Porter. *From Entry Barriers: Conjectural Decisions and Contrived Deterrence to New Competition*. Quarterly Journal of Economics 91 (1976), pp. 421–34.
7. John, A. Pearce II, Richard B. Robinson, JR. *Strategic Management Strategy Formulation and Implementation*. A.I.T.B.S. Publishers & Distributors (Regd.), New Delhi, 2002.
8. Karger, D.W., and Z.A. Malik. *Long–Range Planning and Organizational Performance*." Long Range Planning, December 1975, pp. 60–64.
9. Kudla, R.J. *Elements of Effective Corporate Planning*. Long-Range Planning, August 1976, pp. 82–93
10. Pearce, J.A., II, and W.A. Randolph. *Improving Strategy Formulation Pedagogies by Recognizing Behavioral Aspects*' Exchange, December 1980, pp. 7–10.
11. Robinson, R.B., Jr. *The Importance of Outsiders' in Small Firm Strategic Planning*. Academy of Management Journal, March 1982, pp. 80–93.
12. Brown , Shona L., and Kathleen M. Eisenhardt. *Competing on the Edge: Strategy as Structured Chaos*. Boston, MA: Harvard Business School Press, 1998.
13. Drucker, Peter. *The Theory of Business*. Harvard Business Review 72, no.5 (September-October) , pp. 95-104.
14. Hamel, Gary, and C.K. Prahalad. *Strategic Intent*. Harvard Business Review 71. no. 4 (July – August) , pp. 69–82.
15. Kahaner, Larry. *What You Can Learn From Your Competitors 'Mission Statements*. Competitive Intelligence Review 6, no. 4.(Winter 1995), pp. 35- 40.
16. Lipton, Mark. *Demystifying the Development of an Organizational Vision*. Sloan Management Review, summer 1996, pp. 83-92.

17. Porter, M.E. *Industrial Market Structures and Economic Performance*. Review of Economics and Statistics 61 (1979), pp. 214–27.
18. Caves, R.E., and M.E. Porter. *From Entry Barriers: Conjectural Decisions and Contrived Deterrence to New Competition*. Quarterly Journal of Economics 91 (1976), pp. 421 – 34
19. A.A.Thomson and A.J. Strickland 111, *Strategy Formulation and Implementation Tasks of the General Manager*, Plano, TX: Business Publications,1983.
20. A.A.Thomson and A.J. Strickland, *Strategic Management Concepts and Cases*, Tata McGraw –Hill Publishing Company Limited, New Delhi, 2003
21. Gilmore, Frank. *Formulating Strategy in Smaller Companies*. Harvard Business Review, May–June 1971, pp. 75-85.
22. Glueck, William F. *Business Policy and Strategic Management*. 3rd. ed. New York: McGraw Hill, 1980.
23. Herold, David. *Long-Range Planning and Organizational Performance: A Cross Validation Study*. Academy of Management Review, March 1972, pp. 91–102.
24. Karger, Delmar Karger. *Does Long Range Planning Improve Company Performance*? Management Review, September 1975, pp. 27-31.
25. Schoeffler, Sidney; Robert D. Buzzell; and Donald F. Heany. *Impact of Strategic Planning on Profit Performance*. Harvard Business Review, March–April 1974, pp. 137-45.

Chapter – 6

Internal Environment of the Organization/ Company

CONTENTS

- Introduction
- Internal analysis of the organization/company
- The value of systematic internal assessment
- Identification of strategic factors
- Functional approach
- The value chain approach
- Primary activities
- Evaluation of strategic internal factors
- Quantitative versus qualitative approaches in evaluating internal factors of the Organization.

LEARNING OBJECTIVES

The present chapter aims at:

- Providing the internal analysis of organization
- Providing the detailed process of development of company/organization profile
- Providing familiarity with various approach to identification of internal factors

INTRODUCTION

Environmental analysis is defined as "the process by which strategists monitor the economic, governmental, legal, market, competitive, supplier, technological, geographic, and social cultural settings to determine opportunities and threats to their firms/company/organization".

Exhibit 6.1: IOCL Corporate Indian Oil, the largest commercial enterprise of India (by sales turnover), is India's sole representative in *Fortune's* prestigious listing of the world's 500 largest corporations, ranked 191 for the year 2003, based on fiscal 2002 performance. It is also the 17th largest petroleum company in the world. Indian Oil ranks at 325 in the latest *Forbes*' International listing of 'Global 500' largest public companies. It is also the 17th largest petroleum company in the world. Indian Oil has been adjudged First in petroleum trading listing among the 15 national oil companies in the Asia-Pacific region. Apart from the "Global 500", *Forbes* has also come up with their latest list "Forbes 2000", where Indian Oil is placed at 243rd, and at the top of the 27 Indian firms listed.

Indian Oil has a sales turnover of Rs. 1,19,848 crore (US $ 25.22 billion) and profits of Rs. 6,115 crore (US $ 1,287 million) for fiscal 2002. Indian Oil has been adjudged Second in petroleum trading among the 15 national oil companies in the Asia-Pacific region. As the premier National Oil Company, Indian Oil's endeavor is to serve the national economy and the people of India and fulfil its vision of becoming "an integrated, diversified and transnational energy major." **India's Flagship National Oil Company** Beginning in 1959 as Indian Oil Company Ltd, Indian Oil Corporation Ltd. was formed in 1964 with the merger of Indian Refineries Ltd. (Estd 1958). As India's flagship national oil company, IndianOil accounts for 56% petroleum products market share, 42% national refining capacity and 67% downstream pipeline throughput capacity. To maintain strategic edge in the market place, IndianOil has planned investments to the tune of Rs. 24,400 crore during the X Plan period (2002-07), mainly in refining and pipeline capacity expansions, product quality up gradation, retail operations and diversification projects. IndianOil is an "academy" company with a score of full-fledged training centers across the country building competency, confidence and capability to face the challenges of the market place. Among these, the Indian Oil Institute of Petroleum Management at Gurgaon, the Indian Oil Management Centre for Learning at Mumbai, and the Indian Oil Management Academy at Haldia have emerged as world-class training and management academies.

Source:www.iocl.com

Exhibit 6.2: Indian Oil Corporation Limited Indian Oil Corporation Limited is the country's largest commercial enterprise, with a sales turnover of Rs. 1,19,848 crore (US $ 25.22 billion) and profits of Rs. 6,115 crore (US $ 1,287 million) for fiscal 2002.

Indian Oil is India's sole representative in Fortune's prestigious listing of the world's 500 largest corporations, ranked 191 for the year 2003 based on fiscal 2002 performance. It is also the 17th largest petroleum company in the world. IndianOil has been adjudged first in petroleum trading among the national oil companies in the Asia-Pacific region, and is ranked 325th in the Forbes' "Global 500" listing of the largest public companies. Apart from the Global 500, Forbes has also come out with the "Forbes Global 2000", a comprehensive listing of the world's biggest and most important companies. This list includes 2000 companies from 46 countries.) Twenty-seven Indian firms have been featured in this year's Forbes 2000, a comprehensive ranking measured by a composite of sales, profits, assets and market value. The Indian list is

(Contd...)

headed by Indian Oil Corporation Limited (ranked 243) and followed by State Bank of India (251), ONGC (273), Reliance Industries (303) and Bharat Petroleum (804).

India's Flagship National Oil Company

Beginning in 1959 as Indian Oil Company Ltd., Indian Oil Corporation Ltd. was formed in 1964 with merger of Indian Refineries Ltd. (Estd. 1958).

As India's flagship national oil company, IndianOil alone accounts for 51.2% petroleum products market share among PSU companies, 42% national refining capacity and 67% downstream pipeline throughput capacity.

IndianOil controls 10 of India's 18 refineries with a current combined rated capacity of 49.80 million metric tonnes per annum (MMTPA) or one million barrels per day (bpd). These include subsidiaries Chennai Petroleum Corporation Ltd and Bongaigaon Petroleum Corporation Limited. It owns and operates the country's largest network of cross-country crude oil and product pipelines of 7,575 km, with a combined capacity of 56.85 MMTPA.

IndianOil's countrywide network of over 22,000 sales points is backed for supplies by its extensive, well spreadout marketing infrastructure comprising 184 bulk storage terminals, installations and depots, 93 aviation fuel stations and 85 LPG bottling plants. Its subsidiary, IBP Co. Ltd, is a stand-alone marketing company with a nationwide retail network of over 3,000 sales points.

For the year 2003-04, IndianOil sold 47.264 million tonnes of petroleum products (1.7% growth), its seven own refineries achieved a throughput of 37.6 million tonnes (6.5% increase), and the pipeline network transported 44.50 million tonnes (9.5% increase) of crude oil and petroleum products. IndianOil reaches Indane cooking gas to the doorsteps of about 38 million households in over 2,000 markets through the country's largest network of over 4,100 distributors. The country's leading SERVO brand lubricants from IndianOil, with over 42% market share and 450 grades, are sold through 9,000 retail outlets, besides a countrywide network of bazaar traders.

IndianOil's ISO-9002 certified Aviation Service, with 66.7% market share, meets the fuel and lubricants needs of domestic and international flag carriers, Defence Services and private aircraft operators.

To maintain strategic edge in the market place, IndianOil has planned investments to the tune of Rs. 24,400 crore during the X Plan period (2002-07), mainly in refining and pipeline capacity expansions, product quality upgradation, retail operations and diversification projects.

Indian Oil is an "academy" company with a score of full-fledged training centers across the country building competency, confidence and capability to face the challenges of the market place. Among these, the IndianOil Institute of Petroleum Management at Gurgaon, the Indian Oil Management Centre for Learning at Mumbai, and the IndianOil Management Academy at Haldia have emerged as world-class training and management academies.

R&D Centre

IndianOil's world-class R&D Centre has won recognition for its pioneering work in lubricants formulation, refinery processes, pipeline transportation and bio-fuels. It has developed over

(Contd...)

2,100 formulations of SERVO brand lubricants and greases for virtually all conceivable applications–automotive, railroad, industrial and marine–meeting stringent international standards and bearing the stamp of approval of all major original equipment manufacturers. The Centre has to its credit over 124 national and international patents. The Centre has recently incorporated a subsidiary company–IndianOil Technologies Ltd.—for commercialising its innovations and technologies.

Expanding Horizons

IndianOil is metamorphosing from a pure sectoral company with dominance in downstream in India to a vertically integrated, transnational energy behemoth. The Corporation is making investments in E&P and import/marketing ventures for oil and gas in India and abroad, and is implementing a master plan to emerge as a major player in petrochemicals by integrating its core refining business with petrochemical activities.

Besides this, IndianOil is strengthening its existing overseas marketing ventures and simultaneously scouting new opportunities for marketing and export of petroleum products in foreign markets. Two wholly-owned subsidiaries are already operational in Sri Lanka and Mauritius, and a regional office at Dubai is coordinating expansion of business activities in Middle East region.

The Corporation has launched eleven joint ventures in partnership with some of the most respected corporates from India and abroad — Lubrizol, Nyco SA, Elf, Petronas, Oiltanking GmbH, Marubeni, Mitsubishi, to name a few. SERVO lubricants are being exported to Dubai, Nepal, Bhutan, Kuwait, Malaysia, Bahrain, Indonesia, Sri Lanka, Kyrgyzstan, Mauritius, Bangladesh, etc.

IndianOil has been lending its expertise for nearly two decades to various countries in several areas of refining, marketing, transportation, training and research & development. These include Sri Lanka, Kuwait, Bahrain, Iraq, Abu Dhabi, Tanzania, Ethiopia, Algeria, Nigeria, Nepal, Bhutan, Maldives, Malaysia and Zambia.

IndianOil's sincere commitment to Quality, Safety, Health and Environment is reflected in the series of national and international certifications and awards earned over the years.

The 17th largest petroleum company in the world, IndianOil, is well on its way to becoming an integrated, transnational Energy Corporate.

Source: IOCL website.

Environment diagnosis principally consists of managerial decisions made by strategist for analyzing the significance of the data like strengths, weakness, opportunities and threats of the organization has to design their own strategy for formulation, implementation and controlling the internal environmental factors.

Environmental analysis helps to strategic executive and manager to diagnosis of strategic competitive force and components of strategic management. However, internal environment of the organization is quite essential and important from the point of view of the environment analysis. It is the cornerstone of the new and existing business opportunity analysis too.

For instance, the individual life success depends on his innate capabilities like psychological factors, traits and skills. These are to be coped with the environment then will get success otherwise failure. The survival is the basic element and success of the business organization, it has to depend on its own strengths in terms of resources like money, men, machinery, materials, market and methods as its command. Organization's success depends on effective utilization of physical resource, financial resources and human resource skills. These are adaptability to the business environment.

Every business organization principally consists of internal environment factors and set of external environmental factors. In this chapter, we shall discuss only the internal environment of the organization/company.

Internal environment factors are generally considered as controllable factors of the organization. Internal environment factors are important to business like personal (human) resource department, marketing department, production department, physical facilities, accounting and finance departments and swot analysis. Therefore, the organization controls over these factors, these factors are modified or altered by the organization that suit for the business environment.

INTERNAL ANALYSIS OF THE ORGANIZATION/COMPANY

Formulation of an effective and efficient strategy has based on a clear definition of organization mission, an accurate assessment of the external environment and through internal analysis of the organization. Organization requir success which needs at least three ingredients. They are as listed:

- Strategy must be consistent with conditions in the competitive environment.
- Strategy must place realistic requirements on the organization/company's internal resources and capabilities.
- Strategy must be carefully formulated, implemented, controllable and executed.

Internal analysis of the organization is too difficult and challenging one to strategist. An internal analysis has lead to design a realistic organization profile. It frequently involves tradeoff, value system judgments, educated and skilled guess as well as objective and standardized analysis. A systematic internal analysis leads to main objective of the organization profile. It is essential to develop strategy and design a realistic mission for achievement of the strategy.

Internal analysis of the organization must identify the strategical strengths, opportunities, weakness and threats that are based on organization strategy. Organizational analysis identifies suitable strategy that based on the SWOT analysis.

Internal analysis can be achieved by first identifying key internal factors like value system, mission objectives, management structure and nature, integrated power relationship, human resource, company/organization image and brand equity, physical assets, R&D, technological capabilities, marketing resource and financial resource factors and secondly by evaluating these factors.

THE VALUE OF SYSTEMATIC INTERNAL ASSESSMENT

The value system of internal assessment is essential from the point of view of strategy formulation by the experienced strategist of the organization/company. The value system applies to either large or small business concern. It is critical in developing a successful business strategy. Regardless of the favorable opportunities in the environment, a strategy must be considered the essential internal strengths, weaknesses, opportunities and threats of the organization if such opportunities are to be maximized for accomplishment of goals.

The value systematic internal analysis is particularly essential in small business organizations. Small business organizations face lots of problems like limited resource and markets. These organizations are flexible and capable to capture selected markets and effectively channel their limited resource and maximize these limited market opportunities. *Internal analysis* is the basic objective of the organization.

Steps/Process in the Development of an Organizational/Company Profile

Company/organization profile focus on determination of strengths and weakness of the strategic environment of the business. Identifying and evaluating strategic internal factors are based on accomplishment of organization's future strategy. The major steps are important for the development of an organization/of company profile. They are listed below:

Stage one ---------------------------------- Identification of strategic factors

Stage two ---------------------------------- Using value chain analysis
Stage three ---------------------------------- Evaluations of strategic internal factors

IDENTIFICAION OF STRATEGIC FACTORS

An important identification of strategic factors approach as listed below:

1. Functional approach
2. The value chain approach

FUNCTIONAL APPROACH

Functional approach refers to organizations basic capabilities; characteristics, swot analysis and limitation are the key strategic factors. Functional approach key strategic factors are as follows:

- Marketing
- Finance and accounting
- Production /operation/ technical
- Human resource development
- Organization of general management

Marketing

Marketing deals with the following issues:

- Organization's products/service; product life cycle and marketing strategy.
- Concentration of sales in few products or little customer segmentation.
- Ability to gathere information about the market.
- To know the market share or sub-market share.
- Product/service mix and expansion potential: to know the life cycle of key products; to know the profit or loss of the product/service.
- To clearly know the channel of distribution; number, coverage, and control.
- To maintain effective sales organization: to find out knowledge about the customer needs.
- To improve product/service quality with image and reputation of brand name.
- Efficient and effective utilization of available resource for effective sales promotion and advertising.
- To aware of the pricing strategy and pricing flexibility.

- To effective monitoring and feedback of the marketing functions and expansion of product.
- Effective implementation of after sales service and follow up.
- To keep standards, goodwill and brand loyalty.

Finance and Accounting

Finance and accounting functions are as follows:

- Ability to raise short-term and long-term capital: either debt or equity.
- To maintain good corporate level resource.
- To know the cost of capital relative to industry and competitors.
- Tax consideration.
- To build up effective relationship with owners, investors, financial institution and stock holders.
- To know the leverage position: capacity to utilization financial strategies, like lease or sale and lease back.
- To aware of the cost of entry and barriers of the entry.
- To know the price earning ration.
- Present working capital position of the organization.
- Effective cost control and ability to minimize cost of expenditure for production of goods and service.
- Financial size of the organization.
- Efficient and effective accounting system for cost, budget, and profit planning of the organization.

Production/Operation/Technical

Production or Operation or Technical are as follows:

- To know the present raw material cost and availability.
- Inventory control system of the organization.
- Location facilities; layout and utilization facilities.
- Technical efficiency and effective utilization of technical resource in the organization.
- Effective use and implementation of subcontracting.
- Degree of vertical integration in terms of value added and profit margin of the product.
- To know the efficient and cost benefit of production techniques.
- Effective utilization and implementation of operation control procedure: design, scheduling, purchasing, quality control and efficiency.
- To know the costs and technological competencies relative to industry and competitors.
- Research development, innovative, advance ethnological development.
- Patents, trademarks and similar legal protection for their organization products/service.

Human Resource Development

Human resource development functions are as outlined:

- Effective management of the human resource in the organization.
- Improvement of employee skill and morale.

- Labor relations costs compared to industry and competition from present industry scenario.
- Efficient and effective formulation and implementation and controlling of the policies.
- Effective utilization of incentive to motivate employees' performance.
- To know the ability to level peaks and valleys of employment.
- To regulate employee turnover and absenteeism.
- Specialized skills and experience.

Organization of General Management

Organization of general management functions are listed below:

- To know the organization structure.
- Organization image and prestige to public world.
- Organization record for achieving goals and objectives.
- Effective utilization of resource and overall organization control system.
- To effective monitoring organization cultural climate.
- Effective utilization of systematic procedure and tools and techniques in decision-making.
- To know the top management skills, capabilities and interest.
- Effective implementation strategic planning system.
- To keep and maintain intra-organization synergy (multibusiness)

Some of which would be the focus of internal analysis in most of the business organizations.

Organization is not likely to consider all of the factors potential strengths or weakness. Strategist has to develop or review the factors which are important for the success of the organization.

For the analysis of the organization, firstly, a strategist has to analyze the past trends like sales, costs and profitability. These trends hold the major importance in identification of the internal factors of the organization. Further this identification should be based on a clear picture of the nature of the organization's sales trends. An anatomy of past trends has broken down by product lines channels of distribution of goods and service into different segmentation of key customers, geographical region and sales approach should be developed in detail. A similar anatomy of past trends should focus on costs and profitability. Strategist has to conduct detailed investigation of the organization's performance history that helps isolate internal factors influencing to sales, costs and profitability or their inter-relationships. The above factors are important in future strategy decisions.

Identification of strategic factors also requires an external focus of the organization. Strategist isolates key internal factors through analysis of past and present performance like industry conditions /trends and comparisons with competitors. In addition, strategic internal factors are often selected for in depth evaluation because organizations are contemplating expansion of products or markets, diversification. Strategist carefully scrutinizes the industry under consideration of current competitors. This is a key means of identifying strategic factors, if an organization is evaluating its capabilities more into unfamiliar markets.

THE VALUE CHAIN APPROACH

Value chain approach developed by Michael Porter, he wrote a book "competitive advantage" which identified the value chain approach of the organization. A value chain approach is a systematic way of viewing the serious activities of the organization performs to provide a product to its customers. Figure

6.1 highlights the typical value chain approach of the organization. The value chain disaggregate an organization into its strategically relevant activities in order to understand the behavior of the organization's cost and its existing or potential source of differentiation. An organization gains competitive advantage by performing primary and support activities, these activities are more important strategically.

Every organization can be viewed as value chain approach. Value chain approach as a collection of value activities that are performed to design, produce, market, deliver and support its product. The basic categories of value activities can be grouped into two broad types. They are as listed below:

- Primary activities
- Support activities

PRIMARY ACTIVITIES

Primary activities are those involved in the physical creation of the product and service in the organization. Its delivery of goods and service and marketing to ultimate buyer and it's providing after sales support to buyer. These activities are supporting to organization that provide inputs or infrastructure to the business.

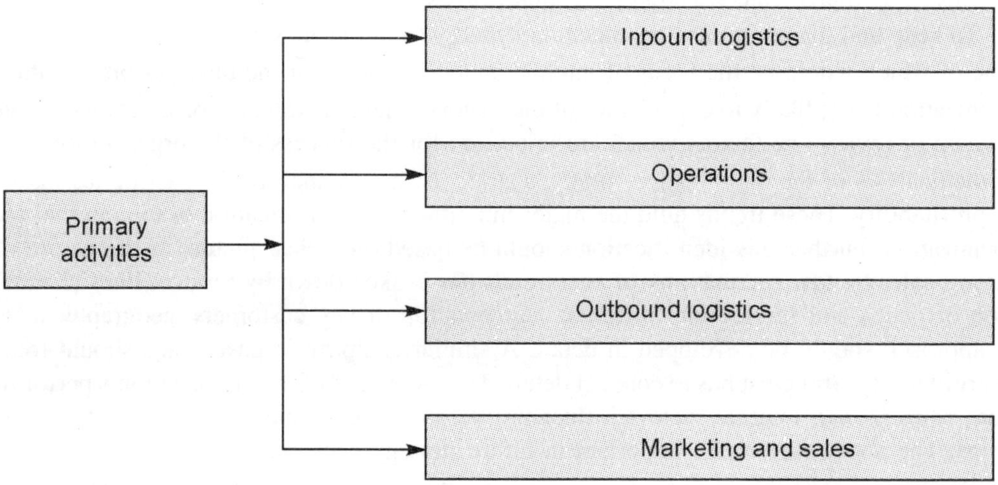

Figure 6.1 Identifying the primary activities of the value chain

Identifying Primary Activities

Primary activities principally composed of five activities. They are as outlined:

- Inbound logistics
- Operations
- Outbound logistics
- Marketing and sales
- Service

Identifying of the primary value activities requires the isolation of activities that are technologically and strategically distinct in the organization. There are five basic categories of the primary activities as listed below:

Inbound Logistics

Inbound logistic activities are associated with receiving, storing and dissemination inputs to the product like material handling, warehousing, inventory control, vehicle scheduling and returns to suppliers.

Operations

Operations activities are associated with transforming inputs into the product form, like machining, packaging, assembly, equipment maintenance, testing printing and facility operations in the organization.

Outbound Logistics

Outbound activities are associated with collecting, storing and physically distributing the product to buyers like finished products warehousing, material handling, delivery vehicle operation, order processing and scheduling.

Marketing and Sales

Marketing and sales activities are associate with providing a means by which buyers can purchase the product and inducting them to do so. Marketing and sales activities are advertising, promotion, sales force, quoting, channel selection, channel relations and pricing strategy of the organization.

Service

Service activities are associated with providing service to enhance or maintain the value of the product. Service activities are like installation, repair, training, and parts supply and product assessment.

The primary activities most deserving of further analysis depend on the particular Industry.

Identifying Support Activities

Support value activities arise in any one of four activities like procurement, technology development, and human resource management and organization infrastructure. These categories can be identified or disaggregated by isolating technologically or strategically distinct activities. Identifying support activities often overlooked as sources of competitive advantage. Support activities are listed below:

- Procurement
- Technology development
- Human resource management
- Organization infrastructure

Procurement

Procurement activities are involved in obtaining purchased inputs like raw materials, purchased services and machinery or so on. Procurement stretches across the entire value chain; therefore, it supports every activity–closely relating to purchased inputs of some kind. Different people typically perform with many discrete procurement activities in an organization.

Technology Development

Technology development activities are involved in desiring the product like creating and improving quality of the products and service. Technological development is closely related to innovation of new products and service of the organization. We shall tend to think of technology in terms of the product or manufacturing process. However, every activity of the organization performs and involves a technology. Organization has developed own research and development department for performing to innovation of new product and service.

Human Resource Management

Human resource management activities are necessary to ensure the recruitment, training and development of employees in the organization. Every activity involves human resources. Therefore, human resource management activities can be controled and managed across the entire chain.

Organization Infrastructure

Organization infrastructure activities are such activities as general management, accounting, legal, finance, strategic planning and all other developed organization specific primary activities or support activities but essential to the entire chain's operation.

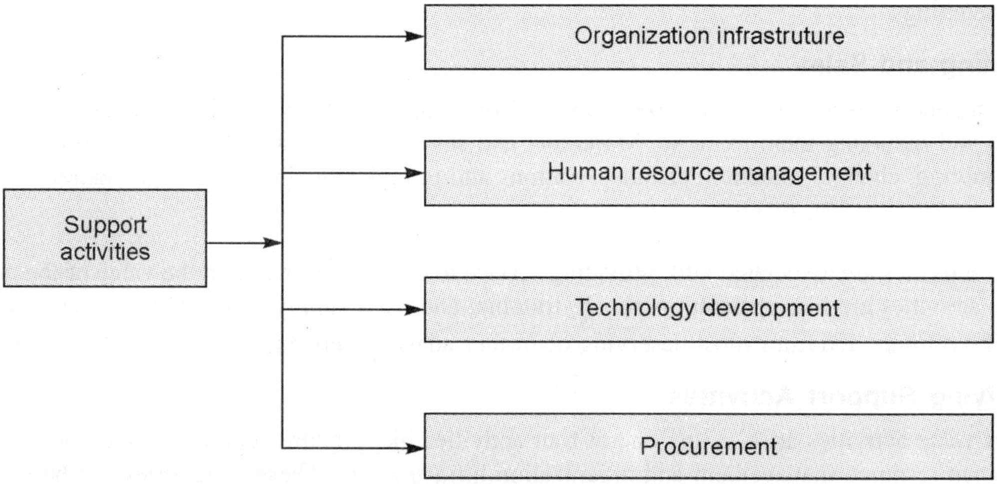

Figure 6.2: Identifying the support activities of the value chain

USING VALUE CHAIN IN INTERNAL ANALYSIS

The value chain provides a useful approach to organization to guide and monitor systematically evaluation of the strengths, weakness, and opportunity and threatens. An organization provides to distinct value activities like primary and supporting activities. The strategist has identified key internal factors for further examination as potential sources of competitive advantage.

EVALUTION OF STRATEGIC INTERNAL FACTORS

The major objective of internal analysis is a careful determination of an organization's strengths and weaknes. An internal analysis generates a long list of resources and capabilities which have provided little to help in strategy formulation. Instead, internal analysis must identify and evaluate a limited number of strengths and weaknesses relative to the opportunities targeted in the organization's present and future competitive environment.

Strategist evaluates the key internal strengths and weaknesses. He has considered four important basic perspectives. They are as follows:

- Comparison with organization's past performance
- Stages of product/market evolution
- Comparison with the competitors
- Comparison with key success factors in the organization's industry

Comparison with Past Capabilities and Performance

Strategist has taken more care about the comparison with past capabilities and performance. However, the historical experience of the organization as a basis for evaluating internal factors. Strategic Managers are most familiar with the organization's internal capabilities and constraints. Therefore, they have been immersed over time in managing the organization's financial, marketing, production facilities, sales organization, financial capacity, control systems, and key personnel. Organization has developed own strategy on the basis of comparison with past capabilities and performance.

Stages in Product/Market Evolution or Product Life Cycle

Product life cycle is the second factor to ascertainment of strengths and weakness of organization. Stages in product life cycle are essential from the point of view of success of the organization. As a result, strategist can use changing patterns associated with different stages in product lifecycle/market evolution as a framework for identifying and evaluating the organization's strengths and weakness.

There are four major stages of product life cycle/market evolution. They are as below:

- Introduction
- Growth
- Maturity
- Decline/Saturation

And typical changes in functional capabilities often associated with business success at each stage of the development of product/market cycle.

Strengths are needed in the growth stage because of rapid growth brings competitor into the market. This stage involves with brand recognition, product or market differentiation and the financial resources to support both heavy marketing expenses and affect the price competition and effective cash flow can be key strengths at this stage.

As the product/market moves through a "shakeout" phases and into the maturity stage, this stage market growth continues but at a decreasing rate the number of market segments begins to expand, while technological change in product.

While the products markets move towards a saturation decline stage, this stage strengths and weakness center on cost advantages, superior supplier or customer relationships and financial control.

Comparison with Competitors

A major focus in determining organization strengths, weaknesses is the comparison with potential competitors. Organization in the similar industry often have different marketing potential skills, financial resources, operating facilities and locations, technical know how, brand image, levels of integration, managerial talent, and so on. These different internal capabilities can become relative strengths or weaknesses depending on the strategy of the organization to select. In selection strategy, strategist should compare the organization's key internal capabilities with those of its rivals, thereby isolating key strengths or weaknesses.

Exhibit 6.3: Comparison With Competitors Growth In Software Industry. With the wave of consolidation sweeping the software industry and small and medium-sized software vendors needing scale to survive, Netkraft's sell-out was anticipated. When queried earlier, both company executives and its VC partners had brushed aside any such happening, saying that there was space for small and medium-sized companies to survive in the current highly competitive market place. Medium sized software vendors, who have recently succumbed to the merger wave, include Kshema Technologies, which was acquired by MphasiS. and iVega which merged with the Kolkata-based TCG Software of the, The Chatterjee Group. Adea Solutions, which has a development centre in Hyderabad, has emerged as a global player with a comprehensive portfolio of services including solutions development and delivery in domains like consulting, retail, finance and healthcare. The firm, which has a widespread global presence, employs around 1,500 people. Adea chief executive Abid H Abedi was awarded the Ernst & Young Entrepreneur of the Year award in 2003. Abedi had earlier stated that, with the expansion of the company's labs in Dallas and Hyderabad, its delivery capabilities are bound to be substantially effective in this competitive marketplace. Netkraft, which has managed to overcome its financial crisis and earn profits, is said to have made around $8 million last fiscal and is expected to touch the $10 million revenue figure this fiscal. The company started operations in 1998 and presently earns around 50 per cent of its revenues from the retail vertical. It recently joined the growing band of Level 5 CMMI certified companies. BANGALORE: US-based Adea Solutions, a global provider of business process and technology consulting services, has pipped a few international software firms to acquire Bangalore-based Netkraft. Netkraft, which focusses on retail, healthcare and banking and finance solutions, is currently owned by private equity firm Actis, US technology fund Jumpstart and employees. Sources said that Ernst & Young was the advisor for Adea on this deal. The deal size could not be confirmed. While Actis holds around 45 per cent, Jumpstart owns around 20 per cent of Netkraft with the employees holding the balance. Netkraft had been in the news when its original promoters, Prashanth Prakash and Atul Jalan, left the company, though they still have a stake in the company, a year ago. Sources added that a Texas-based software multinational firm too was keen to acquire the company. When contacted by The Economic Times, Anand Sudarshan, CEO of Netkraft, declined to comment.

Source: Times News Net Work, June 10, 2004

Success Factors in the Industry

The key determinant success factor in the industry may be used to identify the internal strengths and weaknesses of the organization. By scrutinizing industry competitors, as well as customer needs, vertical industry structures, channels of distribution costs barriers to entry, availability of substitutes, and supplier. A strategist seeks to determine whether organization's current internal capabilities represent strengths or weakness in the new competitive factors.

QUANTITATIVE VERSUS QUALITATIVE APPROACHES IN EVALUATING INTERNAL FACTORS OF THE ORGANIZATION

Numerous quantitative tools are available for evaluating selected internal capabilities of a term. Ratio analysis is useful for evaluating selected financial, marketing and operating factors. The organization's balance sheet and income statement are important sources from which to derive meaningful ratios.

Quantitative tools cannot be applied to all internal factors and the normative judgments of key planning participants may be used in evaluation.

QUESTIONS FOR DISCUSSIONS

1. Discuss the internal analysis of the organization/company.
2. Explain the process in the development of a company/organization profile.
3. Discuss the functional approach and its functions.
4. What is value chain approach? Describe its importance to strategic management.
5. Write short notes on the following
   - Identifying the primary activities
   - Inbound logistics
   - Operations
   - Outbound logistics
6. Explain the evaluation of strategic internal factors.
7. Discuss the product life cycle.
8. Briefly explain the quantitative versus qualitative approaches in evaluating internal factors.

REFERENCES

1. Capon, N.J. Farely, Jr; and J. Hulbert. *International Diffusion of Corporate and Strategic Planning Practices*. Columbia Journal of World Business, Fall 1980, pp. 5–13.
2. Channon, D.F., and M. Jalland. *Multinational Strategic Planning*. New York: AMACOM, 1978.
3. Davidson, W.H. *Global Strategic Management*. New York: John Wiley & Sons, 1972.
4. Neubauer, F. Fredrick, and Norman B. Solomon. *Mangerial Approach to Environmental Assessment*. Long–Range Planning , April 1977, pp. 13–20.
5. Perry, P.T. *Mechanisms for Environmental Scanning*. University of Michigan Business Review, September 1978, pp. 12–17.
6. A.A.Thomson and A.J. Strickland, *Strategic Management Concepts and Cases*, Tata McGraw –Hill Publishing Company Limited, New Delhi, 2003.
7. John, A. Pearce II, Richard B. Robinson, JR. *Strategic Management Strategy Formulation and Implementation*. A.I.T.B.S. Publishers & Distributors (Regd), New Delhi, 2002.
8. Times News Net Work, June 10, 2004
9. John A. Pearce II, *The company Mission as a Strategic Tool*, Sloan Management Review Spring, 1982.
10. A.J. Arjento, *Corporate Planning– Practical Guide*, Allen and Unwin, 1968.
11. B.W. Scott, *Long Range Planning in American Industry*, American Management Association, 1965.

Chapter – 7

External Environment

CONTENTS

- Introduction
- Micro/Operating environment
- Supplier
- Customers
- Competitors
- Marketing intermediaries
- Public
- Macro/Remote environment
- Economic environment
- Political environment
- Socio–cultural environment
- Demographic environment
- Natural environment
- Physical and technological environment
- International environment

LEARNING OBJECTIVES

This chapter, we shall examine external environment factors of the organization. Let us know that the microenvironment consist of supplier, marketing intermediaries, competitors, and customers, public. In addition, macroenvironment consist of economic, political, socio-cultural, demography, natural, physical and technological, international and legal environment.

INTRODUCTION

The concept of external environment is important for every kind of business operation. External environment is an attempt to understand the outside forces of the organizational boundaries that are helping to shape the organization. External environment has played significant role in formulation, implementation and controlling of the business strategy. The external environment can provide both facilitating and inhibiting influences on organizational performance. Key dimension of the external environment principally consists of a micro environment and a macroenvironment.

MICRO/OPERATING ENVIRONMENT

The micro/operating environment consist of the organization's or company's immediate environment that affects the performance of the organization/company. These are as listed below:

- Suppliers
- Marketing intermediaries
- Competitors
- Customers
- Public

It is quite important that micro/operating environment factors are more intimately linked with organization or company than macro/remote environment factors. The micro/operating forces need not necessarily affect all organizations in a particular industry. Some of the micro factors are particular to affect organization. For instance, an organization that depends on a supplier may have a supplier environment that is quite entirely different from that of an organization whose supply source is also different. When competing organizations in an industry have the same microelements, the relative success of the organization depends on their relative effectiveness in dealing with these elements.

SUPPLIERS

Supplier is the important force of the micro/operating environment of an organization or company *i.e.*, the supplier those who supply the inputs like raw materials and components to the organization. The major and important reliable source/sources of supply to the smooth function of a business is very important. Uncertainties are generated by the several supply problems like maintenance of inventory, delay of supply of inventory to organization.

Many organizations give high importance to vendor development, vertical integration for solving the supply problem. Organization depended on a single supplier is a risk factor due to a strike, lockout or any other production problem of the supplier. Always an organization has to depend on several supplier for the same raw material. Similarly, a change in attitude or behavior of the supplier may also affect the organization. Hence, multiple sources of supply often help reduce such risks. The supply management assumes more importance in a scarcity environment.

CUSTOMERS

The major task of business is to create and develop customers. A business can exist only because of its customers. Monitoring the customer's behavior is a prerequisite for the business success.

Organization may have different kinds of customers. They are listed below:

- Individual

- Households
- Industries
- Other commercial establishments
- Governments
- Other institutions

For instance, the customers of an auto-mobile spare parts manufacturing organization may include individual automobile owners, automobile manufacturers, public, private sector transport undertakings and other transport operators.

Organization depending on a single customer is often much a difficult and risky task. Therefore, it may place the organization in a poor bargaining position, apart from the risks of losing business result to winding up of business by the customer or due to the customers switching over to the competitors of the organization.

The strategic choice of the customer segments should be made by considering a number of factors including the relative profitability, dependability, and stability of demand, growth prospects and the extent of competition in organisation.

COMPETITORS

An organizations competitor includes not only the other organization which market the same or similar products but also those who compete for the discretionary income of the customers. For instance, the competition for a organization's cars may not come from other car manufacturers but also from two-wheeler, refrigerators, cooking ranges, stereo sets and so on and from organizations offering saving and investment scheme like financial institutions, companies accepting deposits or issuing shares or debenture to public. This competition among those products may be described as desired competition as the primary task here is to influence to the basic decision of the consumer. Such desires competition is generally very high in countries characterized by limited disposable incomes and many unsatisfied desires because of wants are unlimited.

If the consumer decides to spread his discretionary income and recreation he will still be confronted with a number of alternatives to select from such computer, stereo, two-in-one, three-in-one. The competition among such alternatives that satisfy a particular category of desire is called *generic strategy competition*.

An implication of these demands is that a marketer should strive to create primary and selective demand for his products.

MARKETING INTERMEDIARIES

The immediate environment of an organization may principally consist of a number of marketing intermediaries which are "organizations that aid the organization in promoting, selling and distributing its products and services to final buyers".

The marketing intermediaries are as outlined:

- Middlemen
- Agents
- Merchants
- Marketing agencies
- Advertising agencies

- Marketing research firms
- Media
- Consulting firms

PUBLICS

Public is the one important marketing intermediaries for promoting, advertising, channeling, selling the organization's product into different segmentation. If public accept the product of the organization, definitely it will be successful in the market, suppose product is rejected by the public definitely it will close the company.

MACRO/REMOTE ENVIRONMENT

The macro/remote environment principally consists:

- Economic environment
- Political environment
- Legal environment
- Socio-cultural environment
- Demographic environment
- Natural environment
- Physical and technological environment
- International environment

Macroenvironment force is uncontrollable i.e., uncontrollable factors of business organizations.

ECONOMIC ENVIRONMENT

The economic environment constitutes to economic conditions, economic polices, and the economic system that is the important external factors of business.

The economic conditions of the country include:

- Nature of the economy of the country
- Development process of the country
- Availability of economic resources of the country
- The level of the economic income of the country
- The distribution of income and assets of the country
- Public finance of the country

These are the very important determinants of business strategy in the organization for formulating, implement and controlling of economic policies.

Economic environment refers to the nature and direction of the economy within which business organization is to operate. For instance, in developing country, the low income may be reason for the very high demand for the product and services of the business.

In countries where the investments and income are steadily and rapidly rising, business prospects are generally bright and further investments are encouraged.

In developed economics, replacement demand accounts for a considerable part of the total demand for many consumer durables where as the replacement demand is negligible in the developing countries.

Money is the lifeblood of any business organization and the economic system. The economy consists of microeconomics and macroeconomics. Micro and macro elements are important from the point view of strategic decisions. The critical elements of the macro and microeconomic environment are listed below:

- Economic system
- Nature of the country economy
- The monetary and fiscal policies
- Autonomy of the economy
- Functions of economics
- Factors of productions
- Economic trends and structures
- Economic policy statements and structure
- Economic legislation
- Economic problems
- Import and export policy

Economic environment encourages liberalization, privatization and globalization of the economic policies in the business environment. Every country's development is based on the economic environment activities that withheld to the development process of the country.

POLITICAL ENVIRONMENT

Political environment refers political and government environment. It has close relationship with the economic system and economic policy of the country. For instance; the communist countries had a centrally planned economic system. Communist government countries laws are control investment and related matters. There are number of law that regulates the conduct of the business. These laws cover such matter as standards of business and its production and service.

The democratic governments countries law's/act are passed in the parliament. Then they are regulating rules and regulation of business according to the act.

The political environment is based on the uncertainty. Therefore, democratic countries consist of number of political parties. Political parties aren't got clear majority to form a government. In this situation, industry and commerce collapsed their business activities due to hung government. The political parties are unable to formulate stable government, it affect and fluctuate the government policies. Therefore, business organization and public needed a stable government.

SOCIO-CULTURAL ENVIRONMENT

Socio-cultural environment is an important factor that should be analyzed while formulating company business strategies. If company is ignoring the customs, traditions, tastes and preferences and education are all factors that affect business.

Business organization is successful due to appropriate strategies effective utilization of socio-cultural environmental factors. Social cultural environment is an important for MNC. Therefore, MNC should study the social cultural activities of the region, where they are introducing their own business. Even when the people belong to different cultures, they are used to the same basic product, and the mode of consumption may vary from one culture people to another culture. The socio-cultural vary in terms of the product attributes, method of presentation, promoting product into different market segmentation in business.

The difference in language sometimes poses a serious problem to culture, even necessitating a change in the brand name of the company. The value and beliefs associated with colour vary significantly between different cultures. For instance, white indication death and mourning in China and Korea; but some country it expresses happiness and is the colour of the wedding dress of the bride.

Social practice, beliefs and associated factors come in the way of the promotion of the action of certain products, services or ideas, the success of marketing depends to a vary large extent, on the success in changing social attitudes or value systems.

DEMOGRAPHIC ENVIRONMENT

Demography refers to study of the population. Demographic factors are as below:

- The population size
- Growth rate of population
- Age composition of the population
- Family size
- Economic stratification of the population
- Education levels
- Language
- Caste
- Religion

These factors are relevant to the business for formulating and implementing of strategy for controlling and accomplishment of the objectives of the organization.

Demographic factors like size of the population, population growth, rate, age, composition, life expectancy, family size, spatial dispersal, occupational status, employment pattern etc., affect the demand for goods and service.

The growth of population and income result increases demand for goods and services. A rapidly increasing population indicates that a growing demand for many products. For instance, developing countries like India, Pakistan, etc., with high population growth rate indicates an enormous increase in labor supply.

The occupational and spatial nobilities of population have implications for business. Labor is easily mobile between different occupations and regions. Its supply will be relatively smooth and this will be relatively affect the wage rate.

If a labor is highly heterogeneous in respect of language, caste and religion, ethnicity, etc., personal management is likely to become a more complex task. The heterogeneous population with its varied tastes, preferences, beliefs, temperaments, etc., gives rise to different demand patterns and calls for different marketing strategies.

NATURAL ENVIRONMENT

Natural environment is the study of an important component of the nature *i.e.*, natural environment. Natural environment includes geographical and ecological factors areas below:

- Natural resource endowments
- Weather
- Climate conditions
- Topographical factors

- Location aspects in the global context
- Port facilities are relevant to business.

Difference in geographical conditions between markets may sometimes call for changes in terms of product. place, promotion and price mix. Geographical and ecological factors also influence industries which help material index tend to be located near the raw material sources. Climate and weather conditions affect the location of certain industries like the often textile and sugar industry.

Natural and Ecological factors have recently assumed great importance. The depletion of natural resources, environmental pollution and the disturbance of the ecological balance has caused great concern to society. Government decision relating to protect the environmental purity and ecological balance and conservation of non replenisable resources etc. This resulted in additional responsibilities and problems to business and industry sector. Some of there issues impact on the cost of production and marketing the products and services.

PHYSICAL AND TECHNOLOGICAL ENVIRONMENT

Physical and technological environment factors are as below:

- Geographical factors
- Weather conditions
- Climate conditions

These conditions may call for modifications in the product etc., to suit the environment because these environmental factors are uncontrollable.

Business prospects also depend on the availability of certain physical facilities. Some products like many customer durables have certain used facility characteristics services offered by firm.

Technological factors sometimes pose serious problems to firms. A firm that is unable to cope with technological changes may not survive in terms of growth, and development. Further, the differing technological environment of different markets or countries may be called for product diversification.

Advances in the technologies of manufacturing, processing and preservation, packing etc, have facilitated product improvements and introduction of new products and have considerably improved the marketability of the products and services of the company.

The fast changes in technologies also create problems for enterprises as they render obsolete plants and product. Today, adopt changes in technology to achieve success in business and industry.

INTERNATIONAL ENVIRONMENT

International environment is the very important from the point of view of certain categories of business. It is particularly important for industries directly depending on imports or exports and import competing industries.

QUESTIONS FOR DISCUSSION

1. Explain the micro/operating business environment scenario.
2. Write a short note on
    - Customers

- Competitors
- Marketing intermediaries
- Public

3. Describe the external environment of the corporate scenario.
4. Briefly discuss macro/remote environment.
5. Briefly elucidate economic environment.
6. Describe the soci-cultural environment.
7. Discuss
   - Demographic environment
   - Natural environment
   - Physical environment
   - Legal environment
   - International environment.

REFERENCES

1. Capon, N.; J. Farely, Jr.; and J. Hulbert. "*International Diffusion of Corporate and Strategic Planning Practices*." Columbia Journal of World Business, Fall 1980, pp. 5–13.
2. Channon, D.F., and M. Jalland. *Multinational Strategic Planning*. New York: AMACOM, 1978.
3. Davidson, W.H. *Global Strategic Management*. New York: John Wiley & Sons, 1972.
4. Neubauer, F. Fredrick, and Norman B. Solomon. "*Mangerial Approach to Environmental Assessment*." Long-Range Planning, April 1977, pp. 13–20.
5. Perry, P.T. "*Mechanisms for Environmental Scanning*." University of Michigan Business Review, September 1978, pp. 12–17.
6. A.A.Thomson and A.J. Strickland, *Strategic Management Concepts and Cases*, Tata McGraw –Hill Publishing Company Limited, New Delhi, 2003.
7. John, A. Pearce II, Richard B. Robinson, JR. "*Strategic Management Strategy Formulation and Implementation*. "A. I. T. B.S. Publishers & Distributors (Regd), New Delhi, 2002.
8. Phip Kotler, *Principles of Marketing* (New Delhi, Prentice Hall of India Pvt. Ltd., 1987).
9. Francis Cherunilam, *Business Environment.* Himalaya Publishing House, Mumbai 1999.
10. Philip Kotler, *What Consumerism Means to Marketers*. Harvard Business Review, May-June 1972.
11. George N. Halm, *Economic Systems—an adoption*, Newyork, Fetter and Simons Inc., 1971.
12. Gary Hamel and C.K. Prahalad, *Competing for the future*, Harward Business School Press, 1994.
13. Altred D. Chandler Jr., *Strategy and Structure:*.
14. Kenneth R. Andrews, *The Concept of Corporate Strategy*, Taraporevala Publishing Industries Pvt. Ltd. 1971, Bombay.
15. Frank T. Paine and William, *Organisational Strategy and Policy*, The Dryden Press, 1982.
16. Peter F. Drucker, *Management: Task responsibilities, Practices*, Allied Publishers Pvt. Ltd. 1975.

Chapter – 8

Competitive Advantages

CONTENTS

- Introduction
- Strategic management tools
- Identifying the company or organisation strengths and resource capblities
- An achievement or attribute that plus the company in a position of market advantage
- Competitive advantage
- Low cost and differentiation
- The generic building blocks of competitive advantage
- Distinctive competencies, resources, and capabilities
- The durability of competitive advantage

LEARNING OBJECTIVES

This chapter, we shall examine

- Strategic management tools
- Identifying the company or organization strengths and resource capabilities
- An achievement or attribute that plus the company in a position of market advantage
- Competitive advantage
- Low cost and differentiation
- The generic building blocks of competitive advantage
- Distinctive competencies, resources, and capabilities
- The durability of competitive advantage

INTRODUCTION

"Only firms who are able to continually build new strategic assets faster and cheaper than their competitors will earn superior returns over the long term". C.C. Markides and P.S. Williamson.

Exhibit 8.1: Competitive Advantage of THE SATYAM EDGE

Satyam: The preferred IT services provider

With nearly a decade-and-a-half of experience in servicing global MNCs and Fortune 500 clients with end-to-end IT services, solutions and products, Satyam has come a long way, emerging as the preferred IT services provider for major global business corporations. An innovative organization, Satyam has been a pioneer-of-sorts in the Indian IT industry.

Landmarks

- Pioneered the IT Offshore Development concept in India
- First established a satellite link for communicating with client sites
- Developed the unique Right Sourcing delivery model
- Established India Development Centers for clients
- First to have acquired BVQI's ISO 9001:2000 certificate
- Developed eSCM model for ITES/BPO space with Carnegie Mellon University and Accenture
- **Satyam Infoway (Sify)** India's first Indian Private ISP; India's first Internet firm listed on the NASDAQ (NASDAQ: SIFY) **Advantage Satyam**
- World class processes (SEI CMM® Level 5, ISO 9001: 2000, eSCM)
- Global presence (Operations in 45 countries across 6 continents)
- Long lasting customer relationships (Nearly 80 % of repeat business)
- Flexible engagement models (Right Sourcing delivery model, IDCs, GDCs, JVs)
- Evolved competency and solution-based services
- Technology-led innovator
- Experience in serving top-notch customers that include four of Top 10 Fortune 500 corporations
- Strong Domain knowledge
- Highly qualified IT professionals
- State-of-the-art infrastructure
- Offshore advantage

Source: Satyam Company Website (www. Satyam.com)

"Organization succeed in a competitive market place over the long run because they can do certain things their customers value better than can their competitors".

Robert Hayes, Gary Pisano, and Daid Vpton

STRATEGIC MANAGEMENT TOOLS

Strategic management tools are as listed below:

- Swot analysis
- Value chain analysis

- Strategic cost analysis
- Competitive strengths assessment

These techniques are basic strategic management tools that serve to illuminate a company's resource strengths and deficiencies. Strategic management tools are found out of its best market opportunities and are aware of the outside threats to its future profitability. In addition, these tools stand competitive relative to rivals in the market. Company or organization situation analysis is a precondition for identifying the strategic issues like strength, weakness, opportunity and threats. Strategic tools are needs to address management for tailoring strategy to company resources like men, machine, material, method, market, money and competitive capabilities as well as to industry and competitive conditions.

A stronger a company's financial performance and market position has the result as a well–conceived and well executed strategy.

IDENTIFYING THE COMPANY OR ORGANIZATION STRENGTHS AND RESOURCE CAPABILITIES

Strengths refer to something good characteristic for a company or organization. It enhanced competitiveness in the market. Strengths may be depended on the company resource. Important strengths are as outlined:

- A skill or important expertise
- Valuable physical assets
- Valuable organization assets
- Valuable human assets
- Valuable intangible assets
- Competitive capabilities
- An achievement or attribute that puts the company in a position of market advantage
- Alliance/cooperative ventures

Skill or Important Expertise

Skills refer to expertise service done by the expert in the organization for accomplishment of goals and objectives of the company or organization. Important skills are as outlined:

- Low cost manufacturing capabilities
- Strong e-commerce expertise
- Technological know how
- A proven track record in defect free manufacture
- Expertise in providing consistently good customers service
- Excellent mass merchandising skills
- Unique advertising and promotional talents of the company.

Valuable Physical Assets

Valuable physical assets refer to fixed asset, tangible asset, intangible asset and current asset owned by the organization or company. Valuable physical asset are as outlined:

- State-of-the-art plant and equipment

- Attractive real estate locations
- Worldwide distribution facilities
- Ownership of valuable natural resource deposits cutting edge computer networks and information system
- Sizeable amounts of cash and marketable securities.

Valuable Human Assets

Valuable human assets refer to trained, well experienced people in the organization. Organization consists of the group of people. When these people are well experienced the ultimate result that accomplishment superior objectives of the organization or company. Valuable human assets are as outlined:

- An experienced and capable workforce
- Talented employees in key areas
- Motivated and energetic employees
- Cutting edge knowledge and intellectual capital
- Astute entrepreneurship and managerial know how
- The collective learning embedded in the organization and built-up over time.

Valuable Organizational Assets

Valuable organizational assets are important to organization. Successful organization depends on valuable organizational assets. Valuable organizational assets are as outlined:

- Proven of quality control systems
- Proprietary technology
- Key patents
- Mineral rights
- A base of loyal customers
- Strong balance sheet and credit rating
- Cutting-edge supply chain management systems
- A well functioning company intranet and e-commerce systems for accessing and exchanging information with suppliers and key customers
- Computer assisted design and manufacturing systems
- Systems for conducting for business on the Internet or comprehensive list of customers e-mail address.

Valuable Intangible Assets

Valuable intangible assets reduce the cost of production of products and service. Organizations success depends on the effective utilization of the valuable intangible assets in the company or organization. Valuable intangible assets are as outlined:

- Brand name image
- Company reputation
- Buyer goodwill
- Motivated and energized work force

Competitive Capabilities

Competitive capabilities refer to the competitive strengths of the organization. Competitive capabilities are efficiently curbed the competition from the rival industry. Competitive capabilities are as outlined:

- Short development times in bringing new products to market
- A strong dealer network
- Strong partnerships with key suppliers of raw material
- An R&D organization with ability to keep the company's pipeline full of innovative new products
- A high degree of organizational ability in responding to shifting market conditions and emerging opportunities
- A cadre of highly trained customer service representatives

AN ACHIEVEMENT OR ATTRIBUTE THAT PUTS THE COMPANY IN A POSITION OF MARKET ADVANTAGE

It refers to an achievement made by the organization with the help of human resource in the organization. An achievement or attribute that puts the company in a position of market advantages are as outlined:

- Lower overall costs
- Market share leadership
- A superior product
- A wide product selection
- Strong name recognition
- State-of-the-art e-commerce technologies and practices or exceptional customer service

Alliances/Co-operative Ventures

Alliances or co-operative ventures refer to strategic partnership with competitive firms in a particular industry. It helps the organization to improve their profitability and long term benefits. Alliances are as outlined:

1. Fruitful collaborative partnerships with suppliers and marketing allies that enhance the companies or organization's own competitiveness.

   Figure 8.1 highlights the company resource to produce competitive advantage as outlined:

   - Competitive advantage
   - Stretegic assets and company resource
   - Core and distinctive competencies
   - Competitive capability

   The company or organization resource has importance to produce competitive advantage with effective utilization of a skill or important expertise, valuable physical assets, valuable organization assets, valuable human assets, valuable intangible assets, competitive capabilities, an achievement or attribute that puts the company in a position of market advantage and alliance/cooperative ventures for growth, survival and profitability for very long time in the business.

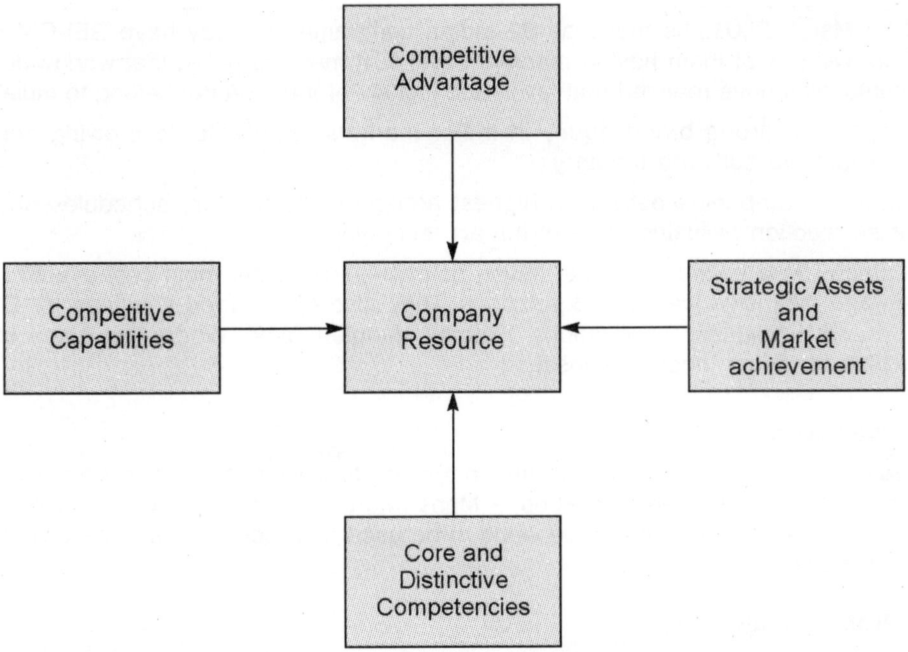

Figure 8.1 Mobilizing Company Resources to Produce Competitive Advantage

COMPETITIVE ADVANTAGE

Competitive advantage refers to organization or companies with how much benefit from the point views of cost and benefit analysis. Every organization has strategically competitive advantage for their business. For example, India's competitive advantage is as listed below:

Exhibit 8.2: Competitive Advantage India

Companies around the world are gaining competitive advantages by using Indian software services that offer high quality, cost effectiveness, time savings, state-of-the-art technologies and above all reliability.

The World Bank funded study compared India with many other countries to analyse India's position vis-a-vis cost and quality. Its findings proved that India is the **best** positioned as a high-quality and cost-effective country for software development. The advantages India offers are tremendous. They include:

- A virtual 12-hour time zone difference between India and USA offers cost and time savings, provides the client with a virtual 24-hour office environment.
- A huge pool of English speaking and computer literate graduate workforce who can continue to cater to the growing demand of professionals for IT Enabled Services.
- India offers the ultimate quality advantage with relatively less costs. India has more than 137 ISO 9000 certified and 147 more companies are in the pipeline to be ISO

(Contd...)

certified by March 2001. As many as 32 Indian companies already have SEI-CMM certification, with six of them having reached Level 5. It must be noted that worldwide, only 12 companies have reached that level, and just six of them do not belong to India.

- India enjoys very strong brand equity in major markets, thanks to its growing and globally competitive software industry.
- Indian software companies believe in highest adherence to delivery schedules and customer satisfaction by using state-of-the-art technologies.
- E-Business and web based solutions: Indian companies offer the most cost-effective, innovative and extensive web-based solutions. They also offer varied solutions for E-commerce and E-business applications. Hotmail, Junglee, Who, Where are some of the examples of Indian innovativeness.

Other Global advantages

One of the unique methods used by Indian software companies to deliver competitive advantage to its clients involves using high-speed (64 kbps, 2 Mbps and above) datacom links, which in turn allow computers situated anywhere in the world to be used by programmers in India on a real-time and on-line basis.

Large Pool of Professionals

Just as the Gulf has its crude oil and South Africa in diamonds, India's natural resource in today's knowledge economy is its abundant technically skilled manpower. India has the second largest assembly of English-speaking scientific professionals in the world today, second only to the US. It also has a growing bank of 4.1 million technical workers, supplied by, among others, over 1,832 educational institutions and polytechnics, which train more than 67,785 computer software professionals every year. This includes the graduates passing out of the prestigious Indian Institute of Technology (IIT), where the quality of technical training is comparable to the best of the educational institutes in the world. NASSCOM every year undertakes a survey to understand the manpower requirements of the industry. The study undertaken in 1999, highlighted the following facts:

- The number of software professionals employed have increased to 250,000 in 1999 compared to 2,00,000 in the preceding year. This includes software professionals in non-commercial organisation as well as software development units in user organisation.
- Almost 67% of the software professionals employed in the industry were in software development and operations, 3% in domain expertise development, 11% in marketing and relationship development, 15% in client support and 4% in other activities.
- The overall median age of the software professionals was about 26.2 years.
- 77% of software professionals in software companies were men, whereas 18% were women. However, this ratio is likely to be 65:35 (male: female) by the year 2003.
- Half of the software professionals possessed 5 years of working experience.
- There was an average of 21% rise in basic salary in 1998 over the previous year. However, rise in total compensation was supported by issuance of stock options to employees. During 1999, as many as 41 software and solutions companies announced employee stock option plans.

- In 1999, although the attribution rate was controlled at 16% (from the earlier turnover rate of 25% in 1992), but it still remained high, fuelled by 50% growth in the revenue for the software industry in 1998-99. This caused the HRD market to tighten considerably.
- Our software professionals were highly rated by their employers for their quality. Most gave an average of close to a 9 on a 10 point rating scale, with 1 being the lowest and 10 being outstanding.
- The skills in demand were in the area of business applications of software development, E-Commerce, Euro, software engineering, Java, ERP, CRM/ ERM, Interactive Integration Services, Datawarehousing, Internet, Client-Networking, BPR, OOPS, client-server, GUI, Windows, project management, quality assurance, technical writing, telecommunications, networking and RDBMS.

Source: NASSCOM

LOW COST AND DIFFERENTIATION

A company or organization has a competitive advantage when its profit rate is higher than the average for its industry. Profit rate defined as some ratio such as return on sales (ROS) or return on assets (ROA).

The most basic determinant of a company's profit rate is its Gross Profit Margin (GPM). GPM is simply the difference between Total Revenues (TR) and Total Costs (TC) divided by total costs.

$$\text{GPM} = \frac{(\text{Unit price} \times \text{Unit sale}) - (\text{Unit cost} \times \text{Unit sales})}{(\text{Unit cost} \times \text{Unit sales})}$$

Gross profit margin is to be higher than the average for the industry, one of the following issues must be occurring:

- The company's unit price must be higher than that of the average company and its unit cost must be equivalent to that of the average company.
- The company's unit must be lower than that of the average company and its unit price must be equivalent to that of the average company
- The company must have both a lower unit and a higher unit price than the average company.

Therefore, to achieve competitive advantages, a company must either have lower costs than its competitors or it must do both simultaneously.

When a company charges a higher unit price than the industry average, it is engaging in premium pricing. From the consumers prospective, consumer is to pay a premium price, the company must add value to the product, in a way that competitors added value requires differentiating the product from those offered by competitors along one or more dimensions like quality, design, delivery time, and after-sales services and support. More precisely, it means achieving superior performance on dimensions such as these.

Building on these basic ideas, Michael Porter has referred to low cost and differentiation as generic business level strategies i.e., the strategies represent the two fundamental ways of trying to obtain a competitive advantage in an industry.

- A low cost strategy highlights the possible to lower unit costs of the product and service.
- A differentiation strategy highlights the possibility to differentiate products from those offered by competitors in order to be able to charge premium.

THE GENERIC BUILDING BLOCKS OF COMPETITIVE ADVANTAGE

There are four factors to build competitive advantage. They are called as generic building blocks of competitive advantage. They are as outlined:

- Efficiency
- Quality
- Innovation
- Customer responsiveness

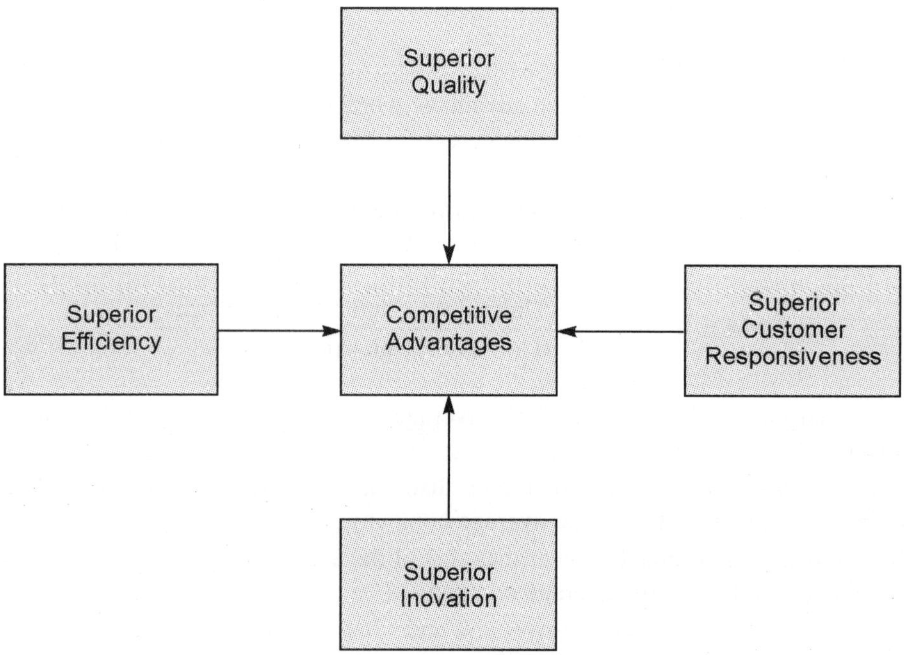

Figure 8.2: Generic building blocks of competitive advantage

Figure 8.2 indicates the generic building blocks of competitive advantage of the organization or company. Superior efficiency, quality, innovation and customer responsiveness represent the four basic ways of lowering costs and achieving differentiation of any company or organization which can adopt regardless of its products and service.

Superior Efficiency

Superior efficiency refers to effective utilization of factors of production for inputs converted into output. Superior efficiency arises due to the following factors:

- A company or organization is a method for transforming inputs into outputs. Inputs are basic factors of production like labor, land, capital, management, technological know-how, and so on.

- Output is the goods and service that a company or organization produces output. The more efficient a company or organization has converted the inputs into outputs at lower cost.
- One of the important keys to achieving high efficiency is to utilize inputs in the most productive way possible the most important component of efficiency for most companies in employee productivity, which is usually measured by output per employee. The company with highest employee productivity in an industry will typically have the lowest costs of production. In other words, that company will have a cost based competitive advantage.

Quality

Quality is another important generic building block of the competitive advantages. Quality product represents goods and services. Quality product can be designed very well. The impact of high product quality on competitive advantage is two fold. They are:

- Providing high quality product creates a brand reputation for company's products. Therefore, this enhanced reputation allows the company to charge a higher price for its product.
- Second impact of quality on competitive advantages comes from the greater efficiency and hence lower unit costs brought about by higher product quality.

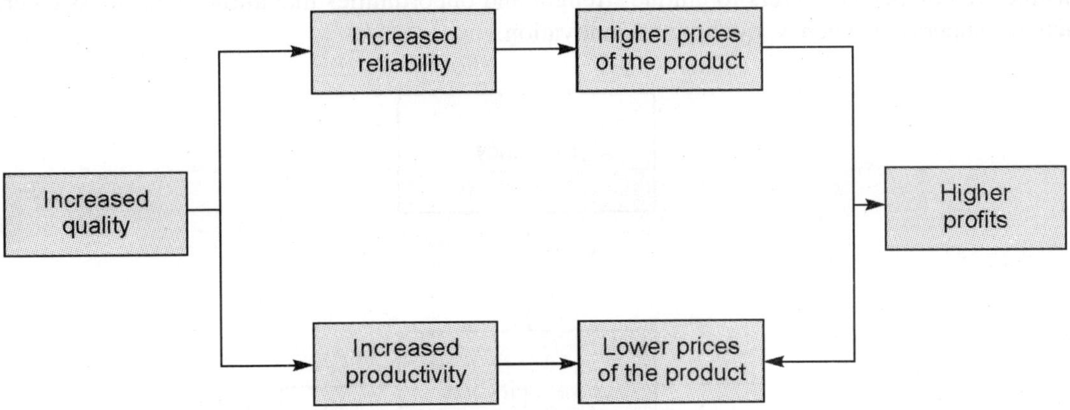

Figure 8.3: The Impact of the Quality on Profits

Figure 8.3 indicates impact of the quality on the products. Increase the quality products, its impact gets increased on the reliability of the products. The organization or company can be charged higher prices for the quality products, therefore, company charges higher price for the quality products ultimately the companies earn huge profits. On the other hand increase the quality, its impact on increased the productivity of the products, hence the company or organization can increase the productivity, therefore, even quality products available at lower cost for the consumers. The importance of quality in building competitive advantage has increased dramatically in recent years.

Innovation

Innovation is another one of the essential generic building blocks of competitive advantage. Innovation refers searching of anything new, the way a company operates or the producing of new products. Innovation includes advances in the kind of products, production process, managerial systems, organizational structures, new customers and marketing strategies developed by a company or organization. Product either success or failure depends on innovation.

Customer Responsiveness

Any business enterprise which has to achieve customer responsiveness, must give its customers exactly what they want when they want it. Consequently, business enterprise must do everything possible to identify customer needs and satisfy them. Customer responsiveness is the basic function of the strategist for achieving superior customer responsiveness; it involves giving customers value for money. In other words, achieving superior efficiency for quality and innovation are all part of achieving superior customer responsiveness of the business enterprise.

Another obvious factor that stands out in any discussion of customer responsiveness is the need to customize goods and services to the unique demands of individual customers.

Another important aspect of customer responsiveness that has drawn increasing attention is customer response time. The time takes for a good to be delivered or a service to be performed. Besides quality, customization and responsive time improves the customer responsiveness. Business enterprise properly and carefully defined customer responsiveness is superior design, superior service, and superior after sales service and support.

DISTINCTIVE COMPETENCIES, RESOURCES, AND CAPABILITIES

A distinctive competency refers to unique strength and opportunities that allows a business enterprise to achieve superior efficiency, quality and innovation.

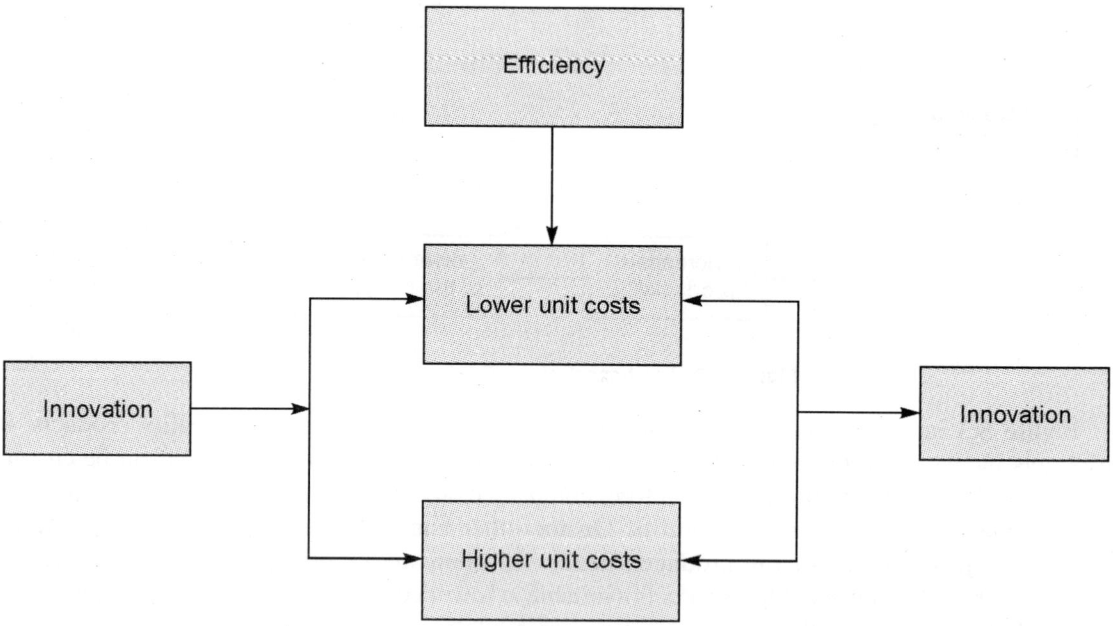

Figure 8.4: The Impact of Efficiency, Quality, Customer Responsiveness, and Innovation on Unit costs and Price.

Figure 8.4 indicates the impact of efficiency, quality, customer responsiveness, and innovation on unit costs and price. These are indicated the distinctive competencies, resources, and capabilities strengths of the business enterprise. A business enterprise with a distinctive competency can charge a premium price for its products and service or achieve substantially lower costs than its rivals. Finally, it can earn a profit rate substantially above the industry average.

Resources and Capabilities

The distinctive competencies of a business enterprise arise from two complementary sources. They are as listed below:

- Resources
- Capabilities

Resources

Resources refer to the financial, physical, human, technological, and organizational resources of the company. These can be divided into two categories. They are as outlined:

- Tangible resources
- Intangible resources

Tangible resources

Tangible resource includes:

- Land
- Building
- Plant
- Equipment

Intangible resource

Intangible resource includes:

- Brand name
- Reputation
- Patents
- Technological
- Marketing

Tangible and intangible resource are distinctive competency of business enterprise. Resources must be both unique and valuable.

Capabilities

Capabilities refer to an enterprise's skill at co-coordinating its resources and putting them to productive use. These skills reside in an enterprise's routines *i.e.*, in the way an enterprise makes decisions by managers, its internal process in order to achieve enterprise objectives. More generally, enterprise's capabilities are the product of its organizational structures and control systems. These specify how and where decisions are made within an enterprise, the kind of behaviors the enterprise rewards, and the business enterprise's cultural norms and values. It is important to keep in mind that capabilities are tangible and intangible resource. Team and individuals interact, cooperate, and make decisions within the context of an organization that is the major capabilities of business firm.

The distinction between resources and capabilities is critical to understand what generates a distinctive competency. A firm may have unique and valuable resources, but unless, it has the capability to use those resources effectively then only successful in business otherwise it may not be able to create or sustain a distinctive competency.

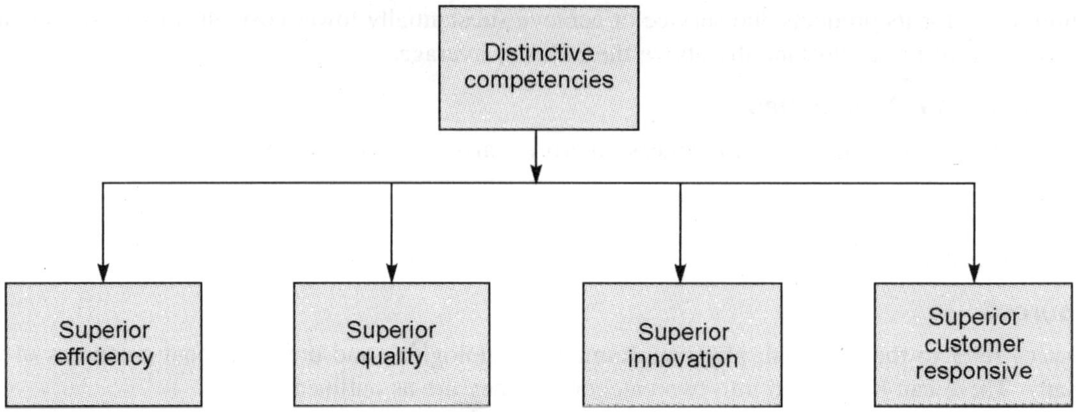

Figure 8.5: The Relationship between Distinctive Competencies and the Building Blocks of Competitive Advantage

Figure 8.5 highlights the relationship between distinctive competencies and the building blocks of competitive advantage. And how it matches the resources and capabilities is important to build a competitive advantage. It is also important to recognize that a firm may not need unique and valuable resources to establish a distinctive competency so long as it has capabilities that no competitor possesses. Ultimate for business firm to have a distinctive competency it must possess two unique factors as listed below:

- A unique and valuable resource and the capabilities skills necessary to extract that resource

or

- A unique capability to manage common resources

A business firm's distinctive competency is strongest when it possesses both unique and valuable resources and unique capabilities to manage those resources.

STRATEGY AND COMPETITIVE ADVANTAGE

The primary objective of strategy is to achieve a competitive advantage. Attaining this goal demands a two prolonged effort. A company needs to pursue strategies that build on its existing resources and capabilities, as well as strategies that build additional resources and capabilities and enhance the company's long-run competitive position.

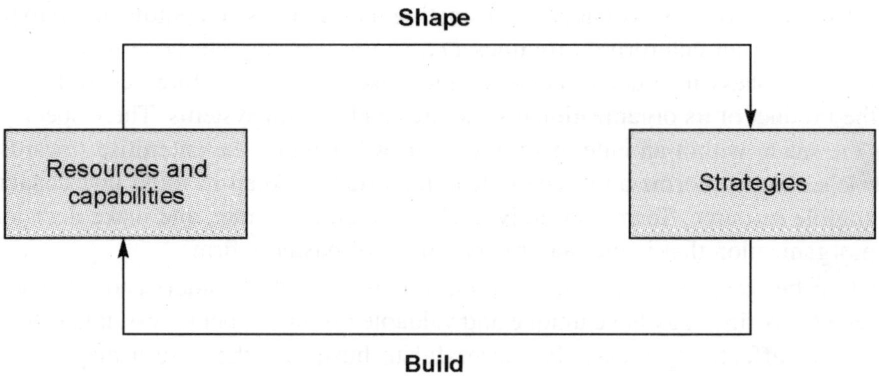

Figure 8.6: The Relationship between Strategies and Resources and Capabilities

Figure 8.6 shows the relationship between strategies and resources capabilities of the business firm. It is important to note that strategist has designed all types of strategies such as functional level strategies, business level strategies, corporate level strategies, and international strategies or, typically, some combination of them.

THE DURABILITY OF COMPETITIVE ADVANTAGE

The durability of a business enterprise's competitive advantages depends on three factors. They are as outlined below:

- The height of barriers to imitation
- The capability of competitors
- The general dynamism of the industry

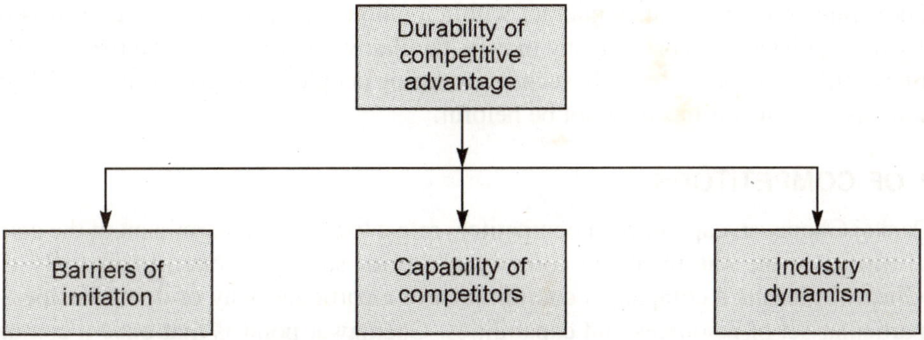

Figure 8.7: Factors influencing the Durability of Competitive Advantage.

Figure 8.7 indicates the factors influencing the durability of competitive advantage. Barriers to imitation, capability of competitors and industry dynamism are the durability of competitive advantage of the business enterprise or company or firm or organization.

BARRIERS TO IMITATION

Barriers to imitation refer to factors that make it difficult for a competitor to copy a firm or company's distinctive competencies. Distinctive competencies allow business firms or companies to earn superior profits; therefore, competitors want to imitate them. However, the greater barrier is to imitation for the more sustainable to firm or company's competitive advantage. It is important to note that ultimately almost any distinctive competency can be imitated by a competitors to intimate a distinctive competency. It is the greater opportunity to firm or company has to build a strong market position and reputation with consumers, which is then difficult for competitors to attack. Moreover, the longer it takes to achieve a limitation, the greater is the opportunity for the imitated firm or company to improve on its competency, or build other firms or companies, thereby, staying one step ahead of the competition.

Imitating Resources

Imitating resources refers to the easiest distinctive competencies for prospective rivals to intimate tend to be those based on possession of unique and valuable tangible resources like buildings, plant and equipment. These resources are visible to competitors can often purchase on the open market.

Intangible resources can be more difficult to imitate, it is particularly true of brand names. Brand names are important because they symbolize a firm's or company's reputation to the heavy, moving equipment industry.

Imitating Capabilities

Imitating capabilities refers to a firm's or company's capabilities tend to be more difficult than imitating its tangible and intangible resources, chiefly because a firm's or company's capabilities are often invisible to outsiders. Since capabilities are based on the way in which decisions are made and processes managed deep within a firm or company. By definition, it is hard for outsiders to discern the nature of a company's internal operation.

The invisible nature of capabilities would not be enough to halt imitation. In theory; competitors still gain insights into how a firm or company operates by hiring people away from that firm or company. However, a firm or company's capabilities rarely reside in a single individual. Rather, they are the product of how numerous individuals interact within a unique organizational setting. It is possible that no one individual with in a firm or company may be familiar with the totality of a firm or company's internal operating routines and procedures. In such cases, hiring people away from a successful company in order to imitate its key capabilities may not be helpful.

CAPABILITY OF COMPETITORS

According to Pankaj Ghemwat, capability of competitors refers to a major determinant of the company's competitive advantage is the nature of the competitor's prior strategic commitments. By strategic commitment, Ghemwat means a company's commitment to a particular way of doing business *i.e.*, to developing a particular set of resources and capabilities. Ghemawat point is that once a company has made a strategic commitment, it will find difficult to respond to new competition if doing so requires a break with this commitment. Therefore, when competitors already have long-established commitments to a particular way of doing business, they may be slow to imitate an innovating firms or company's competitive advantage. Its competitive advantage will thus be relatively durable.

INDUSTRY DYNAMISM

Industry dynamism refers to a dynamic industry environment is one that is changing rapidly. The most dynamic industries tend to be those with a very high rate of product innovation, For example, the consumer electronic industry and the personal computer industry. In a dynamic industries, the rapid rate of innovation means that product life cycles are shortening and that competitive advantage can be very transitory.

QUESTIONS FOR DISCUSSIONS

1. Discuss the company's/organization's strengths and resource capabilities.
2. Explain the competitive advantage.
3. Write short notes on the following:
   - Low-cost differentiation
   - The generic building blocks of competitive advantage

- Efficiency
- Quality
- Innovation

REFERENCES

1. Charles W.L. Hill/Gareth R. Jones, *Strategic Management Theory an Integrated Approach*, All India Publishers and Distributors Regd.2001.
2. A.A. Thomson and A.J. Strickland, *Strategic Management Concepts and Cases*, Tata McGraw –Hill Publishing Company Limited, New Delhi,2003
3. John, A. Pearce II, Richard B. Robinson, JR. *Strategic Management Strategy Formulation and Implementation*. A.I.T.B.S. Publishers & Distributors (Regd), New Delhi, 2002.
4. Taylor, B., *The Return of Strategic Planning — Once More with Feeling*, *Long Range Planning*, vol. 30, no. 3, 1997, pp. 334-344
5. Wernerfelt, B. and A. Karnani, *Competitive Strategy Under Uncertainty*, *Strategic Management Journal*, 8 (2), 1987, pp. 187-194
6. Michael E. Porter, *Competitive Adavatage*, op.cit, pp.1-25
7. William F. Glueck, *Business Polity and Strategic Management*, McGraw-Hill International Book Co., Auckland, 1972.
8. Cited by Leslie W. Rue and Phyllis G. Holland, *Strategic Management*, McGraw-Hill Book Co., Newyork, 1989.
9. Gary Hamel and C.K. Prahalad, *Competing for the future*, Harward Business School Press, Bosten, 1994.
10. Arthur Sharplin, *Strategic Management*, McGraw-Hill Book Co., Newyork, 1985.
11. H.J. Ansoff, *The New Corporate Strategy*, John Wiley & Sons, Newyork, 1988.
12. Alfred Chandler, *Strategy and Structure*, MIT Press, Cambridge, 1962.

Chapter – 9

Value Chain Concept Analysis

CONTENTS

LEARNING OBJECTIVES

This chapter plans to discuss about the value chain, basic concepts of value chain, the value creation process, primary activities, supporting activities, how to achieving superior efficiency in manufacturing, materials management, research and development, infrastructure. In addition, to know total quality management and its concepts, implementation TQM, superior innovation, building competitive steps in innovation.

INTRODUCTION

We shall discuss about the central role played by efficiency, quality, innovation and customer responsiveness in building and maintaining value chain in a competitive advantages. In this chapter, we examine the value chain analysis, the role of functional strategies in achieving efficiency, quality, innovation, and customer responsiveness. Functional level strategies are strategies directed at improving the effectiveness of operations with in a company; take manufacturing, marketing, materials management, research and development, and human resources.

THE VALUE CHAIN

The primary analytical tool of value chain is identifying the separate activities, functions and business process of the organization that are performed in designing, producing, marketing, delivering and supporting a product and service. The chain of value is creating activities like, it takes to provide a product or service activities that starts with raw materials supply and continues on through conversion of the raw material into finished product or service, after the distribution of goods and service to ultimate user of the product or service.

BASIC CONCEPT OF VALUE CHAIN

A company's or organization value chain identifies the primary activities and supporting activities create the value for end user of the product and service.

The value chain of the organization creates the value for the product and service. It is measured by the amount that buyers are willing to pay for a product or service. Organization is profitable, it creates the value for the product or service. The value creation functions are as listed below:

- General administration
- Operations
- Material management
- Research and Development
- Human resource
- Infrastructures
- Procurement
- Marketing

These functions gain to competitive advantage of an organization. Company or organization must perform value creation functions at a lower cost.

THE VALUE CREATION PROCESS

The value creation process chain concept popularized by Michael Porter

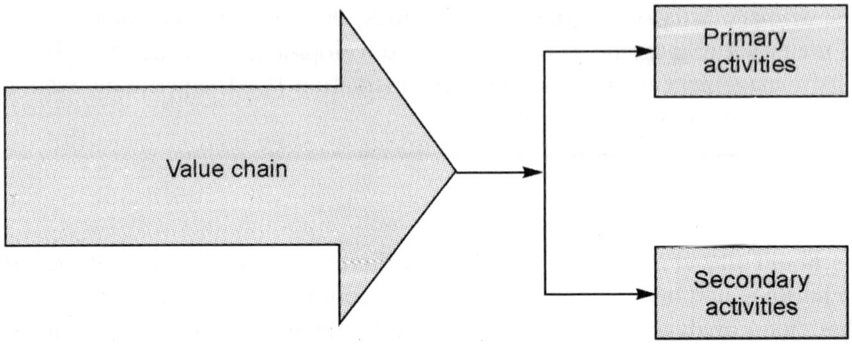

Figure 9.1. The Value Chain Process

The Fig. 9.1 indicates the value-chain process. The value-creation process chain is classified into two processes. They are as outlined:

- Primary activities
- Supporting activities

PRIMARY ACTIVITIES

Primary activities are as listed below:

- Purchased supplies and in-bound logistics
- Operations
- Distributions and out-bound logistics
- Sales and marketing
- Service

Primary activities aim to do with the creation of the physical product.

SUPPORTING ACTIVITIES

Figure 9.2 highlights the supporting activities of the company or organization. It indicates to cross functional goals and value chain. Supporting activities are known as *functional activities* of the organization. Supporting activities are as listed below:

- Research, technology and systems development
- Human resource management
- General administration
- Efficiency
- Quality
- Innovation
- Customer responsiveness

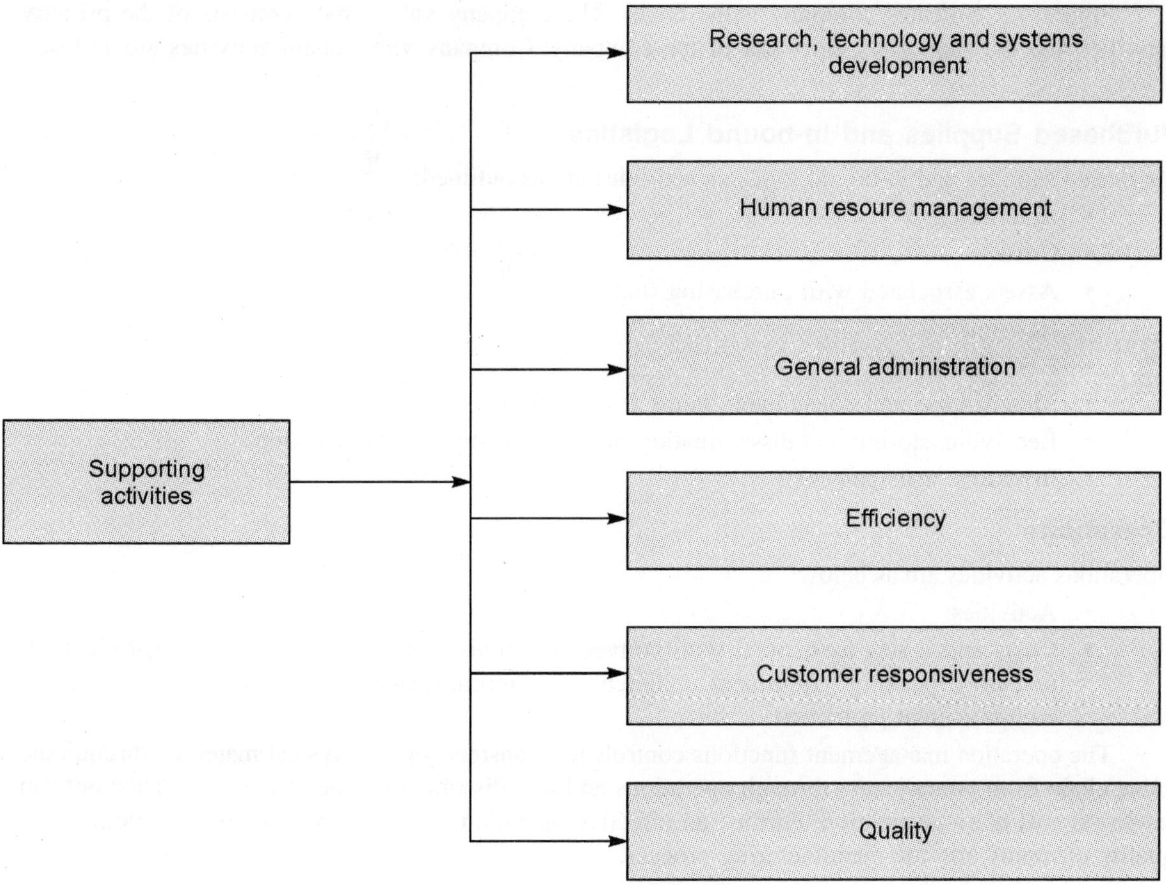

Figure 9.2. Supporting Activities

Value creation activities are as superior efficiency, quality; innovation and customer responsiveness are achieving goals of the company or organization. These activities require strategies for formulation, implementation and monitor, guide and controlling of value-chain activities of the organization or company.

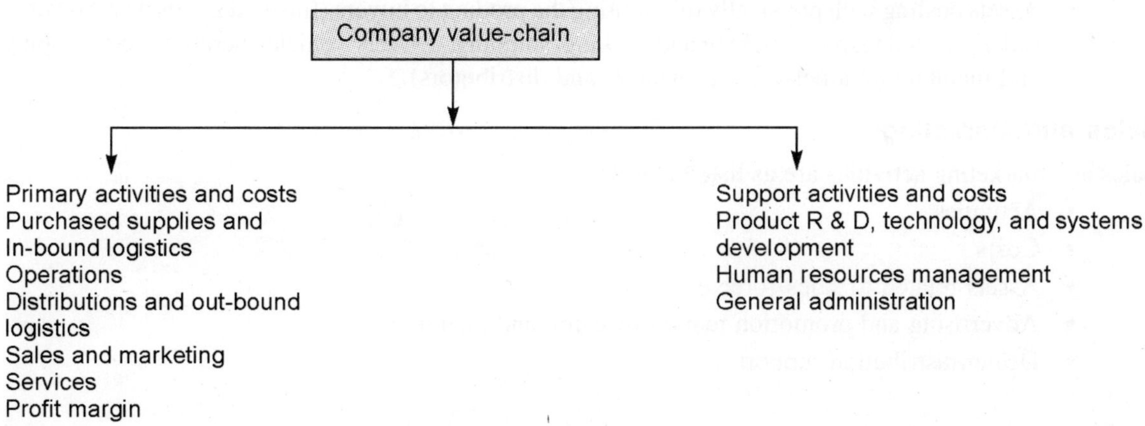

Figure 9.3. Company Value Chain

Figure 9.3 indicates company value chain. The company value chain consists of the primary activities and the supporting activities of the company. Company value chain activities are as listed below:

Purchased Supplies and In-bound Logistics

Purchased supplies and in-bound logistics activities are as outlined:

- Activities
- Costs
- Assets associated with purchasing fuel
- Raw materials
- Past components
- Merchandise and consumable items from vendors
- Receiving, storing and disseminating inputs from suppliers, inspection
- Inventory management

Operations

Operations activities are as below:

- Activities
- Costs and assets associated with converting inputs into final product form (production, assembly, packing, equipment, maintenance, facilities, operations, quality assurance, and environmental protection).

The operation management functions controls the transmission of physical materials through the value chain from procurement through operations and into distribution. The efficiency carried out can lower the cost of value creation. Further, an effective operation management function can monitor the quality of inputs into the manufacturing process.

Distribution and Out-bound Logistics

Distribution and out-bound logistics are as listed below:

- Activities
- Costs
- Assets dealing with physically distributing the product to buyers (finished goods warehousing, order processing, order picking and packing, shipping, delivery vehicle operations, establishing and maintaining a net-work of dealers and distributors).

Sales and Marketing

Sales and marketing activities are as listed below:

- Activities
- Costs
- Assets related to sales force efforts
- Advertising and promotion market research and planning
- Dealer/distribution support

Service

Service activities are as outlined:

- Activities
- Costs
- Assets associated with providing assistance to buyers such as installation, spare parts delivery, maintenance and repair, technical assistance, buyers inquiries and complaints.

Support Activities

Support activities are listed below:

- Research, technology and systems delivered
- Human resource management
- General administration

Research, Technology and Systems Delivered

Research, technology and systems delivered are essential requirement of the company. Research, technology and systems delivered are as outlined.

- Activities
- Costs and assets relating to product R&D
- Process R&D
- Process design improvements
- Equipment design
- Computer software development
- Telecommunications system
- Computer-assisted designs and engineering
- New database capabilities
- Development of computerized support systems.

The R&D function develops new product and its process technologies. Technological innovation result is lower manufacturing costs and result in the creation of more attractive products that demand a premium price. It can affect primary manufacturing and marketing activities, and through them value creation.

Human Resources Management

Human resources management refers to recruitment, hiring, training, development and compensation of the employees of the organization. Human resource management activities are as follows:

- Activities
- Costs
- Assets associated with the recruitment, hiring training, development, and compensation of all types of personnel
- Labor relations activities
- Development of knowledge-based skills and core competencies.

The human resource function ensures that the company or organization has the right to collect the skilled people to perform its value creation activities effectively.

General Administration

General administration refers to administration of the organization. The general administration activities are as listed below:

- Activities
- Costs
- Assets relating to general management
- Accounting and finance
- Legal and regulatory affairs
- Safety and security
- Management information systems
- Forming strategic alliances and collaborating with strategic partners and other overhead functions.

Infrastructure is the final supporting activities of the company or organization value chain. It has a somewhat different character from the other support activities. Infrastructure is the company's or organization wide context within which all the other value-creation activities take place. It includes the company's or organizational structure, control systems, and culture.

Steps in Value-Chain Analysis

Value-chain analysis can be broken down into a three sequential steps as follows:

- Break down a market/organization into its key activities under each of the major headings in the model.
- Assess the potential for adding value via cost advantage or differentiation, or identify current activities where a business appears to be at a competitive disadvantage.
- Determine strategies built around focusing on activities where competitive advantage can be sustained.

ACHIEVING SUPERIOR EFFICIENCY

A company or organization can be viewed as a device for converting of inputs into outputs. Inputs are basic factors of production like labor, land, capital management technology, plant and machinery etc. Output is the goods and services that are produced by the company or organization or business enterprise. Efficiency is measured by the cost of inputs (raw materials) required to produce a given output (finished product and service). The cost of production of the outputs is the lower, the efficient company or organization required to produce a given output. In another words, an efficient managed organization or company shown higher productivity than its rivals. Here, we shall review the various steps for achieving superior efficiency. They are as mention below:

- Economies of scale and efficiency
- Flexible manufacturing and efficiency
- Marketing strategy and efficiency
- Materials management strategy and efficiency
- R&D strategy and efficiency
- Human resources strategy and efficiency
- Infrastructure and efficiency

ECONOMIES OF SCALE

Economies of scale is one way achieving a superior efficiency. It refers to the unit-cost reductions which is associated with large scale of output. An economy of scale is the ability to spread fixed costs that over a large production volume. Fixed cost means that fixed costs are costs that must be incurred to cost include the cost of purchasing machinery, the costs of setting up machinery for individual productions runs, the costs of advertising and R&D. Companies or organization are able to produce output in large volume to achieve a greater division of labor and specialization. It is also another source of scale of economies. Company or organization wishes to effective utilization of resource become more efficient and thereby attain a low-cost position.

FLEXIBLE MANUFACTURING EFFICIENCY

An organization or company produces a standardized product in large volumes. It drives down-unit costs. Flexible manufacturing technologies designed for reduction of unit cost in the following circumstance:

- Reduce setup times for complex equipment in the factory.
- Increase the utilization of individual machines through better scheduling.
- Improve quality control at all stages of the manufacture process of the product and service.

Flexible manufacturing technologies allow the company or business organization to produce a wider variety of output. Company or organization can achieve cost reduction by producing outputs in large volume and it should be standardized output.

Marketing Strategy and Efficiency

Marketing strategy involves the combination marketing mix. They are as mentioned below:

- Product
- Price
- Promotion
- Place

These play a major role in boosting a company's or organization efficiency. Some of the marketing steps leading to greater efficiency are fairly obvious. The most important is the relationship between customer defection rates and unit costs. Customer's loyalty in turn is a function of the ability of a company to satisfy its customers. Another economic benefit of customer long-time loyalty is the free advertising that customer provide for a company. Loyal customers do a lot of talking, and they can dramatically increase the volume of business through refers. Reducing customers' defection rates and building customer loyalty can be a major source of cost saving.

MATERIALS MANAGEMENT STRATEGY AND EFFICIENCY

Material management strategy refers to the activities that are necessary to get materials for conversion of raw material into finished output and these outputs distributed to ultimate customers. Efficient materials management is reducing costs. It can have substantial impact on profitability. Organization or company adopts for Just in Just inventory systems. Just in just inventory system is to improve the efficiency of the materials management function. Raw materials arrive at manufacturing plant just in time to enter the production process that the basic concept of the just in just inventory system. Increasing inventory turnover generates cost saving to organization which reduces inventory holding costs like warehousing and storage costs.

The Disadvantages of Just in Just Inventory Systems

Organization or company depends just in just inventory for manufacturing of output. Therefore, organization has faced major disadvantages of the just in just inventory system as listed below:

- It leaves an organization without a buffer stock of inventory.
- It is expensive to store.
- It can be disruption of supplies from supplier.
- It can be disruption of output.

R&D STRATEGY AND EFFICIENCY

The role of superior research and development strategy is helping a company or organization to achieve greater efficiency. It has two fold as mentioned below:

- The R & D function can boost efficiency by designing innovative products that are easy to manufacture of output. It cuts down cost and the numerous parts and decreased the assembling time of output. It translates higher employee productivity and lower unit costs.
- R & D function like process of innovation helps the company to achieve greater efficiency.

HUMAN RESOURCE STRATEGY AND EFFICIENCY

Human resource strategy refers to employee productivity, is one of the key determinants of an enterprises efficiency and cost structure. The more productivity of human resource of the organization that lowers unit costs. Human resource functions are as outlined:

- Recruitment
- Selection of employee
- Training and development of employees skills
- Performance appraisal and fringe benefits for employees
- Self-managing teams
- Best pay for performance of the employees

These functions help the organization to increase employee productivity.

SUPERIOR QUALITY

Achieving superior quality refers to quality of output produced by organization or company. It has two fold advantages for organization. They are outlined as

- It enhances the reputation for quality, lets the company charge a premium price for its output.
- The elimination of defects from the manufacturing process, therefore, increases quality and hence output available at lower costs to customers.

TOTAL QUALITY MANAGEMENT

The total quality management (TQM) focuses on improving the quality of a company's products and services and stress that all company operations should be oriented toward this goal.

The TQM Concept

The total quality management (TQM) concepts were first developed by a number of American consultants, including W. Edward Deming, Joseph Juran, and A.V. Feigenbaum. The total quality concept is based on the following five steps *i.e.*, "chain reaction", they are as below:

- Improved quality results to decrease costs because of less rework, fewer mistakes, fewer delays, and better use of time and materials. As a result productivity improves.
- Better quality output capture to higher market share and allows the company or organization to raise prices. This increases the company's profitability and allows it to stay in business.
- Quality output captures the market, for this purpose the company creates more jobs.

Implementing TQM

TQM requires close cooperation among all functions in the pursuit of the common goal of improving quality of output. Implementing total quality management function as listed below:

Build Organizational Commitment to Quality

It refers to training of employees to build organizational commitment to improve the quality of the output, this is the major performance of the company.

Focus on Customer

TQM focus on customers as the starting point it raised the whole quality philosophy for customers to identify major role in market role. It needs to identify what the customers want from the goods or service the company provides.

Find Ways to Measure Quality

TQM program is to create some metric that can be used to measure quality. It is simple to measure quality in manufacturing companies, quality measured by defects per million parts. It is more difficult to measure quality in service companies. Top management should take primary responsibility for formulation of different metrics to measure quality.

Set Goals and Create Incentives

Once a quality metric has been devised, the next step is to set a challenging quality goal and to create incentives for reaching that goal.

Solicit Input from Employees

Employees can be an important source of information regarding the source of poor quality. Some framework must be established in the organization for soliciting employee suggestions for improvement of the quality. Self-managing teams are involved in discussing quality improvement tasks.

Identify Defects and Trace Them to Source

TQM main function is to identify defects during the work process and trace them to their source. Manufacturing and materials management typically have primary responsibility to find out what caused them and make corrections. So that, if any uncover defects, they use statistical procedures to pinpoint variations in the quality of goods or service. One variation identified, and traced to their source and eliminated and easily traces defective parts in manufacturing process.

Supplier Relations

A company must work closely with its suppliers if it is going to introduce different inventory system to manage material flows from them. Organization plan to implement good relations with suppliers even maintain good interaction with suppliers. Organization or company is not depending on single suppliers due to lack of supply of inventory which are required for manufacturing of outputs. TQM required two steps necessary for implementation of quality in company or organization. They are as below:

- The supply has to be rationalized to manageable, therefore, the number of suppliers is reduced to manageable proportions.
- There is a need to commit to building cooperative long-term relationships with the suppliers that remain strong focus on supplier relationships.

Design for Ease of Manufacture

Designing products with more parts should make assembling complex and result in larger defects. Designing products with fewer parts should make assembly easier and result in fewer defects. Both R & D and manufacturing functions need to be involved in designing products that is easy to manufacture of outputs.

Break Down Barriers Between Functions

Implementing TQM requires organization, it's wide commitment and substantial cooperation among functions of the organization. R&D has to cooperate with manufacturing to design products that are easy to manufacture of outputs. Marketing has to cooperate with manufacturing and R&D. Organization has identified customer problems in quality output and act to solve marketing problems. Human resource management has to cooperate with all of other functions of the company or organization in order to devise suitable quality training for employees of the organization.

SUPERIOR INNOVATION

Superior innovation is the single-most important building blocks of competitive advantage. Successful innovation of products or process gives a company something same that its rivalry lack. This uniqueness may allow a company to charge a premium price or lower its cost structure below that of its competitor's, rivalries will try to imitate successful innovations. Although, company high barriers to imitation can slow it down.

The High Failure Rate of Innovation

In competitive advantage scenario, 80 to 88 percent new products innovation is failure. Remaining 10 to12 percent of new products actually generate profit when they get to the market place.

Reasons for New Products Failure in the Market

There are four reasons for new products failure to generate an economic return:

- **Uncertainty**

  Introducing new products to market that is uncertain task for organization. Developing new products is risky task since no one can predict the demand although good market research can reduce the risks of failure of new products.
- **Poor Commercialization**

  New product has to fail due to poor commercialization and lack of promotion by the company.

Therefore, there is no demand for new technology products at beginning stage to market. Although, the product technology feature is not well adapted to consumer needs.

- **Less Demand**

  Company produced goods and services which are not having enough demand from the customers. Therefore, company is failed promote its innovative products due to less demand from the customers.

- **Slow the Market Cycle**

  Company's introduced new products to the particular market. The new product is a failure due to the slow market cycle and the company is unable to promote market cycle in a particular market.

BUILDING COMPETENCIES STEPS IN INNOVATION

There are five steps which are an important to build competencies in innovation to avoid failure of the innovative products. They are as listed below:

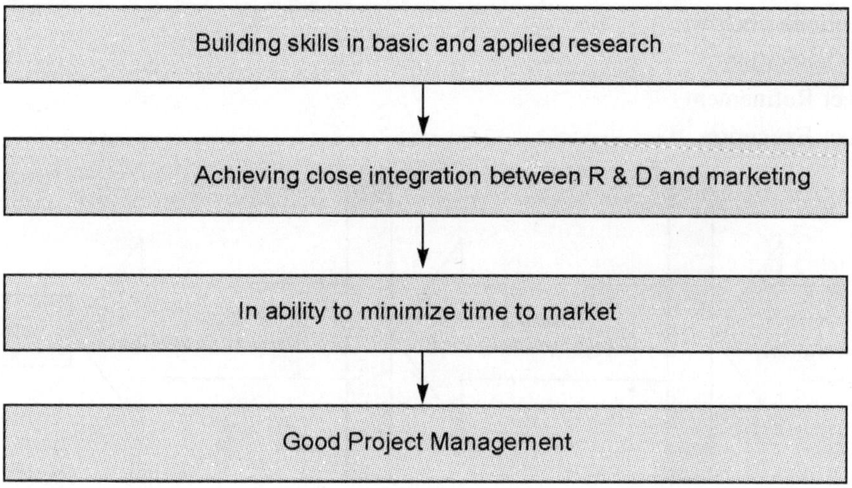

Building Skills in Basic and Applied Research

Building skills in basic and applied research requires the employment of research scientists and engineers of the company. The establishments of excellent work environment that fosters creativity. Top companies try to achieve this by setting applied research department where scientists and engineers are given time to work on their own research projects. Further these applied research projects are directly linked with ongoing projects.

Integrating R & D and Marketing

Time is the second step of building competencies in innovation. Organization or company's marketing function provides valuable information regarding the company's customers; customers are the primary sources of new product idea and identification of customer needs. However integration of R & D and marketing are very important for development of new product. It is to be properly commercialized without integrating research and development and marketing of the company or organization can run the risk of developing products.

Integrating Manufacturing R&D

Integrating Manufacturing and R&D is the third step for building competencies in innovation. Successful innovation also requires close integration between manufacturing and R&D. Integrating manufacturing research and development important task is to design products and is easy to manufacture at lower manufacturing costs along with less defects of outputs of the company or organization. It is designing manufacturing cost at less cost and an increase product quality. It can also help to reduce the development cost of the output.

Reducing Time to Market

Reducing time to market is the fourth step for building competencies in innovation. It is one of the key requirements for reducing time to market and is to achieve cross-functional integration among research and development, manufacturing and marketing departments of the company or organization.

Project Management

A project management is the last step for building competencies in innovation. Project management is the overall management of the innovation process. Project management requires three important skills. They are as mentioned below:

- Idea Generation
- Project Refinement
- Project Execution

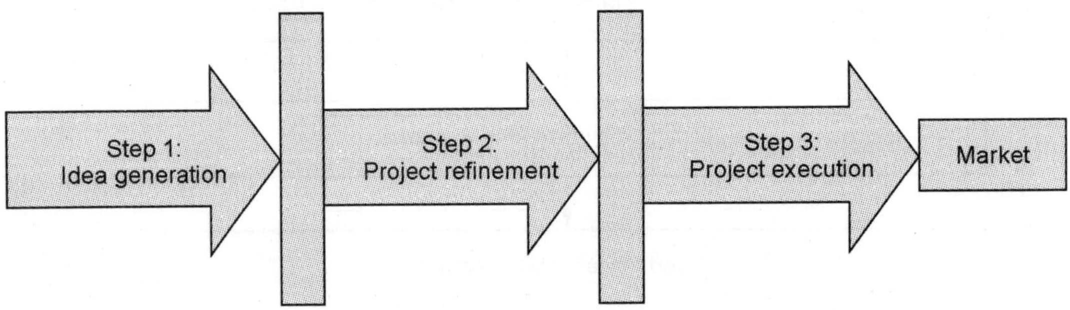

Figure 9.4. The Concept of Project Development.

Figure 9.4 indicates the concept of project development. The project development process is divided into three steps as follows:

- Idea generation
- Project refinement
- Project execution proposed is executed by gross functional team in order to ensure that time to market is minimized.

CUSTOMER RESPONSIVENESS

Achieving superior customer responsiveness refers to company or organization how to response the customer enquiry regarding the quality, sales after service and its products. Organization or company's superior efficiency, quality, and innovation are all parts supporting to achieve superior customer responsiveness. There are two goals achieving superior customer responsiveness of the organization. They are as listed below below:

- Customer focus
- Satisfying the customer needs

Customer Focus

Customer focus is the first step in building superior customer responsiveness in the organization. It is to motivate the whole company to focus on customer. Customer focus involves to the following areas:

- Leadership
- Employee attitudes
- Bringing customers into the company

Leadership

Customer focus must start at the top of the organization. A commitment of superior customer responsiveness involves creating strong leadership qualities in company or organization for focus of customer enquiry regarding products and service.

Employees Attitudes

Employee attitude is essential to organization. All employees in the company must be trained to focus on customer enquiry about the product and service irrespective of their function like marketing, manufacturing, R&D, accounting. Employees carefully identify ways to improve the quality of a customer service from the experience with the company or organization. Employees who are satisfying customer's desire, the company should adopt incentive system and reward for responsible employees of the company.

Bringing Customer into the Company

"Know the customer" is one of the key components to achieving superior customer response of the company or organization and as much as possible bring them into the company. It means that bringing in customers opinion and feed-back from customers about the products and service which offered by the organization or company. Organization or company effective building customer information systems and that communicate the feedback to the responsible employee or department.

Satisfying Customer Needs

Efficiency, quality and innovation all are crucial to satisfying customer desires and needs. Company provides a higher level satisfaction by their product and service. An obvious satisfying customer needs are as listed below:

- Customization
- Response time

Customization

Customization refers to dynamic features of a service to tailor it for the organization or company. It is used to be thought that customization would raise costs.

Responsive time

The responsive time is important to organization or company. It relates to goals and service delivery of a product and service to customers. Reducing response time requires the following areas:

- A marketing department quickly communicates customer requests to manufacturing department.
- Manufacturing and materials management department quickly adjust production schedules in response to unanticipated customer demands.
- Information system department helps to manufacturing and marketing department for this process.

QUESTIONS FOR DISCUSSIONS

1. Discuss the value chain.
2. What are the basic concepts of value chain?
3. What are the steps involved the creation process.
4. Write short notes on the following:
   - Primary activities
   - Secondary activities
5. How to achieve superior efficiency?
6. How to achieve superior quality?
7. Discuss the TQM concept.
8. How to achieve superior innovation?
9. Write short notes on the following:
   - Customer responsiveness
   - Building competitive steps in innovation

REFERENCES

1. Burgelman, Robert A. *Strategy Is Destiny*. New York: The Free Press, 2000.
2. Collins, James C., and Jerry I. Porras. *Building Your Company's Vision*, Harvard Business Review 74, no. 5 (September-October 1996), pp.65–77.
3. Hamel, Gay. *Strategy as Revolution*. Harvard Business Review 74, no. 4 (July-August 1996), pp.69 – 82.
4. Lipton, Mark. *Demystifying the Development of an Organizational Vision*. Sloan Management Review, summer 1996, pp. 83–92.
5. Mintzberg, Henry. Bruce Ahlstrand; and Joseph Lampel, *Strategy Safari: A Guided Tour through the Wilds of Strategic Management*. New York: Free Press, 1998.
6. Caves, R.E., and M.E. Porter. *From Entry Barriers: Conjectural Decisions and Contrived Deterrence to New Competition*. Quarterly Journal of Economics 91 (1976), pp.421–34.
7. John, A. Pearce II, Richard B. Robinson, JR. *Strategic Management Strategy Formulation and Implementation*. A.I.T.B.S. Publishers & Distributors (Regd), New Delhi, 2002.

8. Karger, D.W., and Z.A. Malik. *Long–Range Planning and Organizational Performance.* Long Range Planning, December 1975, pp. 60–64.
9. Kudla, R.J. *Elements of Effective Corporate Planning*. Long Range Planning, August 1976, pp. 82–93.
10. Pearce, J.A., II, and W.A. Randolph. *Improving Strategy Formulation Pedagogies by Recognizing Behavioral Aspects* Exchange, December 1980, pp. 7–10.
11. Robinson, R.B., Jr. *The Importance of 'Outsiders' in Small Firm Strategic Planning*. Academy of Management Journal, March 1982, pp. 80–93.
12. Brown , Shona L., and Kathleen M. Eisenhardt. *Competing on the Edge: Strategy as Structured Chaos. Boston*, MA: Harvard Business School Press, 1998.
13. Drucker, Peter. *The Theory of Business*. Harvard Business Review 72, no.5 (September-October) , pp. 95–104.
14. Hamel, Gary, and C.K. Prahalad. *Strategic Intent*. Harvard Business Review 71. no. 4 (July–August) , pp.69–82.
15. Kahaner, Larry. *What You Can Learn From Your Competitors 'Mission Statements*. Competitive Intelligence Review6, no 4(Winter 1995), pp. 35–40.
16. Lipton, Mark. "*Demystifying the Development of an Organizational Vision*. Sloan Management Review, summer 1996, pp. 83–92.
17. Porter, M.E. *Industrial Market Structures and Economic Performance*. Review of Economics and Statistics 61 (1979), pp. 214–27.
18. Caves, R.E., and M.E. Porter. *From Entry Barriers: Conjectural Decisions and Contrived Deterrence to New Competition*. Quarterly Journal of Economics 91 (1976), pp.421–34.
19. A.A.Thomson and A.J. Strickland 111, *Strategy Formulation and Implementation Tasks of the General Manager*, Plano, TX: Business Publications,1983.
20. A.A.Thomson and A.J. Strickland, *Strategic Management Concepts and Cases*, Tata McGraw –Hill Publishing Company Limited, New Delhi,2003.
21. Gilmore, Frank. *Formulating Strategy in Smaller Companies*. Harvard Business Review, May–June 1971, pp.75–85.
22. Glueck, William F. *Business Policy and Strategic Management*. 3rd.ed. New York: McGraw Hill, 1980.
23. Herold, David. *Long Range Planning and Organizational Performance: A Cross Validation Study*. Academy of Management Review, March 1972, pp. 91–102.
24. Karger, Delmar Karger. *Does Long Range Planning Improve Company Performance?* Management Review, September 1975, pp.27–31.
25. Schoeffler, Sidney; Robert D. Buzzell; and Donald F. Heany. *Impact of Strategic Planning on Profit Performance*. Harvard Business Review, March – April 1974, pp. 137–45.
26. Lawrence R. Jauch and William E. Glueck, *Strategic Management and Business Policy*, McGraw-Hill Book Co., Newyork, 1998.
27. Michael B. Porter, *Competitive Advantage: Creating and Sustaining Superior Performance*, Free Press, Newyork Press, 1985.

Chapter – 10

Business and Investment Level Strategy

CONTENTS

- Introduction
- Customer needs and product differentiation
- Customer groups and market segmentation
- Deciding on distinctive competencies
- Choosing a generic competitive strategy at the business level
- Cost leadership strategy
- Advantage of cost leadership strategy
- Strategic choices
- Disadvantages of cost leadership strategy differentiation strategy
- Strategic choice
- Advantages and disadvantages
- Focus strategy
- Advantages of focus strategy
- Disadvantages of focus strategy
- Investment strategy
- Competitive position
- Life cycle effects
- Embryonic
- Growth
- Shake out
- Maturity and declines

LEARNING OBJECTIVES

In this chapter, we shall discuss customer needs and product differentiation, customer groups and market segmentation, deciding on Customer needs and product differentiation, Choosing a generic competitive strategy at the business level, Cost leadership strategy, Advantage of cost leadership strategy, Strategic choices, Disadvantages of cost leadership strategy differentiation strategy, Strategic choice, Advantages and disadvantages, Focus strategy, Advantages of focus strategy, Disadvantages of focus strategy, Investment strategy, Competitive position, Life cycle effects, Embryonic, Growth, Shake out, Maturity and declines.

INTRODUCTION

This chapter aims to discuss about the customer needs, customer groups and distinctive competencies decisions are the heart of business level strategy choice. Therefore, these are provided the resource of a competitive advantage over its competitors and determine how the company will compete in a business or industry.

CUSTOMER NEEDS AND PRODUCT DIFFERENTIATION

Customer needs and product differentiation are one of the foundations of business level strategy. Customer needs are anything that can be satisfied by means of the future of a product or service. Product differentiation is the step of creating competitive advantage by designing products and service to satisfy customer needs. All companies must differentiate their products and service to certain degree in order to attract customers and satisfy some minimal level of customer needs. Some companies differentiate their products to a much greater degree than others and this difference can give them a competitive edge.

Some companies offer the customer a low priced product without much engaging in product differentiation others seek to create something unique about their product. Therefore, they satisfy customer's needs. Indian companies are concentrated for customer needs and product differentiation, thereby, reducing the cost of production of goods and service.

CUSTOMER GROUPS AND MARKET SEGMENTATION

It is the second decision of foundation of business-level strategy market segmentation. It defined as the way a company decides to group customers; it is based on importance of differences in their needs and preferences in order to gain a competitive advantage. A company can adopt three alternatives strategies toward market segmentation and different customer groups. They are as listed below:

- A company may choose different groups of customers and is not recognize that different groups of customers have different needs and may adopt the approach of serving the average customer.
- A company may have to choose market segment into different states and develop a product to suit the needs of each group.
- A company can choose and recognize the market segment. Therefore, it concentrates on servicing only one market segment or niche.

DECIDING ON DISTINCTIVE COMPETENCIES

It is the third decision of the foundation of business level strategy, it is to decide what distinctive competencies to pursue to satisfy customer needs and groups as we discussed in the competitive advantage chapter. In making business strategy choice, a company must decide how to organize and combine its distinctive competencies to gain a competitive advantage.

CHOOSING A GENERIC COMPETITIVE STRATEGY AT THE BUSINESS LEVEL

Choosing a generic competitive strategy at the business level, it is choosing from three generic competitive approaches. They are as listed below:

- Cost leadership/low cost
- Differentiation
- Focus

These strategies are known as *generic* because of all business or industries can pursue them regardless of whether they are manufacturing, service or not for profit organizations. Each of the generic strategies results from a company making consistent choices on product, market and distinctive competencies.

The product/market distinctive-competing choices and generic competitive strategies at business level industries are listed below:

- Cost leadership
- Differentiation
- Focus

And its choices as listed below:

- Product differentiation
- Market segmentation
- Distinctive competency

COST LEADERSHIP

A company's goal in pursuing a cost leadership or low-cost strategy is to out perform competitors by doing everything. It can pursue goods or service at a cost lower than their competitors. Cost leadership strategy is required strategies choice of product and service into different market segmentation and its competitors.

ADVANTAGE OF COST LEADERSHIP STRATEGY

Exhibit 10.1: Advantage of Cost Leadership Strategy

There are two advantages which occur from cost leadership strategy. They are as mentioned below:

- Cost leadership strategy refers to lower costs of product and service offered by the company, the cost leader is able to charge a lower price than its competitors. The cost leader makes a higher profit than its competitors because of its lower cost of products and service.

(Contd...)

- If industry rivalry increases and companies start to compete on price, the cost leader will be able to withstand competition to compete on price; the cost leader will be able to withstand competition better than other companies because of its lower costs. For both reasons, cost leaders are likely to earn above–average profits.

DISADVANTAGES OF COST LEADERSHIP STRATEGY

Exhibit 10.2: Disadvantages of Cost Leadership Strategy

Important disadvantages of cost leadership strategy are outlined:

- The principal dangers of the cost leadership approach risk in competitors ability to find ways of producing at lower cost and beat the cost leader.
- Competitor's ability to easily imitate the cost leader's method is another threat to the cost leadership strategy.
- The cost leadership strategy carries a risk that the cost leader, the single-minded desire to reduce costs, may lose right to changes in customer tastes.

STRATEGIC CHOICES

The company cost leader strategy is choosing a low level of product differentiation. Differentiation is expensive for company; if the company expands resources to make its product unique then its costs rise. The cost leader aims for a level of differentiation not marketing inferior to that of the differentiator (a company competes by spending resources on product development) but a level obtainable at low cost.

The cost leader also normally ignores the different market segments and positions. Its product is to appeal to the average customer. The main reason is that the cost leader makes its choice by developing a line of products and tailored to the needs of different market segments. It is an expensive proposition. A cost leader normally engages to only a limited amount of market segmentation. Customer is happy when the company normally charges a lower price than its competitors attracts customers to its products and service.

In developing distinctive competencies, the overriding goal of the cost leader must be to develop competencies. It enables to increase its efficiency and lower its costs compared with its competitors. The development of distinctive competencies in manufacturing and material management is central to achieving this goal. Companies pursuing a low-cost strategy may attempt to ride down the experience therefore; they can lower their manufacturing costs. Achieving a low-cost position may also require that the company develop skills in flexible manufacturing and adopt to develop skills in flexible manufacturing and efficient materials-management techniques.

DIFFERENTIATION STRATEGY

Differentiation strategy refers to the differentiated company's ability to satisfy a customer needs. It helps the company to charge a premium price; a price considerable above the industry average. Company ability to increase by charging premium prices (rather than by reducing costs of the output) allows the differentiator to outperform its competitors and gain above-average profits. The premium price is usually substantially above the price charged by the cost leader, and customers pay it therefore, they believe the product-differentiated qualities to be worth the difference.

Advantages of Differentiation Strategy

Exhibit 10.3: Advantages of Differentiation Strategy

Advantages of Differentiation Strategy as outlined:

- The company's unit price must be higher than that of the average company and its unit cost must be equivalent to that of the average company.
- The company's unit must be lower than that of the average company and its units price must be equivalent to that of the average company.
- The company must have both a lower unit and a higher unit price than the average company.

Disadvantages of Differentiation Strategy

Exhibit 10.4: Disadvantages of Differentiation Strategy

Major disadvantages of differentiation strategy are listed below:

- Developing the distinctive competency needed to provide a differentiation advantage is often expensive to company.
- A differential cost usually has higher costs than the cost leader.
- The main problem with the differentiation strategy center on the company's long-term ability to maintain its perceived uniqueness in customers' eye in market.
- A differentiation strategy is the ease to competitors can imitate a differentiators's product and the difficulty of maintaining a premium price.

Strategic Choice of Differentiation Strategy

The differentiation strategy chooses a high level of product differentiation to gain a competitive advantage. Differentiation can be achieved with quality, innovation and responsive a product appeal to customers' psychological desires can become a source of differentiation. A company pursues a differentiation strategy strives to differentiate itself along as many dimensions as possible. The less it resembles its rival, the more it is protected from competition, and the wider is its market appeal.

A differentiator chooses to market segment. Company offers a product to design for each market differentiator, but a company chooses to serve just niches where it has a specific differentiation advantage.

A differentiated company concentrates on the organizational function that provides the source of its differentiation advantage. Differentiation based on the innovation and technological competency depends on R & D function. A differentiator does not want to increase costs unnecessarily.

FOCUS STRATEGY

Focus strategy is the third generic competitive strategy and one of the foundations of business level strategy. Focus strategy is directed towards serving the need of a limited customer group or segment. A focus strategy is the focused company concentrates on serving a particular market niche that may be defined geographically, by type of customer, or by segment of the product line.

Once company has chosen its market segment, a company may pursue a focus strategy through either a differentiation or a low-cost approach. A focused company is a specialized differentiator or cost leader. Because of their small size, few focus firms are able to pursue cost leadership and differentiation simultaneously. If a firm uses a low-cost approach, it competes against the cost leader in the market segment where it has no cost advantage with focus strategy, a company concentrates on small volume custom products, where it has a cost and leaves the large volume standardized market to the cost leader.

If a focuser pursues a differentiation approach, then all the means of differentiation that are open to the differentiators are available to the focused company. The point is that the focused company competes with the differentiator in only one or in just a few segments. Focused companies are likely to develop differentiated product qualities successfully because of their knowledge of a small customer set or knowledge of a region. Further, more concentration on a small range of products. Sometimes allows a focuser to develop innovations faster than a large differentiation. A focused company concentrates on building market share in one market segment and, if successful, may begin to serve more and more market segments.

ADVANTAGES OF FOCUS STRATEGY

Exhibit 10.5: Advantages of Focus Strategy

An important advantage of focus strategy as listed below:

- Focus strategy is protected from competitors to the extent therefore; it can provide a product or service.
- Focus strategy gives the focuser power over its buyer therefore; they cannot get something from anyone also.
- It permits a company stay close to its customers and to respond to their changing needs.
- It can be developed superior skills in customer responsiveness, its based unit's ability to serve the needs of regional customer.

These advantages are focused to efficiency, quality, innovation and customer responsiveness of the company.

DISADVANTAGES OF FOCUS STRATEGY

Exhibit-10.6: Disadvantages of Focus Strategy An important and major disadvantages of focus strategy are listed below:

- Key focuser failure due to powerful suppliers of goods and service. Therefore, the competitor has strong control of market segmentation.
- A large differentiator sometimes has not the experience to focus strategy due to the difficulty of managing a large number of market segments.
- A focuser produces a small volume, its production costs often exceed. Higher cost can also reduce profitability and even loss of the business, so that this factor has one of the important disadvantages of focus strategy.
- The focuser's niche can suddenly disappear because of technological changes in customer tastes.
- Focuser is not concentrated of efficiency, quality, innovation and customer responsiveness. Its impact is to failure of focus strategy in company.

Strategic Choices of Focus Strategy

The specific product/market/distinctive competency choice is made by a focused company. Differentiation can be high or low because the company can pursue a low-cost or differentiation approach. As for customer groups, a focused company chooses specific niches in which to compete, rather than going for whole market, like the cost leader. A focuser may pursue any distinctive competency because it can pursue any kind of differentiation or low-cost advantage.

A focused strategy company can take to develop a competitive advantage explains why there so many small companies in relation to large ones. A focused company has enormous opportunity to develop its own niche and compete against low cost and differentiated enterprises, which tend to be larger. A focus strategy provides an opportunity for an entrepreneur to find and then exploit a gap in the market by developing an innovative product that customers cannot do without.

INVESTMENT STRATEGY

Investment strategy refers to the amount and type of resources in terms of

- Human
- Financial

These must be invested to gain a competitive advantage. Generic competitive strategies are provided competitive advantages to company. Generic competitive strategies are expensive to develop and maintain. Differentiation is the most expensive therefore; a company invests resources in many functions. They are listed below:

- Research and development
- Sales and marketing

These functions are to develop distinctive competencies. Cost leadership is less expensive to maintain once the initial investment in a manufacturing plant and equipment has been made. It does not require like sophisticated research and development of marketing efforts. The focus strategy is cheapest because fewer resources are needed to serve one-market segment than to serve the whole market.

In deciding on an investment strategy, a company must evaluate the potential or existed returns from investing in a generic competitive strategy against the cost of developing the strategy in this way, it can determine whether the strategy is likely to be profitability to company. Two factors are important in choosing an investment strategy. They are outlined:

- Competitive position
- Life-cycle effects

COMPETITIVE POSITION

Two factors can be used to determine the strength of a company's relative competitive position. They are as outlined below:

- The larger a company ~~marked share~~
- Measure of the competitive strength

The Larger a Company Market Share

The larger a company market share, the stronger its competitive position and the greater are the potential returns from future investment. It is, therefore, a large market share suggests that the company has developed own brand loyalty.

Measure of the Competitive Strength

The strength and uniqueness of company distinctive competences are the second measure of the competitive strength. In the cases, it is difficult to imitate a company's research and development expertise, its manufacturing or marketing skills, its knowledge of particular customer segments, or its unique reputation or brand name capital. The company's relative competitive position is strong and its returns from the generic strategy increases. In general, the companies with the largest market share and strongest distinctive competencies are in the best position in the market.

Two factors explain why some companies get stronger and stronger over time. A unique competency leads to increase demand for the company's products. A result of larger market share, the company has more resources to invest in developing its distinctive competency. Companies with a smaller market share and little potential for developing a distinctive competency are in a weaker competitive position. Therefore, they are less attractive sources for investment.

LIFE CYCLE EFFECTS

A life cycle effect is the second main factor which is influencing the investment attractiveness of a generic strategy. Each life cycle stage is accompanied by a particular industry environment, presenting different opportunities and threats, each stage, therefore, as different implications for the investment of resources needed to obtain a competitive advantage.

Stages of Investment Strategy Life Cycle Effecting

Investment strategy life cycle principally consists of the life cycle effecting. They are listed below:

- Embryonic strategy
- Growth strategies
- Shake-out strategies
- Maturity strategies
- Decline strategies

EMBRYONIC STRATEGY

Embryonic strategy refers to the share creation stage of the company. It is the basic stage of investment life cycle.

Feature of Embryonic Strategy

Exhibit 10.7: Feature of Embryonic Strategy

- All companies, weak and strong, emphasise the development of a distinctive competency and a product/market policy.
- During this stage, more investment needs are important because a company has to establish a competitive advantage.
- Many fledging companies are seeking resources to develop a distinctive competency.
- The appropriate industry level investment strategy is a share building strategy.
- The aim is to build market share by developing a stable and unique competitive advantage to attract customers who have no knowledge of the company's product.
- Companies are requiring large amount of capital to build research and developments competences or sales and service competency.
- Company success depends on its ability to demonstrate a unique competency to attract outside investors and venture capitalist.
- If company gains the resources to develop a distinctive competency, it will be relatively stronger competitive position.
- If it fails, its only option may be to exit the industry.

GROWTH STRATEGY

Growth strategy need to survive the company shakeout therefore, the appropriate investment strategy is the growth strategy.

Exhibit 10.8: Feature of Growth Strategy

Important features are identified as below:

- The growth strategy is to maintain a company's competitive position in a rapidly expanding market share. i.e., to grow with the expanding market.
- A company has to invest resources to develop a new sales and marketing competency.
- The growth strategy helps company to increase their market share and also enter with new market.
- In this stage, companies required low-cost to produce goods and service.
- Companies spend a lot of money just to keep up growth in the market, finding an additional resource to develop new skills and competencies is a difficult task for strategic manners.
- Growth strategy is an obvious because of companies growth is based on profits, survival and generation and expansion of market share if company has constraints of growth, that consequence is the exit from the business.

SHAKEOUT STRATEGY

Shakeout strategy is the third stage of investment life cycle effect. It is very important for industry to continue in business or exit from the business.

CHARACTERISTICS OF SHAKE-OUT STRATEGY

Exhibit-10.9: Characteristics of shakeout strategy

An important characteristic of shakeout strategy are identified below:

- In this stage, demand is increasing slowly and competition by price or product characteristics has become intense.
- Companies in strong competitive position need resources to invest in share-increasing strategy to attract customers from weak companies that are exiting the market.
- In this stage, investment in cost control is crucial; therefore, companies are to survive the shakeout stage.
- Investment is likely to be oriented toward marketing and companies are likely to develop a sophisticated after–sales service network.
- If companies differentiators in a weak position reduce their investment burden by withdrawing to a focused strategy.

MATURITY STRATEGIES

Maturity strategies stage is the essential for king of investment. It has emerged in the industry. Companies have learned how their competitors will react to their competitive motives.

Exhibit-10.10: Features of Maturity Strategies

An important feature of maturity strategies are listed below:

- Company's profits have been reinvested in the business and increase in market share.
- Dividend has been small.
- Investors in strong companies have obtained their rewards through capital appreciation.
- Strategic managers need to continue to invest heavily in maintaining the company's competitive advantage.
- Differentiation takes advantage of their strong position to develop flexible manufacturing systems in order to reduce their production costs.

Decline Strategies

The decline stage of the industry life cycle begins when demand for the industry's product start to fail.

Exhibit-10.11: Feature of Declining Strategies

Important features as identified below:

- Foreign competition and production substitution is the major feature for declining of strategies.
- Reducing the customer needs and customer groups and customer responsiveness that the decline stage of the industries.
- Adopt asset reduction strategy.
- Apply to turnaround strategy.

QUESTIONS FOR DISCUSSIONS

1. Discuss the customer needs and product differentiation.
2. Explain the customer groups and market segmentation.
3. Describe deciding on distinctive competencies.
4. How to choose a generic competitive strategy at the business-level?
5. Discuss the cost-leadership strategy.
6. What are the advantage and disadvantage of the cost leadership strategy?
7. Define differentiation strategy? What are the merits and demerits of the cost-leadership strategy?
8. Define the focus strategy. What are the advantages and disadvantages of the focus strategy?
9. Discuss investment strategy.
10. Describe the life cycle effects.
11. Write short notes on the following:
    - Embryonic
    - Growth
    - Shakeout
    - Maturity
    - Decline strategies

REFERENCES

1. Charles W.L. Hill / Gareth R. Jones, *Strategic Management Theory an Integrated Approach*, All India Publishers and Distributors Regd.2001.
2. A.A.Thomson and A.J. Strickland, *Strategic Management Concepts and Cases*, Tata McGraw –Hill Publishing Company Limited, New Delhi, 2003.
3. John, A. Pearce II, Richard B. Robinson, JR. *Strategic Management Strategy Formulation and Implementation*. A.I.T.B.S. Publishers & Distributors (Regd), New Delhi, 2002.

4. P.G. Apte, *International Financial Management*, Tata McGraw, New Delhi, 2004.
5. Y.N. Chong and Fileman Campo-flores, *Business Policy and Strategy*, Good Year Publishing Company, California, 1980.
6. R. M. Srivastava, *Corporate Strategy and Planning*, Tata McGraw-Hill Publishing Company Ltd., New Delhi, 1989.
7. Mayer, Robbert J. *Winning Strategies for manufacturers in Mature Industries*, Journal of Business Strategy 8, No 2 (Fall 1987).
8. Day, George S. *Strategies for Surviving a Shadeout*, Harward Business Review 75, No 2 (March–April 1997). pp 92-102.
9. Feldman, Lawrence P., and Albert L. Page. *Harverting : The Misunderstood Market Exit Strategy*. Journal of Business Strategy 5, No 4 (Spring 1985) pp 79-85.
10. Gordon, Geoffrey L., Roger J. Calantrone, and L. Anthony D., Benedetto. *Mature Markets and Revitalization Strategies. An American Fable*. Business Horizons (May-June 1991) pp. 39-50.
11. Mayer, Robert J. *Winning Strategies for Manufacturers in Mature Industries*. Journal of Business Strategy 8. No. 2 (Fall 1987). pp. 23-31.

Chapter – 11

Industrial Environment Analysis

CONTENTS

LEARNING OBJECTIVES

This chapter presents these issues as Strategy in fragmented industries, Chaining, Franchising, Horizontal merger, Strategy in embryonic and growth industries, Strategy in mature industries, Strategies to manage rivalry immature industries, Price signaling, Price leadership, Non price competition, Capacity control, Focus causing excess capacity, Choosing a capacity control strategy in mature industries, Supply and distribution strategy in mature industries, Strategy in declining industry, Strategy selection in a declining industry.

INTRODUCTION

In this chapter, we shall focus on how companies in fragmented industries try to develop competitive strategies that support their generic strategies. We shall consider the challenges of developing competitive advantage in embryonic and growth industries. We shall concentrate on how a set of companies that have been pursuing successful generic competitive strategies can use a variety of competitive interdependence found in such industries. Lastly, we shall assess the constraints of managing a company's generic competitive strategy in declining strategy.

STRATEGY FRAGMENTED INDUSTRIES

Fragmented industries are one which consists of a large number of small and medium-sized companies or organization or firms or enterprises. There are several reasons why an industry is composed of many small companies rather than a few larger ones. In some industries, there is few scale economies and so large company's do not have advantage overall enterprise. Therefore, some industries are diseconomies of scale. Further more, the lack of scale economies; low barriers to entry characterize many fragmented industries and new entry keeps the industry fragment. Too high transport costs can keep an industry fragmented. An industry-fragmented because of customer needs is so specialized in the market. Small sized industries create only small jobs and produced lots of products required to the market and there is no room for a large volume of production operation to satisfy the customer needs in the market.

Some fragmented industries; competitive strategy and force strategy stands out as a principal choice of the companies. Companies may specialize in the areas of customer groups, customer need, geographical region, therefore, so many small segments of the market. For instance, small service operations like furniture, textiles and food products that cater to particular customer needs in the market. Laundries, restaurants, health clubs, and rental stories, although, service companies make up a large part of the enterprises in fragmented industries. Therefore, they provided personalize service to clients and hence need to be close to clients in the market.

However, entrepreneurs are eager to gain the cost advantage of pursuing a low (generic) cost strategy of a fragmented industry. The required rate of return from consolidating fragmented industry is often huge. Consolidated fragmented strategies may utilize three main strategies. They are as listed below:

- Chaining
- Franchising
- Horizontal merger

Chaining

Chaining is the essential feature of fragmented industries. Chaining establish networks of linked business enterprise or service outlets. They are interconnected with their business function that they function as one of a large business entity. Chaining companies establish their own store chains across the country; it results to capture the amazing buying power of the customer in the domestic market. Chaining company stores allows customer to negotiate large price reducing with supplier and promote their competitive strategy advantage in market. They overcome the problems of high transportation costs by establishing sophisticated regional distribution chaining store centers which minimize the economies on inventory costs and maximize responsiveness to the needs of stores and customers. Chaining companies are realizing economies of scale from point view of sharing managerial skills across the chaining stores in the country and save the advertising cost nationwide.

Franchising

Franchising is the basic element of the fragmented industrial environment. The competitive advantage comes from the business strategy of franchising. Franchising refers to a local store operation in both owned and managed by the same person. Under the franchising, the owner of the outlet acts as manager of the franchising outlet. Therefore, manager is strongly motivated to control the business outlet closely and make sure that quality and standards are consistently high of the output in outlet, so that customer needs are always satisfied. Industries fragment is the very difficult of maintaining control over and the uniqueness of the small outlets. But they must be operated. Franchising avoid this problem. Further more, franchising lessens the financial burden of swift expansion and so permits rapid growth of the company. Franchising allows manager of the outlet to controll costs locally and differentiation can be achieved by marketing on a national level.

Horizontal Merger

Companies have arranged mergers of small companies in an industry in order to create a few large companies. Horizontal merger is the result of the fragment industry. Horizontal merger's main purpose is able to capture small companies market and can be achieved cost leadership or differentiation strategy. Although, small firms merger to big firms in order to avoid competition in the market due to increased profit and reducing the cost of production of goods and service and expansion of their market segmentation through horizontal merger of the small firms.

STRATEGIES IN EMBRYONIC AND GROWTH INDUSTRIES

Embryonic industries are typically created by the innovations of pioneering companies. In most cases, the pioneering company can initially earn enormous profits from its innovation. Therefore, embryonic industry refers to pioneering companies that earned huge profits by innovations of new product and service. These industries attract potential imitators and supporting them to enter the market to earn huge profit. Typically, this type of entry is most rapid in growth stage of industry and may cause the turnover to lose its commanding competitive position in market.

Innovating company's key factor issue in an embryonic industry is how to extract its innovation and build an enduring long run competitive advantage. It is based on low cost or differentiation. There are three strategies available to pioneering company. They are as listed below:

- To develop and market the innovation by itself.

- To develop and market the innovation jointly with other companies through a strategic alliance or joint venture.
- To license the innovation to others and let them develop the market.

The optimal choice of strategy depends of three factors. They are as mentioned below:

- Complementary assets
- Barriers to imitation
- Capable competitors

Complementary Assets

Complementary assets are the assets required by company successfully which extract a new innovation and gain a competitive advantage. The most important complementary assets are competitive manufacturing facilities that capable of handling the innovator. Innovator without encountering production bottlenecks or product quality problems, so that an inability to satisfy demand. Therefore, these problems can create an opportunity for imitators to enter the market place.

Complementary assets as mentioned below:

- Marketing
- Adequate sales force
- Access to distribution systems
- An after sales service
- And support net work

All these assets can help to innovator brand loyalty and also help to innovator achieve market penetration more rapidly. Development of complementary assets is very expensive and it needs large capital for this purpose of the embryonic companies.

Capable Competitions

Competitor's capability to imitate a pioneer's innovations that depends primarily on two factors as listed below:

- R&D skills
- Access to complementary assets

With regards to complementary assets, the access that rivals has to complementary assets like

- Marketing
- Sales
- Manufacturing capabilities

These are the key determinants of the rate of imitation from the competitors. Most of the cases, the imitators have failure to imitate complementary assets and not only do to imitate the innovation. They may also to imitate the innovator's complementary asset. This may be expensive for imitators.

STRATEGY IN MATURE INDUSTRIES

Mature strategy is dominated by small number of large companies in market. Perhaps, it may also contain medium-sized companies and host of small-specialized companies in market. Five competitive forces influence to the large companies that determine the nature of industry competition faced by the company. Therefore, these companies are developed by the most successful generic competitive strategies to manage the industry environment.

During the industry mature stage of the life cycle so many strategic groups of companies adopting generic competitive strategy have emerged by the end of the shakeout stage. These companies have learned the meaning of competitive interdependence of each other.

In mature industries, so many companies choose competitive moves to maximize their competitive advantage within the structure of industry competition. Mature industries should understand business level strategy. Strategist should understand how large companies try to stabilize industry competition to prevent entry/industry overcapacity/cutthroat price competition that would hurt all companies. Companies are using competitive moves and techniques to reduce the threat of each industry competition force.

STRATEGIES TO DETER ENTRY IN MATURE INDUSTRIES

Strategies to deter entry in mature industries refer to deter entry by potential rivals. Therefore, they are maintained and increase industry profitability. .

Table 11.1: Strategies for Deterring Entry

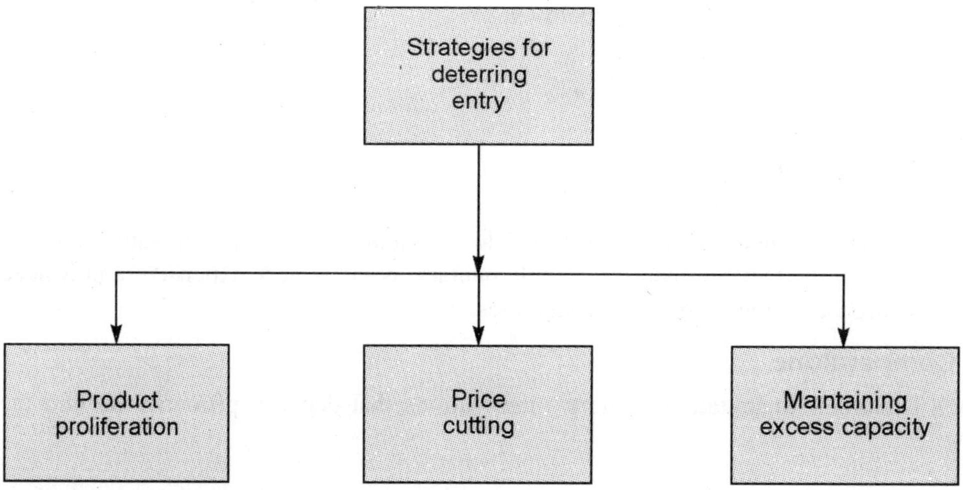

Table 11.1 highlights the strategies for deterring entry. It clearly shows three methods of strategies for deterring entry. They are as listed below:

- Product proliferation
- Price cutting
- Maintaining excess capacity

Product Proliferation

Product proliferation refers to new variety of products introduced by companies. Companies are rare to produce just one product most generally; they produce a variety of products aimed at different market segments. Therefore, they have broad product lines. Sometimes, this reduce the threat from the competitors, companies tailor their wide range of products and introduced the different segmentation and capture market, thus avoid to create a barrier to entry by potential competitors. Company is pursuing a broad product line to deter entry is known as *product proliferation strategy.*

Price Cutting

Price cutting is the important tool to manage competition from the competitors. It refers to pricing strategies involving price cutting can be used to deter entry by other companies. Therefore, it is protecting the profit margins of companies already in an industry. Initial stage price cutting strategy is to charge a high price for a product and seize short term profits. Although, it aggressively cut prices in order to simultaneously build market share and deter potential entrants in the market.

Price-cutting strategy is unlikely to deter a strong potential competitor – an established company that is trying to find profitable investment opportunities in other industries.

Research studies shows that companies first skim the market and charge high prices during the growth stage, maximizing short-run profits. Then they move to increase their market share and charge a lower price to rapidly expand the market, develop a reputation, and obtain economies of scale, driving down costs and barring entry. As competitors do enter, the incumbent companies reduce prices to related entry and give up market share to create a stable industry. Therefore, they can use non-price competitive methods to maximize long-run profits. At the same time, non-price competition becomes the main basis of industry competition and prices are quite likely to rise as competition stabilizes. Therefore, all these price and non-price techniques have reduced the number of new entrants and the level of rivalry.

Maintaining Excess Capacity

A further competitive technique allows companies to deter enter is to maintain a certain amount of excess productive capacity. The excess capacity of production of products and service is a major factor affecting the level of competition in an industry. It may lead to price cutting and reduced industry profitability. Hence, existing companies may prefer to posses some limited amount of excess capacity. It serves to warm potential entrants that if they enter the industry, existing firms can retaliate by increasing output and forcing down prices until entry would become unprofitable to industry.

STRATEGIES TO MANAGE RIVALRY IN MATURE INDUSTRIES

Strategies to manage rivalry in mature industries refer to companies wish to utilize strategies to manage their competitive interdependence and decrease rivalry. Mature industries unrestricted competition results over prices of the output will be reduced and also quality of the output. Ultimately, the mature company's profitability automatically reduces even also stock turnover ratio decreases. So many strategies are available to companies to manage rivalry in mature industry relations. The most important strategies are to manage rivalry in mature industries. They are as listed below:

- Price signaling
- Price leadership
- Non-price competition
- Capacity control

Price Signaling

Price signaling refers to pricing strategy of the mature industries in the market. All industries start out fragmented, with small companies battling for market share, soon, the leading players emerge, and companies start to interpret each other's competitive moves. Companies convey their intention to other companies about pricing strategy and how they will compete in the future or how they will react to the competitive moves of their rivals that representing of the price signaling. There are several ways in which price signaling can help companies defend their generic competitive strategies.

- Companies may adopt price signaling strategy to announce that they will respond vigorously to hostile competitive moves that threaten them. The price signaling products are existing structure of competitive advantage by deterring potential imitators that may attempt to copy of other companies' generic strategies.
- Price signaling strategy indirectly allows companies to coordinate their actions and avoid a costly competitive move that leads to a breakdown in industry pricing policy. It is very important to company, it intends to lower price of output. Because it wished to attract customers were switching of the products of another industry, it means that, price signaling strategy can be used to improve industry profitability.

Price Leadership

Price leadership strategy refers to price setting of the product, this responsibility can be taken by the company. This is another way of using price signaling strategy to enhance the profitability of product and market policy among companies in a mature industry. Industry should follow standard price setting policy for product and service offered by the companies. It can be followed by other companies in similar industry. Price leadership strategy is adopted by the company that is generally the strongest company in the industry. It is one of the best ability to threaten other companies in competition that might cut prices or increase their output to capture more market share.

Formal price leadership strategy helps to differentiators to charge a premium price of output and helps to low-cost companies by increasing their profit margins. Therefore, it makes a combined low-cost or differentiation strategy very profitable to industry.

Price leadership strategy can stabilize industry relations by preventing head-to-head competition. It raises the level of industry profitability, therefore; companies have funds for future investment and good returns to stakeholders. Price leadership strategy has its own dangers; therefore, it helps to companies with high costs and allowing them to survive without becoming more productive and efficient.

NON-PRICE COMPETITION

Non-price competition strategy refers to use of non-price competition to manage rivalry industries. It is the third and very important aspect of product or market strategy in mature industries. It helps to company applying various techniques to try to prevent costly price-cutting and price wars do not prelude competition by product differentiation. Product differentiation is used as the main competitive weapon to prevent competition from many industries for obtaining access to a company' customers and attacking its market share.

Non-price Competitive Strategies

Non-price competitive strategies are important to mature industry for marketing goods and service into different segmentation. They are as listed below:

- Market penetration
- Product development
- Market development
- Product proliferation

These are based on the product differentiation.

Market Penetration

Market penetration strategy refers to advertise to promote and build product differentiation. Company tries to concentrate on expanding market share in its existing product markets. The thrust of advertising is to influence consumer brand choice and create a brand name reputation for the company and its products in a mature industry. In this manner, a company can increase its market share by attracting the customers. Therefore, brand name products often premium prices for product and increasing market share in this situation is very profitable.

Product Development

Product development refers to creation of product or replacement of existing ones. It is the second non-price competitive strategy. Product development is important for maintaining product differentiation and building market share.

Market Development

Market development strategy helps company for finding new market segments for its product. It is third important strategy for non-price competitive strategies. A company pursuing this strategy wants to capitalize on the brand name. Then only, it has developed in one market segment by locating new market segment in which to compete.

Product Proliferation

Product proliferation strategy refers to use to manage industry rivalry and as well as deter entry of new competitors in the market. Product proliferation strategy helps to mature companies to have a product market in each segment and attract customer response for their products and service.

CAPACITY CONTROL

Capacity control strategy helps to mature industries to avoid the cut-throat competition, therefore, it reduces both company and industry levels of profitability and in some industries price competition does periodically breakout. This occurs most commonly when there is industry overcapacity, i.e. companies produce too much output; therefore reducing price is the only route to dispose of it. If one company starts cut price, then the others quickly follow because they fear that the price cutter will be able to sell its entire inventory and they will be left holding unwanted goods. Capacity control strategies can influence the level of industry output.

FACTORS CAUSING EXCESS CAPACITY

Excess capacity may be caused by a shortfall in demand. Company demand is rising; the consequence of each company's decision to increase capacity is a surge industry capacity which drives down prices of output.

Excess capacity problems often derive from technological factor sometimes new, low-cost technology sometimes is to introduce it simultaneously. A capacity problem occurs because the old technology is still being used to produce output. In addition, new technology is often introduced in large industries that generate over capacity; old age of the company's plant is the source of problem.

CHOOSING A CAPACITY CONTROL STRATEGY IN MATURE INDUSTRIES

Choosing a capacity control strategy in mature industries is based on the two choices. They are as listed below:

- Each company must try to prevent its competitors in the market and seize the initiative.
- The companies indirectly co-coordinating with each other. Therefore, they are aware of the mutual effects and their actions.
- Each company must conduct market survey and forecast a large increase in demand in the product market and then move rapidly to establish large-scale operations that will be able to satisfy the predicted demand. By achieving a first mover advantage the company may deter other companies from entering the market.
- This strategy is extremely risky and it involves investing resources in generic strategy before the extent and profitability of the future market are clear.

SUPPLY AND DISTRIBUTION STRATEGY IN MATURE INDUSTRIES

Supply and distribution strategy in mature industries refers to control supplier and distributor relationships. Company can ensure its ability to dispose off its outputs in a timely, reliable manner. Therefore, it can be reduced costs and improve the product quality. Company and its supplier are involved in choosing a distribution/supplier strategy. It is to contrast the situation that exists between a company and its suppliers. The company and suppliers should maintain close relationships that based on long-term personal relationship and trust. This close relationship is more helps to company to get raw input at lower costs and ability to respond to unexpected changes in the customers demand.

A company has many options to choose distributor and decide on the appropriate way to distribute its products to gain a competitive advantage. It may distribute its products to an independent distributor and independent distributor distributes them to retailers. Sometimes, company may distribute directly to retailer or even to customers.

The company distribution strategy is based on the product information and its operation and maintenance of the output. Distribution strategy must support to customer for distribution of products and sales after service to end user of the output. Customer satisfaction is the main objective of the distribution strategy of the company.

A net work of distributors can control distribution. This system is suitable for the large electronics manufactures and the producers of consumers' durables like appliance. Company can choose five or six large distributors per state to control distribution and enhance market share of the products and service. The distributors are required to carry the full time of a company's products and invest in after -sales service facilities to customer. Distributor receives good feedback from the customer about the product quality and future demand for product from the customer. It is help to company to increase and control production of output and service. The company is able to discipline its distributor if they start to discount prices or otherwise threaten the company's reputation.

STRATEGY IN DECLINING INDUSTRIES

Strategy in declining industries refers to sooner or later many industries enter into a decline stage. In this stage, the size of the total market is shrinking, competition tends to intensify in a declining industry, and profit rates tend to fall. The intensity of composition is greater in declining industries where exit barriers are high. The intensity of competition is greater in declining industries where fixed costs are high. Industries start declining for a number of reasons like technological, social trends and demographic changes. Leadership strategy, niche strategy, harvest strategy and divestment strategy are four main strategies that companies can adopt to deal with decline. Decline industries are opposed to new industries in the market.

STRATEGY SELECTION IN A DECLINING INDUSTRY

There are four main strategies available to companies in a declining industry. They are as listed below:

- A leadership strategy
- A niche strategy
- A harvest strategy
- A divestment strategy

Leadership Strategy

Leadership strategy refers to grow in a declining industry by picking the share of companies. They are leaving the industry. This strategy makes most sense to capture market share in a declining industry. In this stage, the speed of decline and intensity of competition in the declining industry is moderate.

Niche Strategy

Niche strategy refers to focus on output demand in the industry. It helps to declining company to keep demand stable or declining less slowly. This strategy makes sense when the company has unique strengths relative to those niches where demand remains relatively strong.

Harvest Strategy

Harvest strategy refers to declining company to cut all new investments in capital equipment, advertising and research and development. This strategy makes the most sense when the company foresees a steep decline and a particularly intense competition or when it lacks strength, relative of remaining pockets of demand in the industry.

Divestment Strategy

Divestment strategy refers to company; it can maximize its net investment recovery from a business by selling its assets early and before the industry has entered into a steep decline. This strategy is appropriate when the company has little strength relative to whether pockets of demand are likely to remain in the industry and when the competition in the declining industry is likely to be intense.

QUESTIONS FOR DISCUSSIONS

1. Discuss the strategy in fragmented industries.
2. Describe the strategy in embryonic and growth industries.
3. Briefly explain the strategy in mature industries.
4. Discuss the strategies to manage rivalry in mature industries.
5. How to choose a capacity control strategy in mature industries?
6. Explain the supply and distribution strategy in mature industries.
7. What are the strategies in declining industry?
8. How to strategy selection in a declining industry?

9. Write short notes on the following
   - Price signaling
   - Price leadership
   - Non-price competition
   - Capacity control

REFERENCES

1. Charles W.L. Hill/Gareth R. Jones, *Strategic, Management Theory an Integrated Approach*, All India Publishers and Distributors Regd. 2001.
2. A.A. Thomson and A.J. Strickland, *Strategic Management Concepts and Cases*, Tata McGraw –Hill Publishing Company Limited, New Delhi, 2003.
3. John, A. Pearce II, Richard B. Robinson, JR. *Strategic Management Strategy Formulation and Implementation*. A.I.T.B.S. Publishers & Distributors (Regd), New Delhi, 2002.
4. Mayer, Robert J., *Winning Strategies for Manufacturers in Mature Industries*, Journal of Business Strategy 8. No. 2 (Fall 1987).
5. Gordon, Geoffrey L., Roger J. Calantrone and Anthony di Benedetto. *Mature Markets and Revitalization Strategies: An American Fable.* Business Horizons (May-June) 1991.
6. Caves, R.E., and M.E. Porter., *From Entry Barriers to Mobility Barriers: Conjectural Decisions and Contrived Deterrence to New Competition*, Quarterly Journal of Economics 91 (1976), pp. 34.
7. Koch, J.V., *Industry Market Structure and Industry Price–Cost Margins*, Industrial Organisation Review, 2 (1974).
8. Scherer, F.M. *Industrial Market Structure and Economic Performance*. 2nd ed. Skokie III, Rand McNally, 1980.

Chapter – 12

Vertical Integration, Diversification and Strategic Alliances

CONTENTS

- Introduction
- Vertical integration
- Upstream/backward integration
- Downstream/forward integration
- Creating value through vertical integration
- Disadvantages of vertical integration
- Strategic alliances
- Short-term contracts and competitive bidding
- Long-term contracting and strategic alliance
- Building long term cooperative relationships
- Diversification
- Types of diversification
- Creating value through diversification

LEARNING OBJECTIVES

We shall discuss the Vertical integration, Upstream/backward integration, downstream/forward integration, creating value through vertical integration, Disadvantages of vertical integration, strategic alliances, short-term contracts, competitive bidding, building long term, cooperative relationships, diversification, and types of diversification and creating value through diversification.

INTRODUCTION

In this chapter, we shall discuss vertical integration, diversification, and strategic alliances of the global scenario. Corporate level strategy is concerned with two main questions as listed below:

- What business areas should a company participate in so as to maximize its long run profitability, survival and growth?
- What type's strategies should a company use to enter into and exist from business areas?

The first question is the focus of this chapter and second question is focus of next chapter (14). A company has several options in choosing business areas to compete in corporate level strategy. Vertically integrate refers to company diversify its business into a number of different business areas.

VERTICAL INTEGRATION

Vertically integration refers to company diversify its business into a number of different business areas. Diversification into a new production line to produce goods and service required as inputs for other main products of the same company. For instance a company diversifies its business into number of different business areas like banking and finance services, energy and utility, health care and insurance, manufacturing retail, telecom. It may be undertaken by a company with the purpose of either maintaining continuous flow of products and service to customer. Vertical Integration Company offer numerous products and service for satisfying customers. A company is opening its own sales and marketing division and showrooms for selling product and service to customer instead of selling through agents and distributors. It can be controlled over the input supply and output distribution also.

Vertical integration further classified into two broad categories. They are listed below:

- Backward or Upstream integration
- Forward or Downstream integration

UPSTREAM OR BACKWARD INTEGRATION

Back integration or upstream refers to company is diversifying the business operation towards some of the raw materials or input supply. Backward integration involves moving into intermediate manufacturing and raw material production.

DOWNSTREAM OR FORWARD INTEGRATION

Forward integration or downstream refers to company is diversifying business operations for marketing sales distribution of products and services and taking up these activities to bring the organization closer to the ultimate customer.

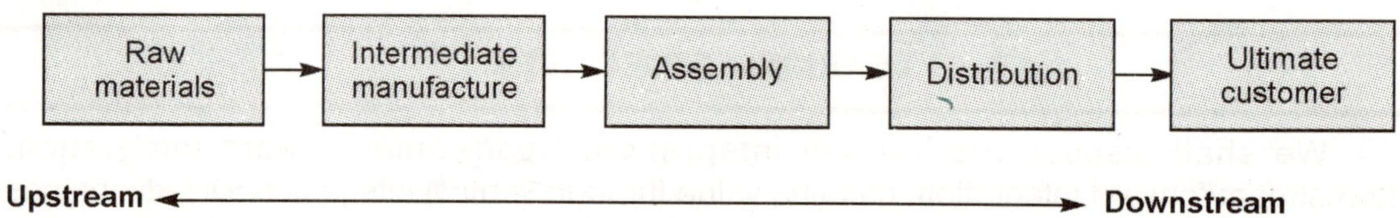

Figure 12.1: Stages in the Raw material to Consumer Production Chain

Table 12.1 highlights the stages in the raw material to customer production chain. It indicates the four steps listed below:

- Intermediate manufacture
- Assembly
- Distribution
- Ultimate customer

Backward integration involves moving into intermediate manufacturing and raw material production. Forward integration involves movement into distribution. At each stage in chain, value is added to the product. It means that a company at that stage takes the product produced in the previous stage, transforms it in some way and then sells the output at a higher price to a company at the next stage in the chain. The difference between the price paid for inputs and the price at which the product is sold is a measure of the value added at that stage.

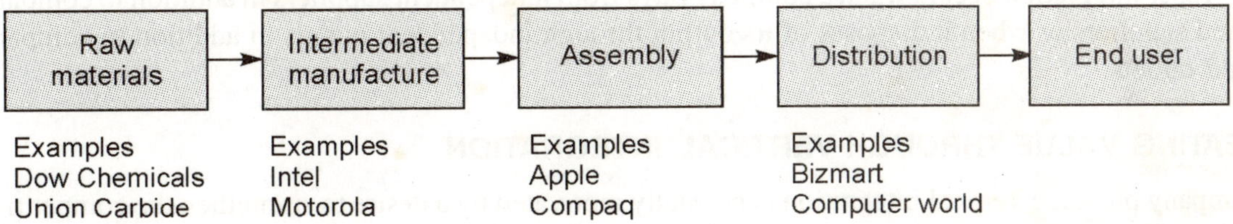

Figure 12.2: The Raw material to Consumer Production Chain in the Personal Computer industry

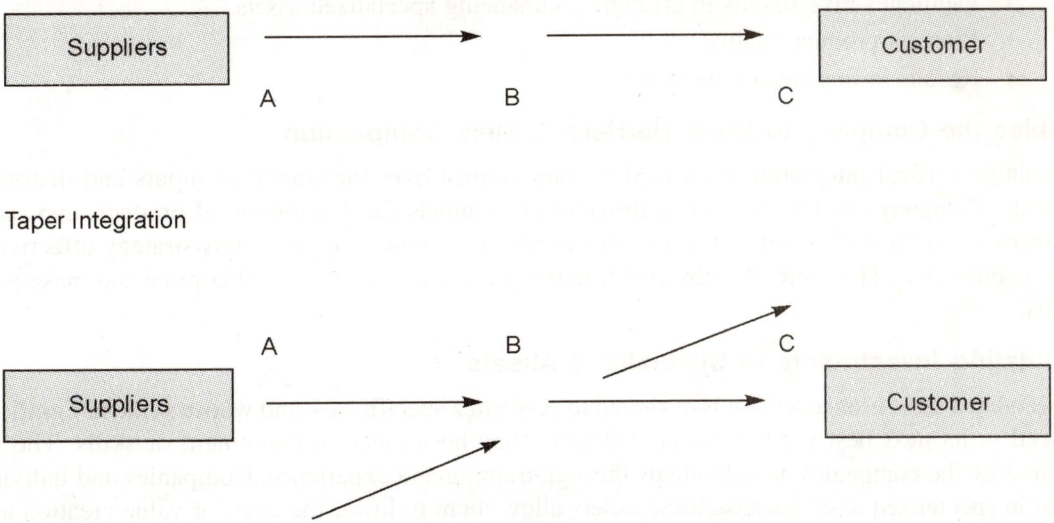

Figure 12.3: Full and Taper Integration

As an example of the value added concept, consider the production chain in the personal computer industry. This figure indicates the raw material to consumer production chain in the personal computer industry. Raw material companies include the manufacture of specialty ceramics, chemicals, and metal such as Dow Chemicals and Union Carbide. These companies sell their output to the manufacturers of intermediate products, the intermediate manufacturers include companies like Intel and Motorola, transform the ceramics, chemicals and metal they purchase into computer components such as micro processors, memory chips, and disk drives. In doing so, they add value to the new materials, they purchase. These components are then sold to assembly companies like Apple and Compaq, which take these components and transform, them into personal computers *i.e.*, add value to the components they purchase many of the personal computers and sell them to final customers. The distribution also is value added to the product by making it accessible to customers, and by providing service and support thus value is added by companies at each stage in the raw materials to consumer chain.

Viewed this way, vertical integration involves a choice about which value added stages of raw material to consumer chain to compete in.

Figure 12.3 indicates the full and tapper integration. A company achieves full integration what it produces all of a particular input needed for it's possess or when it disposes of all of its input through its own operations.

Taper integration occurs when a company buys from independent suppliers in addition to company -owned suppliers or when it disposes of its output through independent outlets in addition to company owned outlets.

CREATING VALUE THROUGH VERTICAL INTEGRATION

A company pursuing vertical integration is normally motivated by a desire to strengthen the competitive position of its original or core business. There are four vital arguments for pursuing a vertical integration strategy. They are as listed below:

- Enables the company to build barriers to new competition
- Facilitates investments in efficiency-enhancing specialized assets.
- Protects product quality
- Results in improved scheduling

Enables the Company to Build Barriers to New Competition

Company's vertical integrating backward to gain control over the source of inputs and distribution channels. Company can build effective distribution channels for distribution of products and service. Company build barrier to new entry into its industry to extent to apply to this strategy effectively to avoid competition. Therefore, thereby enabling the company to charge a higher price and make greater profits.

Facilitating Investments in Specialized Assets

A specialized asset is an asset that is designed to perform a specific task and whose value is significantly reduced in its next best use. A specialized asset may be a piece of equipment or skills. The skills acquired by the companies or individuals through training and experience. Companies and individuals invest in specialized asset because these assets allow them to lower the costs of value creation and to better differentiate their product offering from that of competitors, thereby, facilitating premium pricing. These specialized assets use very specialized purposes. Companies always invest in specialized equipment because it enables it to lower its manufacturing costs and increase its quality. Secondly it invests in developing highly-specialized technological knowledge because it develops better products than their rivals. Therefore, specialization can be achieving a competitive advantage at the industry level.

A company may find it very difficult to persuade other companies' in adjacent stages in the raw material to consumer production chain to undertake investments in specialized assets. As result, companies or individuals are to realize the economic gains associated with investments. It may have to vertically integrate into such adjacent stages and make the investment itself.

Protecting Product Quality

Companies' main aim is protecting product quality. Vertical integration enables a company to become a differentiated player in its core business. If company is integration, therefore it can protect product quality without affecting standard of the product quality.

Improved Scheduling

Strategic advantages arise from the easier planning, coordination and scheduling of adjacent processes. It made possible in vertically-integrated organizations or companies can be particularly important in companies trying to relate the benefits of just in time inventory systems.

DISADVANTAGES OF VERTICAL INTEGRATION

Exhibit 12.1: Disadvantages of vertical integration

- Cost disadvantages
- Technological changes disadvantages
- Demand uncertainty disadvantages
- Others.

Cost Disadvantages

Cost is the main factor of the company to gain a production cost advantages. Meanwhile vertical integration can raise costs, if a company becomes committed to purchasing inputs from company owned suppliers when low cost external sources of supply exist. Company owned might high operating costs compared with the independent suppliers.

Technological Changes

Technological changes are other disadvantages of the vertical integration. When technology is changing fast and outdated its plants and equipment. Therefore, it is also major disadvantages of the company.

Demand Uncertainty

It can also be extremely risky in unstable or unpredicted demand condition. In this case, it is very difficult to achieve their activities in company.

Others

- Vertical integration poses problems of balancing capacity at each stage in the value chain.
- Integrating forward or backward often calls for radically different skills and business capabilities.
- Backward vertical integration into the production of parts and components can reduce a company's strength.

STRATEGIC ALLIANCES

Strategic alliances refers to company which can enter into long-term co-operative relationships with their trading partners. Such long-term relationship is typically known as *strategic alliances*. Sometimes, company can enter short-term contracts with their trading partners. First, we shall discuss the problems associated with short-term contracts. Then we shall look at long-term contracts.

SHORT-TERM CONTRACTS AND COMPETITIVE BIDDING

Short-term contract is one in which period is one or less than a year. Many companies use short-term contracts to structure the purchasing of their inputs or the sale of their outputs. It forces suppliers to keep down their prices of inputs, this is the major benefit of short-term strategic alliance.

In other words, the strategy of short-term contracting and competitive bidding due to the lack of long-term commitment to its suppliers on the part of the company will make it very difficult for that company to realize the gains associated with vertical integration. It is not a problem when there is minimum need for close cooperation between the company and its suppliers to facilitate quality inputs, investments in specialized assets like inputs, improve scheduling in product quality in such case competitive biding may be optional for industry.

LONG-TERM CONTRACTING & STRATEGIC ALLIANCE

Long-term contracts are developed to long-term cooperative relationships and partnership between two companies. Therefore, it refers as strategic alliance. Typically in these arrangements, one company agrees to supply and the other company agrees to continue the purchasing from supplier. Both companies make commitment to jointly seek ways of lowering the costs of inputs or raising the quality of inputs. Long-term strategic alliance helps to company and supplier to commitment of long-term relationship and coordination in business. Therefore, in this way both companies are participating value creation process.

Exhibit 12.2: Reliance announces Strategic Alliance with BRPL

Reliance Industries Ltd. (RIL) has formed a strategic alliance with Bongaigaon Refinery & Petrochemicals Ltd. (BRPL), a subsidiary company of Indian Oil Corporation Ltd.

The agreement following an open tender for a strategic alliance was signed in Mumbai, in the presence of Mr. B.K. Gogoi, Chairman & Managing Director of BRPL and Mr. Nikhil R. Meswani, Executive Director, RIL. The agreement was signed on behalf of BRPL by Mr. R. M. Hazarika, Director (Operations) and by Mr. Subodh Sapra, President (Polyester Business), RIL.

The alliance covers the petrochemicals facilities of BRPL site at Dhaligaon, Assam consisting of 34,200 MT per annum of PSF capacity together with 45,000 MT per annum of Dimethyl Terephthalate (DMT) capacity, which is used as feedstock for PSF production. Under this alliance, RIL will provide technical and manufacturing support for achieving both full capacity utilisation and quality excellence. In addition, RIL will be responsible for marketing the entire output.

This strategic alliance will help BRPL to turnaround its petrochemical businesses, which have been closed for the last two years. BRPL will also get instant access to the state-of-the-art

(Contd...)

technological and manufacturing skills developed successfully by RIL in the last 20 years of Polyester operations.

RIL already sells 450,000 MT per annum of PSF to a vast customer base, both in India and many overseas markets. With current annual capacity of a million tonnes, RIL is already the world's second largest polyester fibre and yarn producer. It markets the output of Polyester capacities located at eight different sites, utilising the world's leading technologies including DuPont, Zimmer, Inventa, and Toray. Reliance will gain additional volumes from this alliance, and will strengthen its market position further. It will also share the benefits of this alliance on equitable terms.

The polyester users in the remote North Eastern part of the country will benefit from this new strategic alliance of polyester manufacturing.

Background information

Reliance Industries Ltd. (RIL) is India's largest private sector company on all major financial parameters with gross turnover of Rs 65,061 crore (US$ 13.7 billion), cash profit of Rs 7,565 crore (US$ 1.6 billion), net profit of Rs 4,104 crore (US$ 864 million), net worth of Rs 30,327 crore (US$ 6.4 billion) and total assets of Rs 63,737 crore (US$ 13.4 billion). RIL features in the Forbes Global list of world's 400 best big companies and in FT Global 500 list of world's largest companies.

RIL has emerged as the 'Best Managed Company' in India in a study by Business Today and A.T. Kearney. RIL was named in the World's Most Respected Companies list published by Financial Times based on a global survey and research conducted by Pricewater house Coopers. RIL also emerged as the most respected among Indian companies and amongst the 10 most respected energy and chemical companies in the world.

Reliance Group

The Reliance Group founded by Dhirubhai H. Ambani (1932-2002) is India's largest business house with total revenues of Rs 80,000 crore (US$ 16.8 billion), cash profit of over Rs 9,800 crore (US$ 2.1 billion), net profit of over Rs 4,700 crore (US$ 990 million) and exports of Rs 11,900 crore (US$ 2.5 billion). The group's activities span exploration and production (E&P) of oil and gas, refining and marketing, petrochemicals (polyester, polymers, and intermediates), textiles, financial services and insurance, power, telecom and infocom initiatives. Reliance has emerged as India's Most Admired Business House, for the third successive year in a TNS Mode survey for 2003.

Source: Reliance

BUILDING LONG-TERM COOPERATIVE RELATIONSHIPS

Companies can take specific steps to ensure a long-term cooperative relationship with their partner. It can build long-term strategic alliance with partner to enter on agreement. The agreement should involve the specific steps listed below:

- Hostage taking
- Credible commitments
- Maintaining market discipline

Hostage Taking

Hostage taking refers to the company to make investment in specialized assets to demand from its partner. It is essential to company give guaranteeing to partner for supply of valuable resources which are required by the partner. In these cases, companies and with partner are mutually dependent.

Credible Commitments

Credible commitments are the second factor to build long-term cooperative relationships with companies and their partner in the business. A credible commitment is a believable commitment to companies and its partner for support the development of a long-term relationship.

Maintaining Market Discipline

Maintaining market discipline is the third important factor of building long-term cooperative relationships. Maintaining market discipline is needful for both companies. Therefore, companies and their partner are essential to maintain market discipline because of to avoid competition from the rivals companies in the market. For this purpose, companies enter into a cooperative long term relationships must be able to held market share in the market. Maintaining market discipline is based on the two important factors as listed below:

- Long-term contracts are generally for four to five years. Therefore, a partner should know the advantages and disadvantages of long-term commitment.
- Some companies engaged in long-term relationships with suppliers to get quality input at lower cost and maintain supply of inputs for long time. Both partners are entering agreement for the supply of inputs and investment in special assets.

DIVERSIFICATION

Diversification refers to company diverting the business focus from the existing traditional areas to new promising areas. Since technology is changing day by day, 'customer' demands are changing accordingly. Company introduced new and substitute products and service available in the market to meet the customer's expectations and to draw their attention. These changing attitudes of the customers, the company has been opening more and more new areas of promising business. Diversification may involve internal or external, related or unrelated, horizontal or vertical, active or passive dimensions. The change of business focus may be either in terms of customer function, customer group and new alternative technologies.

TYPES OF DIVERSIFICATION

- Related diversification
- Unrelated diversification
- Internal diversification
- External diversification
- Horizontal diversification
- Vertical diversification
- Active diversification
- Passive diversification
- Concentric diversification

Related Diversification

Related diversification is diversification into new business activity that is linked to company's existing business activity, normally these activities are common between one or more components of each activity's of existing business activity of value chain. Normally these linkages are based on manufacturing, marketing or technological commodities.

Unrelated Diversification

Unrelated diversification is diversification into a new business area that has no obvious connection with any of the companies existing areas.

Internal Diversification

Diversification business activities with in the company such is known as internal diversification. It means that a company ready to introduce new products with the same geographical areas.

External Diversification

External diversification involves diversification of the business activities like manufacturing, production, marketing, technological changes diversified with the other companies to save to operating cost of the goods and service.

Horizontal Diversification

Horizontal diversification is undertaken in order to increase market share by expansion of same product lines with more varieties to serve customers in different areas, of different types and affluence levels. Horizontal diversification may be taken up to expand business geographically in new territories by taking up an increased market share and an improved business volume.

Vertical Diversification

Vertical diversification means diversification into a new production line to produce items required as inputs for other main products of the same company.

Concentric Diversification

Concentric diversification is to concentrate the direction of business for expansion and diversification is to concentrate the direction in the same and attendant product lines. Concentric diversification may take the form of marketing-related or technology-related diversification.

Active diversification is the long-term expansion of the business activities. Passive diversification is short termed and has negative impact to continuous long-term contracts with partners.

CREATING VALUE THROUGH DIVERSIFICATION

Most companies first consider diversification when they are generating financial resources, therefore, it is excess to maintain competitive advantage in their original or core business. The diversified company can generate value in three main routes. They are listed below:

- Acquiring and restructuring
- Transferring competencies
- Economies of scope

Acquiring and Restructuring

Acquiring and restructuring involved by acquiring and restructuring of poorly-run enterprises. A restructuring strategy rests on the presumption that an efficiently-managed company can create value by acquiring inefficient and poorly-managed enterprises and improving their efficiency. This approach can be considered diversified because the acquired company does not have to be in the same industry as the acquiring company for the strategy to work. Improvements in the efficiency of an acquired company can come from a number of sources. They are listed below:

- The acquiring company usually replaces the top management team of the acquired company with more aggressive top management team.
- The new top management team is encouraged to sell-off any unproductive assets like executive's jets and elaborate corporate head-quarters and to reduce staffing levels.
- The new top management team is also encouraged to intervene in the running of the acquired business to seek out routes of improving the unit's efficiency, quality, innovativeness, and customer responsiveness.
- To motivate the new top management team and other employees of the acquired unit to undertake such actions, increases in their pay may be linked to industries in the performance of the acquired unit.
- The acquiring company often establishes performance goals for the acquired company.

Exhibit 12.3: Reliance to acquire German firm Trevira for Rs 440 crore

RELIANCE Industries Ltd. on Thursday announced it would acquire German polyester producer, Trevira GmbH, for 80 million euros (roughly Rs 440 crore). The acquisition will make RIL the world's largest polyester fibre and yarn producer. Trevira, former division of multinational Hoechst, which operates polyester plants in Germany, Belgium and Denmark, will add 1.3 lakh tonnes to RIL's existing polyester capacity. This will take RIL's polyester capacity, combined with its expansion plans in India, to 1.8 million tonnes - the largest in the world. "This European acquisition will transfer the entire intellectual property portfolio of Hoechst to India," Mr Mukesh Ambani, RIL's Chairman and Managing Director, told reporters, on the sidelines of RIL's annual general meeting, here today. This is the second overseas acquisition of RIL after it acquired the US-based Flag Telecom last year. According to RIL, Trevira is a highly-specialised polyester producer with several valuable patents and technologies and strong R&D. The company has been adding polyester capacity through major acquisitions since 2002 when it acquired IPCL followed by the acquisition of the NOCIL petrochemicals division earlier this year. Over the next three years, RIL intends to hike its total petrochemical capacity to 15 million tonnes from the present 12.4 million tonnes. Responding to queries, Mr. Ambani said Reliance Industries' plans to retail transport fuels have been delayed. However, the company will be adding 300 to 400 new retail outlets every quarter, starting from the second quarter this fiscal. "We are in the 75-outlets zone at the moment," Mr Ambani told reporters. He said the company would put up its planned 5,800 retail outlets over the coming three to five years. Of these, 5 to 10 per cent would be set up in the rural areas. The company will also focus on setting up highway outlets. RIL stock today closed at Rs 422.80, up Rs 11.75 on BSE today. Around 56 lakh shares changed hands.

Source: Reliance Industries Limited

Transferring Competencies

Companies diversification strategy on transferring competencies seek out new business, related to their existing business by one or more value creation functions, for instance, manufacturing, marketing, materials management and R&D. They want to create value by drawing on the distinctive skills in one or more of their existing value creation function in order to improve the competitive position of the new business. It can improve the efficiency of their existing business.

Economies of Scope

It arises when two or more business units share resources like;

- Manufacturing facilities
- Distribution channels
- Advertising
- R & D costs

Each business unit utilized their capacity better and reduced to operating cost.

QUESTIONS FOR DISCUSSIONS

1. Define vertical integration.
2. Define upstream/backward integration.
3. Define forward/downstream integration
4. Discuss the creating value through vertical integration.
5. What are the disadvantages of vertical integration?
6. Discuss the strategic alliances.
7. Explain the short-term contracts and competitive bidding.
8. Describe the building long-term cooperative relationships.
9. Describe the types of diversification.
10. How to create value through diversification?

REFERENCES

1. Charles W.L. Hill/Gareth R. Jones, *Strategic Management Theory an Integrated Approach*, All India Publishers and Distributors Regd. 2001.
2. A.A.Thomson and A.J. Strickland, *Strategic Management Concepts and Cases*, Tata McGraw –Hill Publishing Company Limited, New Delhi, 2003.
3. John, A. Pearce II, Richard B. Robinson, J.R. *Strategic Management Strategy Formulation and Implementation*. A.I.T.B.S. Publishers & Distributors (Regd.), New Delhi, 2002.
4. Ansoff, H.I., *Strategies for Diversification*, Harvard Business Review, September-October 1957.
5. Steiner, G.A., *Strategic Planning*, Newyork, Freepress 1979.

6. Barney, Jay B. *Gaining and Sustaining Competitive Advantage*. MA, Addison–Werly 1997.
7. Goold, Michael, and Kathleen Luchs, *Why Diversify? Four Decades of Management Thinking*, Academy of Management Executive 7. No. 3 (August 1993).
8. Doz. Yver L., and Gary Hamel, *Alliance Advantage, The Art of Creating Value through Partnering*, Boston, Harward Business School Press, 1998.

Chapter – 13

Acquisitions and Joint Ventures

CONTENTS

- Introduction
- Acquisitions versus internal new ventures as entry strategies
- Failure of acquisitions
- Guidelines for successful acquisition
- Advantages of acquisition strategy
- Disadvantages of acquisition strategy
- Pitfalls of internal new venture
- Joint venture
- Recommendations in success of internal new venturing
- Advantages of joint venture
- Disadvantages of joint venture
- Life cycle of a joint venture
- Joint ventures as an entry strategy
- Drawbacks of joint-ventures arrangements

LEARNING OBJECTIVES

Let us discuss about the issues as entry strategy, failure of acquisitions, guidelines for successful acquisition, advantages of acquisition strategy, disadvantages of acquisition strategy, pitfalls of internal new venture, joint venture, advantages of joint venture strategy, disadvantages of joint venture strategy, joint venture as an entry strategy, life cycle of joint venture, drawback of joint-ventures arrangements.

INTRODUCTION

In this chapter, we shall discuss the acquisitions, advantages and disadvantages of acquisition strategy, internal new ventures, joint venture, advantages and disadvantages of joint venture, life cycle of a joint venture and how to make joint ventures successful. Acquisition involves buying an existing business; internal ventures involve starting a new business from scratch. Joint ventures typically involve starting a new business from scratch with the assistance of a partner.

ACQUISITIONS VERSUS INTERNAL NEW VENTURES AS ENTRY STRATEGIES

A company is to enter into a new business area through acquisition. It involves purchasing an established company's all facilities like plant and equipment, human resource and financial resource. Entry into new business area through internal new venturing, it means that starting a business from scratch; building facilities, purchasing equipment, recruiting personnel, operating and opening up distribution outlets. There is the choice between acquisition and internal new venturing as the preferred entry strategy for the company. It is influenced by five factors. They are listed as below:

- Barriers to entry
- Relatedness
- Speed and development costs
- Risk of entry
- Industry life cycle factor

Barriers to Entry

It arises from several factors associated with product differentiation/brand loyalty, absolute cost advantage and economies of scale of the output. These points are already discussed. Therefore, the barriers are substantial to a company is to find entering an industry through internal new venturing. It is very difficult to enter a company have construct an efficient scale manufacturing plant. It undertakes massive advertising to break down established brand loyalties and quickly buildup distribution outlets in major cities. These are hard problems to achieve goals; therefore, it involves substantial expenditures. An established company is acquiring an enterprise which already benefits from substantial scale economies and brand loyalty.

Relatedness

The company can acquire the more related business operations enterprises. Therefore, its advantages for the lower barrier to enter and the more likely it is the experience with the same business operations. These factors heighten the attractiveness of new venturing. If it happens to unrelated business operations, the company's learning process can be lengthy and expensive. The company should fully understand its new business venturing then acquire it.

Speed and Development Costs

The internal new venturing takes years to generate substantial profits from the business operations. Establishing a significant market presence can be both costly and time-consuming process for the company. Acquisition is a much quicker way to establish a significant market presence and generate profitability from the business operations.

Risks of Entry

New venturing creates uncertain problems like low profitability of profit or may be losses of the business operations in the market. A company makes an acquisition to the other company. It should know profitability, revenues and the market share of the acquiring venture; therefore, it reduces uncertainty. Essentially internal new venturing involves the establishment of a business venture with a very uncertain future. Whereas acquisitions allow a company to buy an established business with a track record. Therefore, many companies favor acquisitions for expansion of business operations.

Industry Life Cycle Factors

Industry life cycle factors are already discussed. Industry life cycle factors influence the choice between acquisitions and internal new venturing. Barrier to entry are typically lower in embryonic and growing industries. There is more risk to entry by internal new venture during the early stage of industry life cycle. Internal new venturing is more favored in embryonic and growing industries. Therefore, many of the most successful internal new ventures have been associated with entry-emerging industries.

FAILURE OF ACQUISTIONS

There are so many reasons for failure of acquisitions. There are four reasons to failure of acquisitions as below are:

- Integration
- Overestimating economic benefits
- Expenses of acquisitions
- Inadequate preacquisition's screening

Integration

Integration refers to business operation is joining from the acquired and the acquiring company to share management, financial control systems, information system and human resource. It creates unexpected problems like loss of management talents and expertise and constant tension between the acquired and acquiring company in business operations and harmful performance of the acquired unit.

Overestimating Economic Benefits

It is the second pitfall of the company or organization. It creates an impact on acquisition due to overestimating of the economic benefits and pay more for the target company. It reduces profitability of the acquired company in future because of overestimating resource of the acquiring company.

The Expense of Acquisitions

It is third pitfalls of the company or organization. Acquisitions tend to be very expensive to the company. Therefore, acquisition companies stock is publicly traded tends to be very expensive. When a company bids to acquire the stock of another enterprise, the stock price frequently gets up in the acquisition process.

Inadequate Preacquisition's Screening

It is the fourth pitfall of the company or organization. Companies often don't adequately screen their acquisition targets therefore, one reason for acquisitions failure due to inadequate attention to pre acquisition screening by the company.

GUIDELINES FOR SUCCESSFUL ACQUISITION

To avoid pitfalls and make successful acquisitions, three guidelines for successful acquisition are involved. They are listed below:

- Screening
- Bidding strategy
- Integration

Screening

It increases a company's knowledge and potential takeover targets. Target screening leads to a more realistic assessment of the problems involved in executing and integrating the new business operations in the market. The screening should begin with a detailed assessment of the strategic resource for making the acquisition and identification of acquisition process of the enterprise that would make an ideal acquisition candidate.

Next, the company should scan a target population of potential acquisition candidates, evaluating each according to detailed set of criteria. Screening focuses on the following factors:

- Financial position
- Product market position
- Competitive environment position
- Management capabilities and efficiency position
- Corporate culture position

Screening should evaluate these factors for the company to identify the strengths and weaknesses of each candidate, the extent of potential synergies between the acquiring and the acquire companies and aware of potential integration problems. In addition, the compatibility of the corporate cultures of the acquiring and acquired companies.

The companies should then reduce the list of candidates to the most favored ones and evaluate them further. At this stage, investment bankers' opinions may be important and who may be able to give valuable insights about the efficiency of target companies.

Bidding strategy

Bidding strategy is the second guideline for successful acquisition. The objective of bidding strategy is to reduce the price that a company must pay for and acquisition candidate.

Integration

Integration is the third and major important guideline for successful acquisition. Despite good screening and bidding, an acquisition will fail unless positive steps are taken to integrate the acquired company into the organizational structure of the acquiring one. Integration should center on the source of the potential strategic advantages of the acquisition – for example, marketing, manufacturing, procurement, research development, financial and management synergies. Steps to eliminate any duplication of functions should also accompany integration; any unwanted activities of the acquired company should sell. Finally, if the different business activities are closely related, they will require a high degree of integration.

ADVANTAGES OF ACQUISITION STRATEGY

Exhibit 13.1: Advantages of Acquisition Strategy

- The company immediately gets the ownership and control over the acquired firm's factories, employees, technology, brand names and distribution network.
- The company can formulate suitable strategy and generate more revenues.
- If the industry already reached the stage of optimum capacity level or overcapacity level in the host country. This strategy helps the economy of the host country.

DISADVANTAGES OF ACQUISITION STRATEGY

Exhibit 13.2: Disadvantages of Acquisition Strategy

- Acquiring a firm in a foreign country is a complex task involving bankers, lawyers, regulations and mergers and acquisitions specialists from the two countries.
- This strategy adds no capacity to the industry.
- Sometimes host countries imposed restrictions on acquisition of local companies by the foreign companies.
- Labor problems of the host country's company are also transferred to the acquired company.

PITFALLS OF INTERNAL NEW VENTURES

There is an important pitfall of internal new ventures. There are three reasons, which are quite important for high failure rate of internal ventures. They are listed below:

- Scale of entry
- Commercialization
- Poor implementation

Scale of Entry

Ventures fail because of the companies which enter a new market on too small scale. Large-scale entry into a new business is the best way for an internal venture to succeed. Indeed, in the short run, large-scale entry requires significant development costs and faces substantial losses; in the long run it brings greater returns than small scale entry. Successful small-scale entry involves lower losses, but that in the long-run-scale entry generates greater returns. Therefore, the cost of large-scale entry and the potential loses if the venture fails, many companies prefer a small-scale entry strategy. Acting on the preference can be a major mistake for the company fails to build up the market share necessary for long-term success.

Commercialization

Many internal new ventures are highly technological operations to be commercially successful. Science based innovation must be developed with the market requirements in mind. Many internal new ventures fail therefore; a company ignores the basic needs of the companies market. A company can become blinded by the technologies possibility of a new product and fail to analyses market opportunity properly. Thus, a new venture may fail due to lack of commercialization otherwise; there is no demand for their products in the market.

Poor Implementation

Ventures fail due to the poor implementation of the strategic decisions in the company. It is the third factor which indicates managing the new ventures process. It raises different organizational issues.

RECOMMENDATIONS FOR SUCCESS OF INTERNAL NEW VENTURING

Exhibit 13.3: Recommendations for Success of Internal New Venturing

- A company should adopt a structural approach to managing internal new venturing. New venture typically begins with effective capacity use of research and development. It spells out its strategic objectives and then communicates them to its scientists and engineers and operation workforce of the organization, after it is undertaken in areas relevant to strategic goals.
- A company should close links among the R&D, marketing personnel, and manufacturing personnel. A company ensures to manufacturing of any proposed new products. It can be increasing the probability of commercial success.
- Many companies successfully integrate different functions by setting up project teams. Such teams' representatives of the various functional areas. The task of these teams is to oversee the development of new products.
- Another advantage of such teams is that it significantly reduces the time. It helps in development of a new product.
- Effective utilization of the resources in the company is to devise a selection process for choosing only the ventures that demonstrate the greatest probability of commercial success.
- Once company has selected the project, the management needs to monitor the progress of the venture. It is the most important criterion for evaluating a venture during its first four to five years, it is marked as share growth rather than profitability/cash flow. In the long run, the most successful ventures are those that increase their market share. A company should have clearly-defined market share objectives for an internal new venture.
- Finally, the association of large scale entry with greater long-term profitability. A company can construct efficient scale of manufacturing, facilitates ahead of demand, large marketing expenditures, and commitment by corporate management to accept initial large losses as long as market share is expanding.

JOINT VENTURE

Two or more firms join to create a new business entity to achieve a common purpose. It is legally separated and distinct from its parents. Joint venture are established as corporations and owned by the funding partners in the predetermined proportions. Joint ventures involve the local companies. It acts to improve the local image in the host country and satisfies the governmental requirements regarding joint ventures. In fact, support of host country's government is essential for the success of the joint venture.

Rationale for Joint Venture

What motivates the formation of a joint venture? The common reasons for setting-up joint ventures are as follows:

- Pooling of complementary resources
- Access to raw materials or new markets
- Diversification of risk
- Economies of scale
- Cost reduction
- Tax shelter

ADVANTAGES OF JOINT VENTURE

Exhibit 13.4: Advantages of Joint Venture

- Joint venture provides large capital funds. It is suitable for major projects.
- Joint venture spread the risk between or among partners.
- Different parties to the joint venture bring different kinds of skills like technical skills, technology, human skills, expertise, marketing skills or marketing networks.
- Joint venture makes to provide synergy due to combined efforts of varied parties.

DISADVANTAGES OF JOINT VENTURE

Exhibit 13.5: Disadvantages of Joint Venture Joint venture has also potential for conflicts. They result in disputes between or among parties due to varied interests. For example, the interest of host country's company in developing countries would be to get the technology from its partner while the interest of a partner of an advanced country would be to get the marketing expertise from the host country's company.

- Inadequate pre-planning for joint venture.
- Failure to develop the hope for technology.
- The parties delay the decision making once the dispute arises. Then the operations become irresponsive and inefficient.
- Decision-making is normally slowed down in joint ventures due to the involvement of a number of parties.
- Scope for collapse of a joint venture is more due to entry of competitors, changes in the partners' strength etc.
- Differences in the strategic vision of partners.
- Refusal of the partners to share control or reach compromises on difficult issues.
- Life cycle of a joint venture is hindered by many causes of collapse.

LIFE CYCLE OF A JOINT VENTURE

Joint venture formation stages are listed below:

- Exploratory phase
- Growth phase
- Stability phase
- Renegotiation phase

These are the important life cycle phases of a joint venture. The first stage of the life cycle of a joint venture begins with exploratory stage. During this stage, the prospective partners start making:

- Alliances
- Project collaborations
- Feasibility studies

After making alliance, the growth phase of the joint venture takes place. If the interests of the parties vary at this stage, they will lead to collapse of the joint venture in this phase. If the partners work together, this phase leads to stability of the joint ventures. Even in the stability stage, the joint venture may collapse. If not, the changed interests of the parties force them to renegotiate regarding their interests and shares. If the renegotiation is not successful, the joint venture may collapse. The main reasons for collapse as mentioned below:

- Entry of new competitors
- Changes in partners strengths
- Changes in business environment
- Today's partners may become tomorrow's competitors
- Changes in partners' interest

Partners in the Joint Ventures

Different types of partners join the joint ventures. They include:

Host Country's Governments

Host country's government normally acts as local partners in joint ventures. These are most effective joint ventures in developing and socialistic pattern of countries. This type of joint venture is called *public private venture.*

Public and Private Venture

Public-private joint venture is involving the partnership between a government and private company. This type of joint venture is created under the following circumstances:

- When the priority of the government for development matches with competence of a private company.
- When a country allows entry of foreign companies only through joint ventures with the government.
- Firms enter centrally-controlled economies like China and Sweden only through joint ventures with the government. For example, Alcatel's joint venture with the ministry of Posts and Telecommunications, Shanghai Bell, China

Private Partners

Many companies would like to have joint venture with private companies. Local private partners provide marketing knowledge, cultural know how, information regarding financial companies, creditors, employee work culture, trade unions etc. Active partners participate in ownership and management. Silent (sleeping) partners provide local acceptance and local knowledge.

Joint Ventures between Multinational Companies

These types of joint ventures are quite common. Joint ventures are formed with special skills of the two multinational companies.

How to Make Joint Ventures Successful

It is indicated that joint ventures mostly fail due to potential problems and cultural variations. Harrigan suggests the following measures to make the joint ventures successful:

- Don't accept a joint venture agreement too quickly.
- Get to know a partner by initially doing a limited project together; if a small project is successful, bigger projects are more feasible.
- Small companies are vulnerable to have their expertise lost to large joint venture partners; small companies must structure such deals with great care and guard against potential losses.
- Companies with similar culture and relatively equal financial resources work best together; keep this in mind when looking for an appropriate partner.
- Protect the company's core business through legal means, such as unassailable patents; if this is not possible, don't let the partner learn your methods.
- The joint enterprise must fit the corporate strategy of both parents, if this isn't the case, there will inevitably be conflicts.
- Keep the mission of the joint enterprise small and well defined; ensure that it does not compete with the parents.
- Give the joint enterprise autonomy to fluctuation on its own and setup mechanisms to monitor its results; it should be a separate entity from both parents.
- Learn from the joint enterprise and use this in the parent organization.
- Limit the time frame of the joint enterprise and review its progress frequently.

JOINT VENTURES AS AN ENTRY STRATEGY

A company prefers internal new venturing to acquisition as an entry strategy into new business areas yet hesitates to commit itself to an internal new venture because of the risks and costs of building a new operation. A company's possibility of establishing a new business in embryonic or growing industry, in this situation joint ventures face more risks and costs associated with the project. The company may prefer to enter joint venture with another company and use the joint venture as a vehicle for entering the new business era. Such an arrangement enables the company to share the substantial risks and costs involved in a new project.

With the embryonic nature of the industry, the venture faces substantial risks. A number of competing technologies are on the horizon. In addition, a joint venture makes sense when a company can increase the probability of successfully establishing a new business by joining forces with another company. Company has specialized assets and skills that are necessary to another company required for formulation of joint ventures, it may increase the probability of success.

DRAWBACKS OF JOINT VENTURES ARRANGEMENT

Exhibit 13.6: Drawbacks of Joint Ventures Arrangement

- A joint venture allows a company to share the risks and costs developing a new business, but it also requires the sharing of profit or loss of the new business.
- A company enters into a joint venture when it risk the partner left from the joint venture.

The venture partners have different business philosophies, time horizons, reinvestment preferences, substantial problems. It fails due to partner conflicts.

QUESTIONS FOR DISCUSSIONS

1. Discuss the acquisitions versus internal new ventures as entry strategies.
2. Describe the failure of acquisitions.
3. What are the advantages and disadvantages of acquisition strategy?
4. Explain the guidelines for successful acquisition.
5. What are the pitfalls of internal new ventures?
6. Discuss the joint venture life cycle.
7. What are the merits and demerits of joint venture?
8. Explain the drawbacks of joint ventures arrangement.
9. Discuss the acquisition life cycle.

REFERENCE

1. W.L. Charles Hill/Gareth R. Jones, *Strategic Management Theory an Integrated Approach*, All India Publishers and Distributors Regd. 2001.
2. A.A. Thomson and A.J. Strickland, *Strategic Management Concepts and Cases*, Tata McGraw –Hill Publishing Company Limited, New Delhi, 2003.
3. A. John, Pearce II, B. Richard, J.R. Robinson, *Strategic Management Strategy Formulation and Implementation*. A.I.T.B.S. Publishers & Distributors (Regd), New Delhi, 2002.
4. Kenichi Ohmae, *Global Logic of Strategic Alliance*, Harward Business Review, March-April, 1989.
5. Jet Magsaysay, *Strategic Alliance, Why Compete? Collaborate*, world executive is bigest, October 1989, p. 34.
6. Rechard H. Holton, Making International Joint Ventures Work, paper presented at the seminar in the management of headquarters/subsidiary relationships in transaction at corporation, Stockholur School of Economics, June 2-4 1980 p. 4.
7. William A. Dymsza, Multinational Businees Strategy, McGraw Hill, Newyork 1972.

8. Kathriyis Readie Harrigan, *Joint Ventures and Global Strategies*, Columbia Journal of World Business 19 (Summer 1984) pp. 7-16.
9. Yankelovick, Skedly and White, *Collaborative Ventures: A pragmatic approach to business expansion in the Eighties*, Coopers and Lybrand, Newyork, 1998.
10. United Nations, Guidelines for Foreign Direct Investment, Newyork, 1975.

Chapter – 14

Strategies for Competing in Globalizing Marketing

CONTENTS

LEARNING OBJECTIVES

This chapter aims to provided as Globalization market, feature of globalization market, reasons for globalization, advantages of globalization, disadvantages of globalization, why companies expand into foreign markets, The difference between competing internationally and competing globally, cross country differences in cultural, demographic and market conditions, multi-global/global country competition, strategy options for entering and competing in foreign markets, difference between multicountry strategy and global strategy, pursuing competitive advantage by competing globally, strategic alliance and joint venture with foreign country partners, strategies for local companies in emerging markets and competing in emerging foreign markets.

INTRODUCTION

"You have no choice but to operate in a world shaped by globalization and information revolution. There are two options; Adapt or Die"

– Andrew S. Grove, Chairman Intel Corporation

"You do not choose to become global. The market chooses for you; it forces your hand"

– Alain Gomez, CEO, Thomson, S.A

This chapter examines the globalization of markets, feature, and reasons for globalization of markets, advantages and disadvantages of globalization market. Strategies for competing in globalizing market, issues companies face in crafting strategies suitable for multinational and globally competitive indirect environment. We will be introducing a number of new concepts like profit sanctuaries, cross-market subsidization and the distinction between multicountry competition and global competition. Small firms enter into global market and growing alliance with foreign partners.

GLOBALIZATION OF MARKETS

Globalization of markets refers to the process of integrating and merging of the distinct world markets into a single market. This process involves the identification of some common norm, value, taste, preference and convenience and slowly enables the cultural shift towards the use of a common product or service.

A number of consumer products have global acceptance. For example, coca-cola, Pepsi, McDonald's Music of Madonna, MTV, Sony Walkmans, Levis jeans, Indian masala dosa, Indian Hyderabadi biryani, Citicorp credit cards etc.

FEATURE OF GLOBALIZATION OF MARKETS

Exhibit 14.1: Feature of Globalization of Markets

- The size of the company need not be too large to create a global market. Even small companies can also create a global market. For example, Harry Ramsden – small British company with an annual sale of US $16 million is trying to sell its product of fish 'n' chips in Japan based on the Japanese culture.

(Contd...)

- The distinctions of national markets are still prevailing even after the globalization of markets. These distinctions require the companies to formulate different strategies for each market. For example, Coca Cola, Levis jeans, and MacDonald employ separate strategies for each country.
- Most of the foreign markets are the markets for non-consumer goods like industrial products, machinery, equipment, raw materials, computers, software, financial products etc.
- The global business firms compete with each other frequently in different national markets including home markets. For example, Coca-cola is the global rival of Pepsi. Similarly, Ford and Toyota, Boeing and Airbus, Caterpillar and Komatsu. Though these companies compete with each other they create a global market.

REASONS FOR GLOBALIZATION

Exhibit 14.2: Reasons for Globalization

- Large-scale industrialization enabled mass production. Consequently, the companies found that the size of the domestic market is very small to suffice the production output and thus opted for foreign markets.
- Companies in order to reduce the risk diversity of portfolio of countries.
- Companies globalize markets in order to increase their profits and achieve goals.
- The adverse business environment in the home country pushed the companies to globalize their markets.
- To cater to the demand for their products in the foreign markets.
- The failure of the domestic companies in catering the needs of their customers pulled the foreign countries to market their products.

ADVANTAGES OF GLOBALIZATION MARKET

Exhibit 14.3: Advantages of Globalization Market

- Free flow of capital and increase in the total capital employed.
- Free flow of technology from developed countries to developing countries. Increase in industrialization.
- Spread production facilities throughout the global.
- Balanced development of world economies.
- Increased in production and consumption of outputs.
- Commodities available at lower price with high quality.
- Cultural exchange and demand for a variety of products in foreign market. Increased in jobs opportunities and income.
- Balanced in welfare and prosperity of the country's economy.

DISADVANTAGES OF GLOBALIZATION MARKET

Exhibit 14.4: Disadvantages of Globalization Market

- Globalization kills domestic small business firms
- Exploits human resources in global firms
- Leads to unemployment and underemployment in developing countries
- The customer demand decline in domestic products
- Decline the income because of unemployment
- Widening gap between rich and poor
- National sovereignty at stake
- Leads to commercial and potential colonialism to poor countries

WHY COMPAINES EXPAND INTO FOREIGN MARKETS

There are four main reasons opt to expand into foreign markets. Important reasons are outlined:

- To gain access to new customers
- To achieve lower costs enhance the firms competitiveness
- To capitalize on its core competencies
- To spread its business risk across a wider market base

To Gain Access to New Customers

This is the first reason to companies expand into foreign market. It offers potential for increased revenues, profits and long-term growth and becomes an especially attractive option when a company's home markets is mature. Mature industries plan to enter new market, therefore, to access to new customer for their products and service.

To Achieve Lower Cost Enhance the Firms Competitiveness

This is the second reason to domestic companies opt to expanding their market in outside countries. Many companies are driven to sell their products and service in more countries because the sales volume achieved in their own domestic markets is not large enough to fully capture manufacturing economies of scale and experience curve effects and thereby substantially improve a firm's cost competitiveness.

To Capitalize on its Core Competencies

This is the third factor to companies expand their domestic market into international market. A company with competitively-valuable competencies and capabilities may be able to leverage them into a position of competitive advantage in foreign market as well as just domestic markets.

To spread its Business Risk across a Wider Market Base

This is the last reason opted by the companies to expand their domestic market into international market. A company spreads its business risk by operating in a number of different foreign countries rather than depending entirely on operations in its own domestic market.

Except in a few cases, companies in natural resource-based industries such as oil and gas, minerals, rubber and lumber often to find it necessary to operate in the international arena because of attractive raw material suppliers are located in foreign countries.

Exhibit 14.5: The Difference between Competing Internationally and Competing Globally

Competing internationally	Competing globally
• A company competes in a select few foreign markets. It is an international/multinational *i.e.*, competing internationally.	• A company competes in virtually the entire world's major countries and global competitor is pursuing a market presence on cost continents.

CROSS COUNTRY DIFFERENCES IN CULTURAL, DEMOGRAPHIC AND MARKET CONDITIONS

Small firms competing in foreign markets where there are significant cross-country variations in market conditions. It poses a much bigger strategy making challenge than just competing at home.

Small firms enter into foreign market before to know the responsiveness to cross-country difference in cultural, demographic and market conditions. It complicates the task of competing in the world market. This is the difficult and challenging task for small firms enter into foreign market and is to balance pressures to be responsive to local situations in each country against pressures for lower costs and prices of the products and service.

The Potential for Locational Advantages Stemming from Country to Country Cost Variations

Company's potential for gaining competitive advantage based on where it located its foreign activities or being at a disadvantage. Therefore, rivals have lower-cost locations is a matter of considerable strategic concern.

Fluctuating Exchange Rate

The volatility of exchange rates greatly complicates the issue of geographic cost advantages currency exchange rates often to fluctuate as much as 20 to 40 percent annually, changes of this magnitude can totally wipe out a country's low-cost advantage or transform a former high-cost location into a competitive cost location.

Domestic Government Restrictions and Requirements

Domestic government enacts all kinds of measures affecting business conditions and the operation of foreign countries in their markets. Domestic government may set local content requirements of outputs made inside their borders by foreign-based companies, impose tariffs or quotas on imports, put conditions and restrictions on export to ensure adequate local suppliers, and regulate the prices of imported and locally-produced goods. In addition, outsiders may face a rules and regulations regarding technical standards, product certification, and prior approval of capital spending projects withdrawal of funds from the country and minority/majority ownership by local citizens. Some government, anxious to obtain new plants and jobs, offer foreign companies a helping hand in the forms of subsidies, privileged market access, and technical assistance.

MULTI-COUNTRY COMPETITION OR GLOBAL COMPETITION

Multi-country or multi-domestic competition exists when competition in one national market is independent in another national market where there is no 'international market' just collection of self-contained country markets.

Global competition exists when competitive conditions across national markets are linked strongly enough to form a true international market when leading competitors compete head-to-head in many different countries.

In multi-country competition, rival firms vie for national market leadership. In globally competitive industries, rival firms vie for worldwide leadership.

For a company to be successful in foreign markets, its strategy must be different to one country to another country business and competitive environment into account.

STRATEGY OPTIONS FOR ENTERING AND COMPETING IN FOREIGN MAREKET

Strategic options for a company entering and competing in foreign market that decides to expand outside its domestic market and compete internationally or globally. Important strategic options for a company competing in international market are listed below:

- Export strategies
- Licensing strategies
- Franchising strategies
- A multicountry strategy or global strategy
- Pursuing competitive advantage by competing multinationally
- Strategic alliance and joint ventures with foreign partners

Export Strategy

Company is manufacturing products and service for exporting to foreign markets. It is an excellent initial strategy for pursuing international sales. It minimizes both the risk and capital requirements. With an export strategy, a manufacturer can limit its involvement in foreign markets by contracting with foreign wholesalers who are experienced in importing to handle the entire distribution and marketing of outputs and marketing function in their countries regions of the world. If it has more advantages to company and has to domination to the control over these functions. In this case, a manufactures can establish its own distribution and sales organization in some or all of the target foreign markets. Either way, a firm minimizes its direct investments in foreign countries because of its home-based production and export strategy.

Whether an export strategy can be pursued successfully over the long run depends on the relative cost competitiveness of a home country production base. In some countries, firms gain additional sale economies and firm centralizing production on several giant plants whose output capability exceeds demand in any country market. An export strategy is open for firms when the manufacturing costs in the home country are substantially higher than in foreign countries where rivals have plants or when it has relatively high-shipping costs. Unless an exporter can keep its production and shipping costs competitive with rivals having low-costs plants in location close to end user markets, its success will be limited.

Licensing Strategy

License foreign firms to use the company's technology or produce and distribute the company's products and service. Licensing mode carries low financial risk to the licensor. Licensing also has the advantage of avoiding the risks committing resource to country markets that are unfamiliar, present considerable economic uncertainty or are politically volatile. By licensing the technology or the production rights to foreign-based firms, the firm does not have to bear the costs and risk of entering foreign markets on its own. Licensee escapes himself from the risk of product failure yet it is able to generate income from royalties.

Advantages of Licensing Strategy

Exhibit 14.6: Advantages of Licensing Strategy.

- Licensing mode carries low financial risk to the licensor.
- Licensor can investigate the foreign market without many efforts on his part.
- Licensor gets the benefits with less investment on research and development.
- Licensee escapes himself from the risk of product failure.

Disadvantages of licensing strategy

Exhibit 14.7: Disadvantages of Licensing Strategy

- Licensing agreements reduce the market opportunities for both the licensor and licensee.
- Both the parties have the responsibility to maintain the product quality and promoting the product. Therefore, one party can affect the other through their improper acts.
- Costly and tedious litigation may crop up and hurt both the parties and the market.
- There is scope for misunderstanding between the parties despite the effectiveness of the agreement.
- There is a problem of leakage of the trade secrets of the licensor.
- The licensee may develop his reputation.
- The licensee may sell the product outside the agreed territory and after the expiry of the contract.

Franchising Strategies

Franchising strategies is better suited to the firm that entered to global business and expanded its products and service to international market. Franchising is a form of licensing. The franchising can exercise more control over the franchised compared to licensing. Under the franchising, an independent organization called the *franchisee* operates the business under the name of another company called the *franchiser*. Under this agreement, the franchisee pays fees to the franchiser. The franchiser provides the following service to the franchisee:

- Trade marks
- Operating systems
- Continuous support systems like advertising, employee training, reservation services and quality assurance programmes.

Franchising Agreements

The franchising agreement should contain important items as listed below:

- Franchisee has to pay a fixed amount and royalty based on the sales to the franchiser.
- Franchisee should agree to adhere to follow the franchiser's requirements like appearance, financial reporting and operation procedures and customer services etc.
- Franchiser helps the franchisee in establishing the manufacturing facilities, service facilities, provide expertise, advertising and corporate image etc.
- Franchiser allows the franchisee some degree of flexibility in order to meet the local tastes and preference.
- For example, in India NIIT has the franchised computer training centers in entire India.

Advantages of Franchising

Exhibit 14.8: Advantages of Franchising

- Franchiser can enter global markets with low investment and low risks.
- Franchiser can get the information regarding the markets, culture, customs and environment of the host country.
- Franchiser learns more lessons from the experiences of the franchisees, which he could not experience from the home country's market.
- Franchisee can early start a business with low risk as he selects an established and proven product and operating system.
- Franchisee gets the benefits of R & D with low cost.
- Franchisee escapes from the risk of product failure.

Disadvantages of Franchising

Exhibit 14.9: Disadvantages of Franchising

- International franchising may be more complicated than domestic franchising.
- It is difficult to control the international franchisee.
- Franchising agents reduce the market opportunities for both the franchiser and franchisee.
- Both the parties have the responsibility to maintain product quality and product promotion.
- There is scope for misunderstanding between the parties. There is a problem of leakage of trade secrets.

A Multicountry Strategy or A Global Strategy

A multicountry strategy is suitable for industries where multicountry competition dominates and domestic responsiveness is essential. A global strategy works best in markets. Therefore, it is globally competitive or beginning to globalize.

DIFFERENCE BETWEEN MULTICOUNTRY AND GLOBAL STRATEGIES

	Multicountry Strategy	*Global Strategy*
• **Strategic arena**	Selected target countries and trading areas of business.	Most countries where there is high demand for the products and service.
• **Business strategy**	Business strategies to fit the conditions of each domestic country situation; there is little or no strategy coordination across countries.	Business basic strategies are the same worldwide and it fluctuates from one country to another country; it is the basic requirement.
• **Product-line strategy**	It adapted to local culture and the particular desire and expectations of local buyers.	Mostly standardized quality products and service sold worldwide.
• **Production strategy**	Plants widespread across many home countries, each producing products and service are suitable for the surrounding local.	Plants located on the basis of maximum competitive advantage for the products and service for the firm.
• **Source of supply of raw materials**	Supplier in domestic country preferred (local sources required by home government)	Attractive supplier from anywhere in the world.
• **Marketing and distribution**	It adapted to practices and culture of each home country.	Much more worldwide coordination; minor adoption to home country situations if required for the business.
• **Cross-country strategy connections**	It helps to transfer ideas, technologies, competencies, and capabilities that work successfully in one country whenever such a transfer appears advantages.	It helps to use much the same technologies, competences and capabilities in all country markets, but new strategic initiatives and competitive capabilities that prove successful in one country are transferred to other country markets.
• **Company organization**	From subsidiary companies to handle operations in each home country, each subsidiary operates more or less autonomously to fit home country.	All major strategic decisions are closely coordinated at global headquarters; a global organizational structure is used to unify the operations in each country.

PURSUING COMPETITIVE ADVANTAGE BY COMPETING GLOBALLY

There are three ways a company can gain competitive advantage by expanding outside its domestic markets.

- It exploits a multinational or global competitor's ability to develop R&D, parts manufacture, assembly, distribution centers, sales and marketing, customer service centers and other activities among various countries in manner that lower costs. Therefore, it's achieving a greater product differentiation.
- It involves efficient and effective transfers of competitively-valuable competencies and capabilities from its domestic markets to foreign markets.
- It draws on a multinational or global competitor's ability to deepen or broaden its resources strengths and capabilities and to coordinate its dispersed activities in ways that a domestic-only competitor cannot.

Achieving Locational Advantage

Building and achieving location advantage, a company must consider two issues. They are as follows:

- Whether to concentrate each activity it performs in a few selected countries or disperse performance of the activity to many nations.
- In which countries to locate particular activities companies tend to concentrate their activities are significantly their activities in a limited number of locations.
- When the costs of manufacturing or other activities are significantly lower in particular geographic locations than in others.
- When there are significant scale economies in performing the activities – the presence of significant economies of scale in components production or final assembly means that a company can gain major cost savings from operating a few super efficient plants as opposed to a host of small plants scattered across the world.
- When there is step learning associated with performing an activity in a single location.
- When certain locations have superior resources allow better co-ordination of related activities, or offer other valuable advantages – a research unit or a sophisticated production facility may be situated in a particular nation because of its pool of technically-trained personnel.

Transferring Competencies and Capabilities across Borders

Domestic companies are entered to outside market that purpose they are successfully competing host country markets and growing sales and profits in the process. Transferring competencies capabilities and resources strengths from country to country contributes to the development of broader or deeper competencies and capabilities. It is ideally helping a company achieve dominating depth in a competitively valuable capability or resource or value chain. These are strong basis for sustainable competitive advantages over other multinational or global competitors and especially so over small domestic competitors in host countries. Domestic companies are usually not able to achieve dominating depth because a one-country customer base is too small to support a resource buildup, therefore, their market is just emerging and sophisticated resources have not been required.

Coordinating Cross-Border Activities

Coordinating company activities located in different country. It contributes to sustainable competitive advantage to companies in several different ways. Companies can compete in multiple locations across the world, can select where and how to challenge competitors. Multinational or global competitor may decide rival, may decide to retaliate against an aggressive rival in the country market, where the rival's financial resources for competing in other country markets, capturing greater market share, subsidizing greater market share and subsidizing any short-term losses with profit earned in other country.

Profit Sanctuaries

It refers to company earn huge profits from host country because of its strong market position. Multicountry or global companies may also enjoy huge profit position in other nations where they have a strong competitive position like big sales volume, capture market share and attractive profit margins.

Cross-Market Subsidization

Global company has the flexibility of low prices for products and service in domestic market and capture market share at the domestic company's expenses subsidizing razor-thin margins or losses with healthy profits earned in its sanctuaries, this practice called as cross market subsidization.

STRATEGIC ALLIANCES AND JOINT VENTURE WITH FOREIGN PARTNERS

Strategic alliance can help multinational companies in globally-competitive industries strengthen their competitive positions while still preserving their independence. Strategic alliances refer to agreement between companies to do business in host country market and international market. Companies will make strategic alliance and cooperative agreement towards another company to enter foreign market. It increases strength of the strategic partner in the world markets. More recently, companies from different parts of the world have formed strategic alliances and partnership arrangements to strengthen their mental ability and partnership arrangements to serve whole continents and move toward more global market. Strategic alliances are more effective in helping establish new opportunity in world markets.

Making the Most of Strategic Alliance with Foreign Partners

A company realizes the potential strategic alliance with collaborative partnerships with foreign enterprises. It seems to be six factors as functions as listed below:

- Picking a good partner in global market.
- Being sensitive to cultural differences in local market.
- Strategic alliance must be benefiting and sharing the information both parties.
- Ensuring that both parties live up to their commitments and gets benefits from the business.
- To make decisions process very fast and actions can be taken immediately when technological changes in business.
- Both parties can be managing the learning process and then adjusting the alliance agreement.

COMPETING IN EMERGING FOREIGN MARKETS

Companies racing for global leadership have to consider competing in big and emerging country markets like India, China, Brazil, Indonesia, Mexico and other developing countries. Firms entered to global market, it is an opportunity for economic growth and increases standard of life of the employees of the global firm.

Emerging foreign markets earn huge profits quickly and easily. Therefore, new entrants have to be very sensitive to local conditions. They will be willing to invest resource for the development of market for their products and service over the long term and be patient in earning a profit.

STRATEGIES FOR LOCAL COMPANIES IN EMERGING MARKETS

Local companies are seeking resources and opportunity. However, rich companies are looking to enter the markets of emerging countries. What are the strategy options for local companies in emerging markets and wishing to survive against the entry of global giants? An important strategy for local companies in competing against global challenges are as listed below:

- Defending against global competitors by using home field advantage
- Transferring the company's expertise to cross border markets
- Dodging global entrants by shifting to a new business model or market niche
- Contending on a global level

Defending Against Global Competitors by Using Home-Field Advantage

It refers that the global competition is weak and a local firm has competitive strengths that well-suited to local market and earned huge profits. Local firms cater customer who prefer a local touch and accept the loss of customer attracted to global brands products and service. A local company may be able to utilize local resource and produce quality products and enjoys a significant cost advantage over global rivals and allowing it to compete on the basis of a lower price. Its global competitors often aim their products and service attracted to upper and middle income urban buyers.

Transferring the Company's Expertise to Cross-Border Markets

It refers to company's resources, strengths and capabilities that are suitable for competing in other country markets. They are launching initiatives to transfer its expertise to cross-border markets becomes a viable strategic option for entering the foreign market.

Dodging Global Entrants by Shifting to a New Business Model or Market Niche

It refers to companies strength in terms of resources. They enter to global market with the following options:

- Shift the business to a piece of the industry value chain where the company's expertise and resources provide competitive advantage.
- Enter into a joint venture with a globally-competitive partner.
- Sell out (acquired by) a global entrant into the home market who concludes the company would be on good entry vehicles for their business.

Contending on a Global Level

A local company emerging to global market has transferable resources and capabilities for launching of new products and service in foreign market. It can sometimes launch successful initiatives to meet the pressures for globalization and start to compete on a global level itself.

QUESTIONS FOR DISCUSSIONS

1. Discuss why the companies expand into foreign market.
2. Explain the difference between competing internationally and competing globally.
3. Describe the global country competition.
4. Explain the strong options for entering and competing in foreign markets.

5. What're the difference between multi-country strategy and global strategy?
6. Explain the pursuing competitive advantage by competing globally.
7. Describe the strategic alliance and joint venture with foreign partners.
8. What are the strategies for local companies in emerging markets.
9. Describe the competing in emerging foreign markets.
10. What are merits and demerits of joint venture?
11. What are the advantage and disadvantages of franchising?
12. What are the merits and demerits of licensing strategy?

REFERENCES

1. W.L. Charles Hill / Gareth R. Jones, *Strategic Management Theory an Integrated Approach*, All India Publishers and Distributors Regd. 2001.
2. A.A.Thomson and A.J. Strickland, *Strategic Management Concepts and Cases*, Tata McGraw –Hill Publishing Company Limited, New Delhi, 2003.
3. A. John Pearce II, Richard B. Robinson, JR. *Strategic Management Strategy Formulation and Implementation*. A.I.T.B.S. Publishers & Distributors (Regd), New Delhi, 2002.
4. Campbell, Andrew; Michael Goold;and Marcus Alexander. *Corporate Strategy: The Quest Parenting Advantage*. Harvard Business Review 73, no.2 (March–April 1995).
5. Collis, David J., and A. Cynthia Montgomery. *Creating Corporate Strategy*. Harvard Business Review 76, no.3 (May–June 1998), pp.70-83.
6. Eisenhardt, Kathleen M., and Shona L. Brown. *Patching : Restitching Business Portfolios in Dynamic Markets*. Harvard Business Review 77. no.3 (May-June)pp.72-82.
7. Haspeslagh, Phillippe C., and David B. Jamison. *Managing Acquistions: Creating Value through Corporate Renewal*. Newyork: Free Press,1991.
8. Day, S. George, *Strategies for Surviving a Shakeout*. Harvard Business Review 75, no .2. (March–April) , pp,92–102.
9. Feldman, Lawrence P., and Albert L. Page. *Harvesting : The Misunderstood Market Exit Strategy*. Journal of Business Strategy 5, no.4 (Spring 1985), pp 79-85.
10. Finkin, F. Eugene *Company Turnaround*. Journal of Business Strategy 5, no.4 (Spring 1985).
11. L. Gordon Geoffrey L; Roger J. Calantrone; and C Anthony di Benedetto. *Mature Markets and Revitalization Strategies : An American Fable*. Business Horizons (May–June1991) pp,39-50.
12. John D. Daniels, Earnest W. Ogram, Jr. and Lee, H. Ralegangh, *International Business: Environments and Operations*, Reading mass, Addison werley, 1976.
13. Franklin R. Hoot, *Entering International Markets*, in Handbook of International Business, John wiley and Sons, 1988.
14. William A. Dymsza, *Multinational Business Strategy*, Mc-Graw-Hill, Newyork, 1972.
15. Yankelovick, Skelly and White, *Collaborative sentures. A pragmatic Approach to business expansion in the eighties*, Coopers and Cybrand, Newyork, 1998.

Chapter – 15

Strategy Framework and Restructuring the Corporation

CONTENTS

LEARNING OBJECTIVES

This chapter aims to provide

- Long term objectives of the company
- Successful qualities of long-term objectives
- Portfolio framework, how to utilize for corporate strategy
- BCG matrix
- Limitations of BCG matrix
- Mckinsey's 7s framework
- Restructuring
- Turnaround strategy
- Main elements of successful turnaround strategies

INTRODUCTION

This chapter has to discuss in detail the concept of formulation long-term objectives, grand strategies, portfolio framework for corporate strategy, the BCG growth/share matrix, McKinney's 7s framework, restructuring and turnaround strategy of the corporation.

LONG-TERM OBJECTIVES

Short-run profit maximization is rarely based on the best approach to achieving sustained corporate growth and profitability of the firm. It is recognized by the strategic managers of the firm. Therefore, to achieve long-term prosperity purpose strategic managers designed long-term objectives. Long-term objectives of the firm or company or organization as listed below:

- Profitability
- Productivity
- Competitive position
- Employees development
- Employee relationships
- Public responsibility
- Technological leadership

Profitability

Profitability is an important functional area of the long-term objectives of the firm. The ability of any business to operate in the long run depends on attaining on acceptable level of profits. Strategically managed firms characteristically have a profit objective usually expressed in return on equity.

Productivity

Productivity is an essential need for each strategist in the corporation. Strategic managers try to improve the productivity of their systems. Companies that can improve the input-output relationship normally increase profitability. Productivity objectives are sometimes stated in terms of desired decreases inmost. This is an equally effective way to increase profitability.

Competitive Position

Competitive position can increase profitability and productivity of the company. Companies or firms or organization's competitive position reduces the cost of production of the output. The corporate success depends on the firm's competitive position. It is strongly dominated in the market.

Employee Development

It refers to experienced employees are the asset of the organization. For long-term purposes, the company's employees need training for further course of action that effectively and efficiently managed to produce productivity in the competitive position. Therefore, it is one of the major long-term objectives of the organization.

Employee Relationships

All companies actively seek good employee committed relations with organizational environment. Strategic manager should know the employee needs and expectations. Strategic managers take a decision to welfare programme for the employees of the companies. It is only that improved employee's relationship in the organization.

Technological Leadership

Technological leadership gives clear picture of the organization goals and objectives for the long term changes in the business scenario. Many companies state their objectives in terms of their technological leadership.

Public Responsibility

Business recognizes their social responsibilities towards customer and society. Public responsibility is building up long-term images in the society through providing social work to public.

QUALITIES OF LONG-TERM OBJECTIVES

Acceptable

Acceptable measures in companies are likely acceptable by the strategic managers to pursue objectives. Quality objectives are consistent with perceptions and preference of the company mission and vision. Even if certain long-term objectives are frequently designed to be acceptable to major interest groups external to the company.

Flexible

Long-term objectives should be modifiable in the event of the extraordinary changes due to environmental forecasts. At the same time, flexibility is usually increased at the expenses of specific events of the firms. Like wise, employee confidence may be tempered; therefore, adjustment of a flexible objective may affect their job.

Measurable

Objectives must clearly and precisely measurable in business. It clearly state what will be achieved and with what time frame. Objectives should be measurable because of misunderstanding of long-term objectives of the company.

Motivating

Research studies indicate the people are most productive when objectives are set at a motivating level. This is the major problem to individuals and groups. Therefore, they are different in their perceptions of high enough. One valuable recommendation to strategic managers is to develop multiple objectives to motivating individual and specific groups in the company.

Figure 15.1 indicates the qualities of long-term objectives of the company.

Suitable

Long-term objectives are suitable to the broad aims of the organization or company. It clearly expressed in the statement of company mission. Each objective should be a step toward attainment of overall goals.

Understandable

Strategic managers clearly understand at all levels in organization for accomplishment of objectives. They should understand major criteria for monitoring and evaluating the organizational mission.

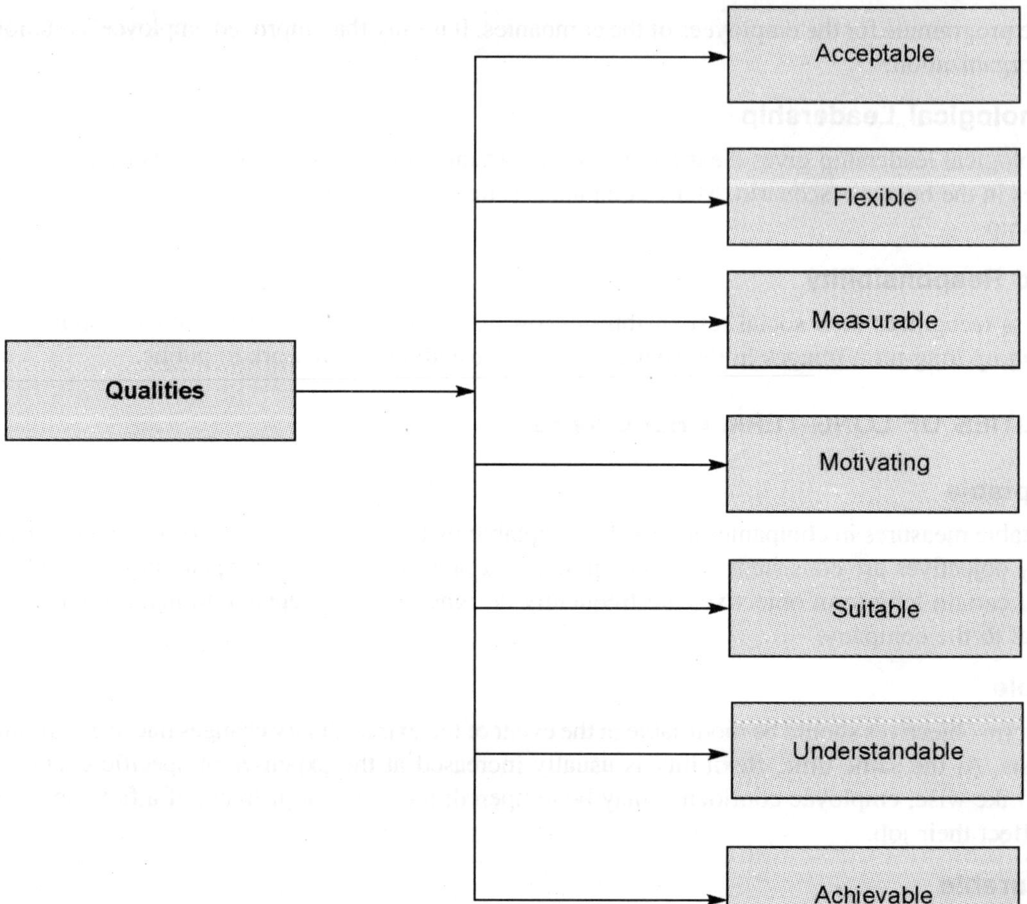

Figure 15.1: Qualities of long-term objectives

Achievable

It is the last long-term quality objectives of the organization. Achievable strategies always focus on mission and vision of the organization or company. It is a very difficult task for a strategist to face complex external difficulties in the business. Strategist designs a suitable strategy for implementation for the achievement of the goals and objectives of the company or firms or organization.

Grand Strategies

Grand strategies are also called as *master or business strategies* that are intended to provide basic direction for strategic actions. Grand strategies aim is the long-term sustainable development and growth of the organization.

Grand strategies indicate how long-range objective will be achieved. Thus, grand strategy can be defined as a comprehensive general approach that guides major actions.

Grand strategies serve as the basis for achieving major long-term objectives of a single business; concentration market, market development, product development, innovation, horizontal integration, vertical integration, joint venture, concentration diversification, conglomerate diversification, retrenchment, turnaround, divestitute and liquidation. Grand strategies usually combine all strategies of the organization or company arena.

PORTFOLIO FRAMEWORK FOR CORPORATE STRATEGY

BCG MATRIX

Portfolio analysis is a significant exercise for corporate strategic planning. Investment and financial decisions should take into consideration the entire portfolio of the firm. It presents a framework for proper assessment of the capability of various operations of company.

During the 1960s, a number of management consulting companies developed a serious of conceptual techniques whose stated purpose was to help the top officers of diversified better management portfolio of business. These techniques are known as *portfolio planning techniques*. Portfolio matrix first time developed by the Boston Consulting group which is named after them as BCG matrix.

The main objective of the Boston Consulting Group (BCG) technique is to help senior manager to identify the cash-flow requirements of the different business in their portfolio. The BCG approach involves three main processes. They are:

- Dividing a company into Strategic Business Units (SBUs) and assessing the long-term prospects of each.
- Comparing strategic business units.
- Strategic complications.

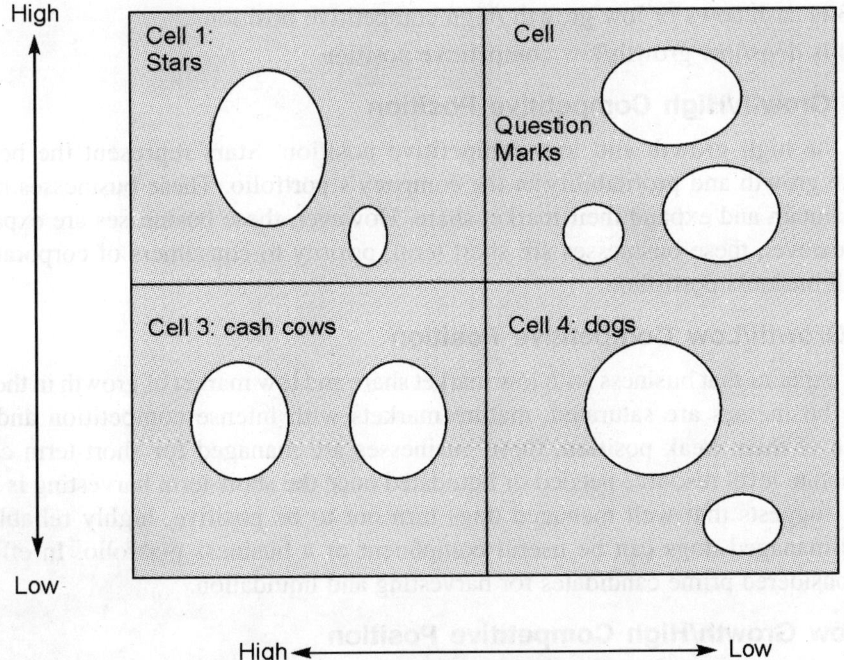

Figure 15.2: BCG growth /Share matrix

Figure 15.2 indicates the BCG Growth/Share market, it identifies the cash-flow requirements of the different business in their portfolio.

Defining and Evaluating Strategic Business Unit

According to this BCG matrix Fig. 15.2, a company can relate a SBU for each economically-distinct business area. Top managers can define SBUs; top managers, then assess each, based on two criteria listed below:

- The SBUs relative market share
- The growth rate of SBUs industry/Market growth

Figure 15.2 represents the BCG matrix for a company with nine businesses. Each circle represents the proportion of corporate revenue generated by that business unit. It provides visualization of the current importance of each revenue generator.

Comparing Strategic Business Units

The next step of the BCG approach is comparing SBUs against each by means of a matrix based on two dimensional areas mentioned below:

- Relative market share
- Industry/market of growth/rate

Figure 15.2 provides the vertical dimension measures the industry/market growth rate. The horizontal dimension measures relative market share.

The matrix is divided into four cells they are:

- Cell 1is stars or high growth/high competitive position
- Cell 2 is question marks or high growth/low competitive position
- Cell 3 is cash cows or low growth /high competitive position
- Cell 4 is dogs/low growth/low competitive position

Stars or High Growth/High Competitive Position

Stars represent the high growth and low competitive position. Stars represent the best long-run opportunities like growth and profitability in the company's portfolio. These businesses require huge investment to maintain and expand their market share. However, these businesses are expanding their market share. However, these businesses are short term, priority to consumers of corporate resources within the overall business portfolio.

Dogs or low Growth/Low Competitive Position

The BCG matrix explains that business with low market share and low market of growth in the company's portfolio. These businesses are saturated, mature markets with intense competition and low profit margins, because of their weak position, these businesses are managed for short-term cash flow to supplement corporate level resource needed or liquidated once the short-term harvesting is maximized. Recent research suggests that well managed dogs turn out to be positive, highly reliable resources generators. Well-managed dogs can be useful component of a business portfolio. In effective dogs should still be considered prime candidates for harvesting and liquidation.

Cash Cows/Low Growth/High Competitive Position

Cash cows are high market share business in maturing, low growth markets or industries because of their strong position and minimum investment requirements for growth; these businesses often generate cash in excess of their needs. Cash cows are yesterday's stars and remain the current foundation of their corporate portfolios; they provide the cash to pay corporate overhead and dividends and provide debt capacity.

Question Mark/High Growth/Low Competitive Position

Question mark business has considerable appeal because of their high growth rate yet present questionable profit potential because of low market share. Question mark businesses are known, as cash guzzlers because their cash needs are high as a rapid growth, while their cash generation is low due to a small market share.

LIMITATIONS OF THE BCG MATRIX

Exhibit 15.1: Limitations of the BCG Matrix

- It is cleary defining a market is very difficult task as a result, accurately measuring share and growth rate can be a problem. This creates the potential manipulation or distortion.
- Dividing the matrix into four cells is based on a high/low classification scheme. It does not recognize the markets with average growth rates or the business with average market share.
- The relationship between market share and profitability underlying BCG matrix.
- The BCG matrix is not particularly helpful in comparing relative investments opportunities across different business units in the corporate portfolio.
- Strategic evaluation of a set of business requires examination of more than relative market shares and market growth.

McKINSEY'S FRAMEWORK

The McKinney Company developed the 7s frameworks towards the end of 1970s, it is a very reputed management consultancy firms in the USA, to diagnose the causes of organizational problems and formulating progammes.

According to Waterman and others, organizational change is not simply a matter of structure, although structure is a significant variable in the management of change. Again, it is also not a simple relationship between strategy and structure although strategy is a critical aspect. In their view, effective organizational change may be understood to be a complex relationship between strategy, structure, systems, style, skills, staff, and subordinate goals.

Structure basically, organizational structure prescribes the formed relationship among various positions and activities, arrangements for reporting relationship and what rules and procedures exist to guide the various activities performed by members are all part of the organizational structure. It performs four major functions. They are as outlined below:

- It reduces external uncertainty through forecasting research and planning in the organization.
- It reduces internal uncertainty arising out of variables, unpredictable, random human behavior within the organization through control mechanisms.
- It undertakes a wide variety of activities through devices like departmentalization, specialization, and division of labor and delegation of authority.
- It enables the organization to keep its activities co-ordinate and to have to focus it the midst of diversities in pursuit of its objectives.

The design of organization structure is a critical task for the top management. The Mckinsey consultants strongly felt that in today's changing business environment, structural changes to cope with specific strategic tasks without abandoning basic structural divisions throughout the organizations.

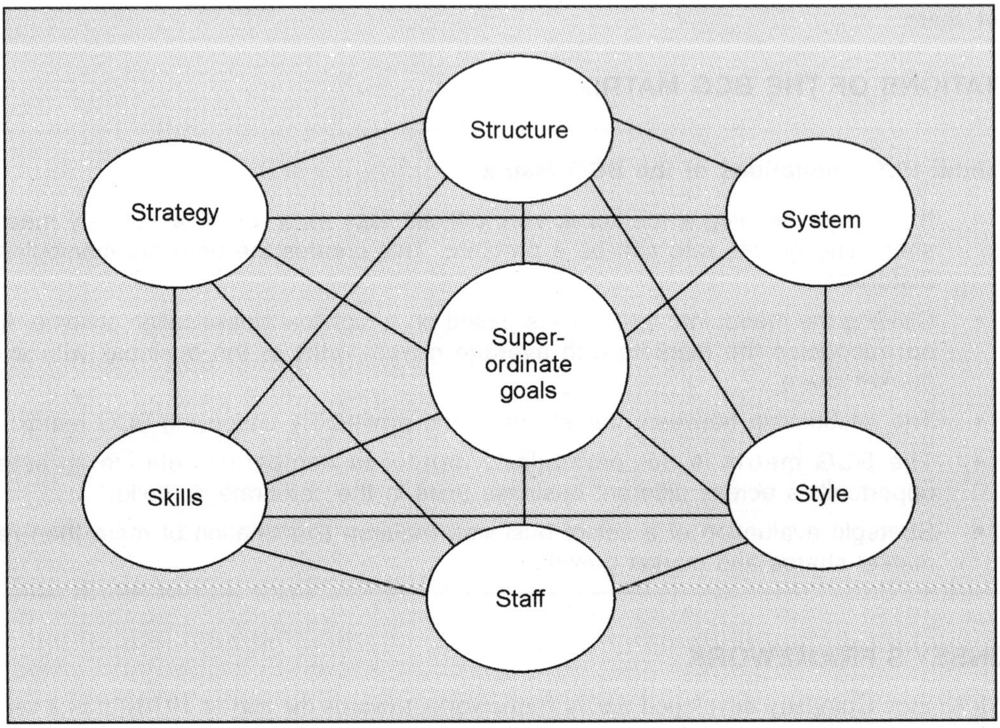

Figure 15.3: McKinney's 7s Framework

Figure 15.3 highlights the 7s framework. They are as listed below:

- Strategy
- Systems
- Style
- Staff
- Skills
- Super-ordinate goal

Strategy

The concept of strategy includes purposes, mission's objectives, goals and major action plans and policies. The 7s model emphasizes that in practice, the development of strategies poses less of a problem than their execution.

Systems

Systems include all those procedures and methodologies, which are framed by the organization and followed by the operating personnel in the respective functional areas. Example, financial accounting system, materials planning and inventory control system, quality management computerization, etc., in all these functional areas some traditional system may be in existence which needs to be reviewed and changed, as per requirements, in view of advanced technology and process developed.

Style

Style is one among the seven levers, which top mangers can use to bring about organizational change. With the change of systems and procedures, the style of functioning in different work places and situations will automatically changed in fact, the old and outdated style of work can hardly bring any result or play any role for material contribution in today's competitive and sophisticated business world. The Mckinsey framework considers the style as more than the style of top management. Aspects of organizational culture also seen to be encompass by the term style.

Staff

Staffing is the process of acquiring human resources for the organization and assuring that they have the potential to contribute to the achievement of organizational goals. Staffing involves placement of the right person for right job. Since the job profile can change so that it requires training and updating knowledge and skills of the different categories staff of the office, it results in increased productivity and efficiency.

Skills

The operating system can change to desired efficient skillful human being for operation of the new techniques in the new technology. Skills development has raised the productivity of the employees of the company. Skill development is needed to training for inadequate skill persons in the organization. However, nowadays, company has never neglected the skills development programmes for employees. It leads to an organization which help in establishing goodwill and image in the business world.

Superordinate Goals

Superordinate goals are the fundamental ideas around which a business is built. They are of main values. They are the broad notions of future direction. According to Mckinsey superordinate goals refers to: a set of values and aspirations that goes beyond the conventional formal statement of corporate objectives. All targets and attention of all activities and exercises of the six levers of any organization should be directed towards accomplishment of the best possible goals. This is the ultimate and terminal point where the organization will have to reach. Superordinate goals have deep meaning within the organization.

RESTRUCTURING

So far, we focused on strategies for expanding the scope of a company into new business areas like diversification enters global market etc. We turn now to their opposite. Strategies is reducing the scope of the company that by existing from business areas. In recent years, reducing the scope of a company through restructuring has become an increasing popular strategy.

Why Restructuring?

- So much restructuring in recent years has been earlier over diversification. Company performance declined due to Bureaucratic inefficiencies, it has created so many constraints by expanding the scope of a company business areas. When company performance declined, therefore, the stock price of many of diversified business areas of company also declined.

- A second important factor driving the current restructuring trend initiate from the 1980 onwards, many diversified companies found their core business areas under attack from new competition.
- A final important factors like innovations in management process and strategy or diversification. In response, companies have reduced the scope of their activities through restructuring and divestments.

Exist Strategies

Exist strategies are listed below:

- Divestment
- Harvest
- Liquidation

Companies can choose above three main strategies for existing business areas: These strategies are discussed in the earlier chapter.

TURN-AROUND STRATEGY

Many companies restructure their operations divesting themselves of their diversified activities, because they wish to focus more on their core business area An integral part of restructuring, therefore, is the development of strategy for turning around the company's core or remaining business areas.

In this section, we shall review in some detail the various steps to be taken by companies for turn-around troubled business areas. We shall first look at the causes of corporate decline and then discuss the main elements of successful turn-around strategies.

The Causes of Corporate Decline

The seven causes are important for the corporate decline. Figure 15.4 indicates the seven causes impact of the corporate declines. They are listed below:

- Poor management
- Over expansion
- Inadequate financial controls
- High costs
- New competition
- Unforeseen demand shifts
- Organizational inertia

Poor Management

Poor management involves a multitude of sins; it is ringing from sheer incompetence to neglect of core businesses and an insufficient number of good managers. Therefore, these things are not necessarily a bad thing. Research study shown that in the presence of a dominant and autocratic chief executive with a passion for empire building strategies characterizes involved for many failing companies.

Over Expansion

Rapid expansion and extensive diversification, these diversifications tend to be poorly conceived and adds little value to a company. Its impact on company in terms of unable to control and inability to cope with recessionary conditions. Moreover, companies expand rapidly their business, involve large amounts of debt financing. Adverse economic conditions can limit a company's ability to meet its debt requirements and can precipitate a financial crisis.

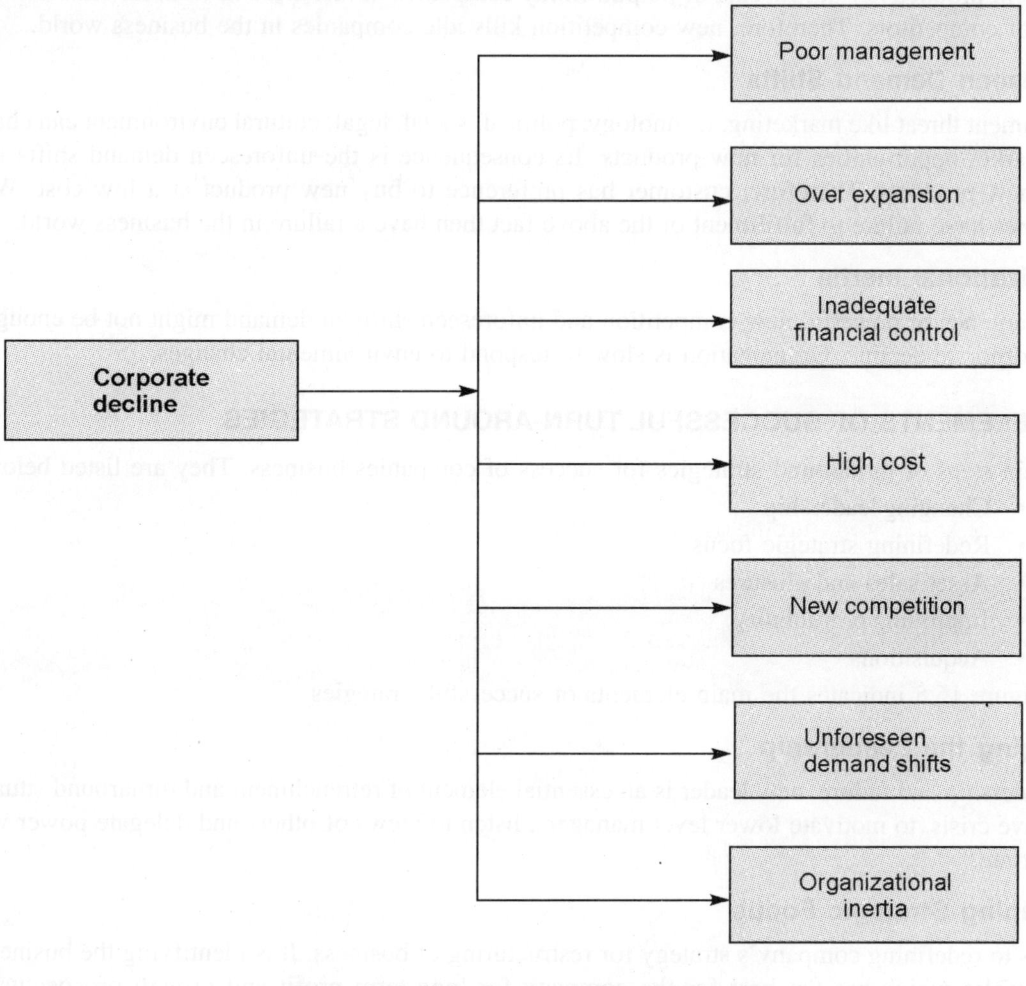

Figure 15.4: Major Causes of Corporate Decline

Inadequate Financial Controls

It is the common trend of the business. Financial manager is a failure to assign profit responsibility for the financial consequences of their actions, it can encourage to mid level mangers to employ excess staff and spend resource beyond what is necessary for maximum efficiency of the company.

High Costs

Inadequate financial control can lead to high costs. Its common cause like low-labor productivity and management has failure to introduce new labor saving technologies and high rate of wages for employees. These are important factor for companies competing on costs in the global market and have a failure to realize economy of scale, therefore, it results impact on companies' low-market share.

New Competition

New competition is essential to companies for competition in the industrial world. A company ready to tackle competition from rivals. Because of new technology made huge cut-throat competition and increase in productivity at low cost of output. Many companies have failure because of unable to face threats of competitors. Therefore, new competition kills idle companies in the business world.

Unforeseen Demand Shifts

Environment threat like marketing, technology, political, social, legal, cultural environment can change open market opportunities for new products. Its consequence is the unforeseen demand shifts from old to new products. Therefore, customer has preference to buy new product at a low cost. When companies have failure to fulfillment of the above fact then have a failure in the business world.

Organizational Inertia

The emergence of powerful new competition and unforeseen shifts in demand might not be enough to cause corporate decline. Organization is slow to respond to environmental changes.

MAIN ELEMENTS OF SUCCESSFUL TURN-AROUND STRATEGIES

The main steps of turnaround strategies for success of companies business. They are listed below:

- Changing leadership
- Redefining strategic focus
- Asset sales and closures
- Improving profitability
- Acquisitions

Figure 15.5 indicates the main elements of successful strategies.

Changing the Leadership

Old leadership had failure, new leader is an essential element of retrenchment and turnaround situation to resolve crisis, to motivate lower level managers, listen to views of others and delegate power when appropriate.

Redefining Strategic Focus

It refers to redefining company's strategy for restructuring of business. It is identifying the business in the portfolio which has the best for the company for long-term profit and growth prospectus and concentrating investment there.

Assets Sales and Closures

Having redefined its strategic focus, a company should divest as many unwanted assets as it can find buyer for and liquidate whatever remains. It is important not to confuse unwanted assets within profitable assets.

Improving Profitability

Improving profitability involves number of steps to improve efficiency, quality, innovation and customer responsiveness. It involves in the following issues:

- Layoffs white and blue collar employee

- Investments in labor saving equipment
- Assessment of profit responsibility to individuals and subunits within the company, by a change of organizational structure if necessary.
- Tightening financial controls
- Cutting back on marginal products
- Re-engineering business process to cut costs and boost productivity, and
- Introducing total quality management

Acquisitions

Turn-around strategy involves making acquisition primarily to strengthen the competitive position of a company's remaining core operations.

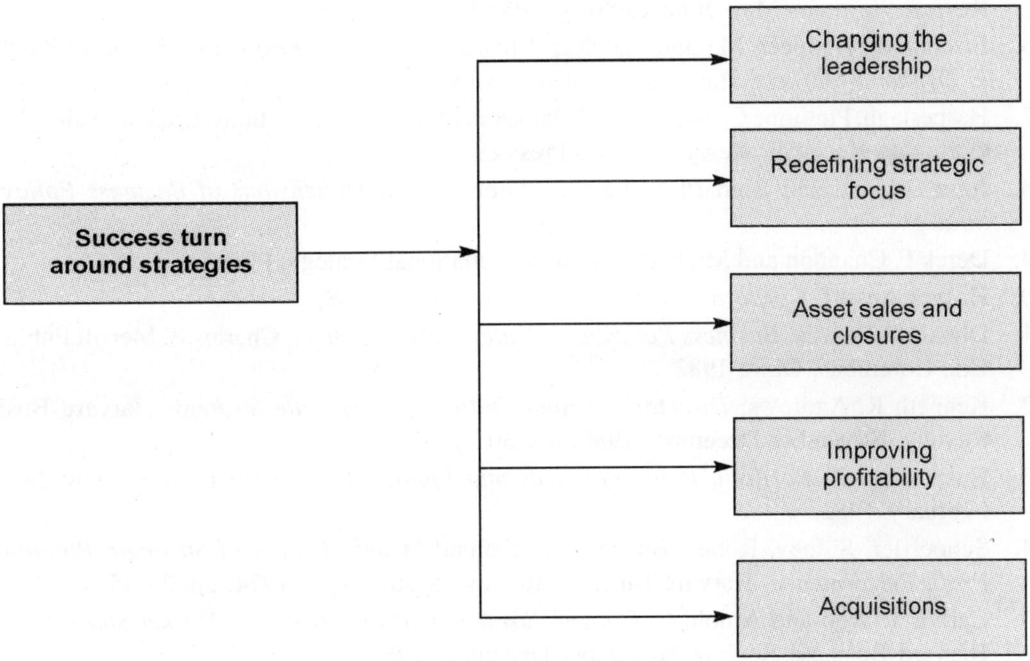

Figure 15.5: Main Elements of Successful Turnaround Strategies

QUESTIONS FOR DISCUSSIONS

1. Briefly discuss the turnaround strategy.
2. Briefly explain the McKinney's 7s framework.
3. Briefly, explain the main elements of successful turnaround strategy.
4. Discuss the BCG matrix and its limitations.
5. Discuss the long-term objectives and qualities of long-term strategy.

REFERENCES

1. Charles W.L .Hill / Gareth R. Jones, *Strategic Management Theory an Integrated Approach*, All India Publishers and Distributors Regd. 2001.
2. A.A.Thomson and A.J. Strickland, *Strategic Management Concepts and Cases*, Tata McGraw –Hill Publishing Company Limited, New Delhi, 2003.
3. John, A. Pearce II, Richard B. Robinson, JR. *Strategic Management Strategy Formulation and Implementation*, A.I.T.B.S. Publishers & Distributors (Regd), New Delhi, 2002.
4. Campbell, Andrew; Michael Goold; and Marcus Alexander. *Corporate Strategy: The Quest Parenting Advantage*, Harvard Business Review 73, no.2 (March–April 1995).
5. Collis, David j., and Cynthia A. Montgomery. *Creating Corporate Strategy*. Harvard Business Review 76, no.3 (May–June 1998), pp.70-83.
6. Eisenhardt, Kathleen M., and Shona L. Brown. "*Patching : Restitching Business Portfolios in Dynamic Markets*. Harvard Business Review 77. no.3 (May–June)pp.72-82.
7. Haspeslagh, Phillippe C., and David B. Jamison. Managing Acquistions: Creating Value through Corporate Renewal. Newyork: Free Press,1991.
8. John Garland and Richard N. Farmer, *International Dimensions of Business Policy and Strategy*,
9. Derek F. Channon and Michael Jallard, Multinational Strategic Planning
10. H. Igor Ansoff, *Corporate Strategy*, McGraw – Hill, 1968,
11. Donald F. Harvey, *Business Policy and Strategic Management*, Charles E. Merrill Publishing Co., Columbus, Ohio, 1982.
12. Kenneth R. Andrews, *Director's Responsibility for corporate Strategy*, Harvard Business Review, November-December 1980, pp. 30.
13. Hasperlagh P., *Portfolio Planning: Uses and Limits.* Harvard Business Review, January-February 1982.
14. Schoeffler, Sidney, Robert Buzzel; and Donald Heany, *Impact of Strategic Planning on Profit Performance.* Harvard Business Review, March-April 1974, pp. 34-45.
15. Carlyn Y. Woo and Arnold C. Cooper, *Strategies of Effective Low Market Share Business.* Harvard Business Review, November-December 1982, pp. 106-13.
16. Anil K. Guptha and V. Govindarajan, *Build, Hold, Harvest: Converting Strategic Intentions into Reality.* Journal of Business Strategy, March 1984, pp. 34-37.
17. Hax, Arnoldo C., and Nicolas S. Majluf. *The use of the Growth– Share Matrix in Strategic Planning.* Interfaces 13, no 1 (1983), pp. 8-21.

Chapter – 16

Strategic Change Management

CONTENTS

- Introduction
- Nature of strategic change management
- Organizational politics and power
- Source of organizational politics
- Power
- Sources of power
- Organizational conflict
- Process of the organizational conflict model
- Managing conflict strategically
- Conflict resolution strategies
- Implementing strategic: change steps in the change process

LEARNING OBJECTIVES

In this chapter, we shall look at strategic change management, organizational politics and conflict affect of an organization to overcome inertia. It influences decision-making and change its strategy and structure. This chapter has focused on political indication of the decision making for success or failure of the organization.

This chapter considers the sources of the organization change in politics and discusses how individuals, departments and division seek to increase their power so that they can influence the organizational decision-making. Soon after we investigate of the nature of the organizational conflict and make note how managers must deal with conflict to make better strategy structure choice available.

INTRODUCTION

In this chapter, we shall look at strategic change management, organizational politics and conflict affect of an organization of overcome inertia. It influences decision-making and change its strategy and structure. This chapter focuses on political indication of the decision making for success or failure of the organization.

This chapter considers the sources of the organizational change in politics and discusses how individuals, departments, and divisions seek to increase their power so that they can influence the organizational decision-making. Soon after we investigate the nature of the organizational conflict and make note how managers must deal with conflict to make better strategy structure choice available.

NATURE OF STRATEGIC MANAGEMENT CHANGE

To change is to move from the present to the future, from known information to relatively unknown information. Therefore, change can be defined as "to make or become different, give or begin to have a different form". For example, post-war recovery of Iraq and Afganistan. Change also refers to dissatisfaction with the old values, beliefs and systems and hence adapts to new values, beliefs and systems. The deficiency also reflects the inability of the system to respond to environmental changes. Change signifies a qualitatively different way of perceiving, thinking and behaving to make improvement over the past and present trends of the business management.

Change line context of an organization can be termed as a process of bringing about relatively enduring alteration in the present status of an organization or its components or interrelationships among the components and their differentiated and integrated functions in totality or partially. Therefore, changes in organization have attained greater adaptability and viability with reference to the current and emerging environmental developments in the world.

Strategic change in organization has signifies alteration in the objectives, goals and strategies, procedures for converting input into outputs, its specified features, structures and human resource. Changes in these are, however, inter-related in organization. Thus, it may include product and process restructuring, mergers and alliances, diversification and installing new systems. It may also mean change in attitudes and skills of organizational human resource, tasks and technology of the enterprise, alteration in customs responsive, norms and culture. These changes are essential and needed to business enterprise.

In view of its pervasive nature, change at anyone level is interrelated with changes at other levels of the enterprise. Therefore, it is essential for the management to assess organization with wide implications of any change is going to be affected. Further, these changes need to be reviewed on continuous basis to cope with ever changing environmental developments in business enterprise.

All changes are happened either in reaction to it as driving forces or a proactive. Changes have been planned and initiated by an organization. Therefore, reactive change happens in response to an event or series of events relating to business. The failure of existing process or system is a powerful mode for change in business. Reactive change being unplanned is hardly welcomed because it usually results in poorly coordinated, inefficient management. It plays havoc with virtually any strategic plan. Proactive changes take place when an organization's managers have concluded that a change would be beneficial to business. Proactive change is more orderly, more efficient because it is planned, structured and organized.

A change in organization is directed at the micro level. It focused on units /subunits /components within an organization and brought in gradually are incremental changes. It is beneficial to an organization and built new skills and beliefs in the organization. These changes are efficient and acceptable by an organization. Many argue that such incremental development can be proactively managed; organization will keep in touch with the environment development and anticipate needs for change. This can be achieved through process of changing of current operating business system. Others argue that while it is not always possible to anticipate the need for major strategic changes, therefore, organizations react to external competitive or environmental pressures. Corporate managers may not perceive the need for major changes. In addition, adapt the existing paradigms and extent ways of operations.

However, incremental time changes may not be beneficial to the organization. Because such changes are based on the condition by the existing paradigms and routines of the organization even when the environmental developments are so cataclysmic and forceful systems and procedures in terms of basic assumptions, culture, technology etc., of the organization. These changes are transformational in character. Therefore, transformational change refers to change that cannot be handled within the existing paradigms and organizational change; it may be taken from the granted assumptions. Transformational change may also be taken from as result of either reactive or proactive process. If strategic drift has occurred or if external stakeholders are not happy due to the adequacy of current objective and strategy to meet external threat of the organization. For this situation, management may be in a forced transformational position. Likewise, if other changes happened in the organizational environment are very powerful to the business issues. The organization is constrained to go for transformation change. Where managers anticipate the need for transformational change, meanwhile they get time to act upon the desired change.

Change can be distinguished on basis of the degree of innovative previously done in the organization. Innovation is brought changes in the organization. Innovation is different from change. Innovation occurs when an organization is the first time or early user of an innovative idea among its set of similar organizations in the business. Change brings modification of operating system of organization. Since innovation provides more excitement in change management. It is highly organized and systematic approach. It is exclusively concerned with reasoning what triggers change in the existing operating system and how affect the change in business. The management process programme is proactive, it monitors the continuously environmental developments for identifying the emerging opportunities and find out the suitable existing policies, strategies and programmes to exploit of these opportunities.

Another distinguishing characteristic of change management programme, it is engagement of the entire organization in the change process because people have always been and will remain important. Organization wide involvement of organizational people is crux of change management.

ORGANIZATIONAL POLITICS AND POWER

Organizational Politics

Organizational politics defines as the tactics but interdependent individuals and groups seek to obtain and use power to influence the goals and objectives of the organization to further their own interests. Organizational politics process is listed below:

- Source of organizational politics
- Source of power
- Strategic change

These processes are used for decision making in the organization.

SOURCE OF THE ORGANIZATION POLITICS

There are two major sources of organizational politics. They are as follows:

- Rational view
- Political view

Rational View

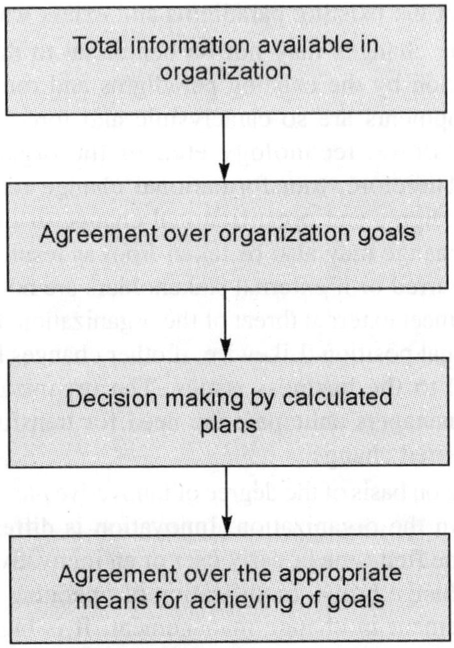

Figure 16.1: Rational Views of Decision Making

Figure 16.1 indicates the rational views decision making. These factors are important from the point of view of decision-making. Rational view factors are listed below:

- Total information available in the organization
- Agreement over organizational goals
- Agreement over the appropriate means for achieving goals
- Decision making by calculated plan

These figures indicate the formulating mission, setting policies and goals. Strategic managers are to achieve strategic goals and to maximize corporate wealth.

Political View

Political is the sound sources of the organizational politics and power. Political view factors are identified below:

- Selected information available to organization
- Disagreement over organizational goals
- Disagreement over the appropriate means for achieving goals
- Decision making by negotiation, bargaining and compromise

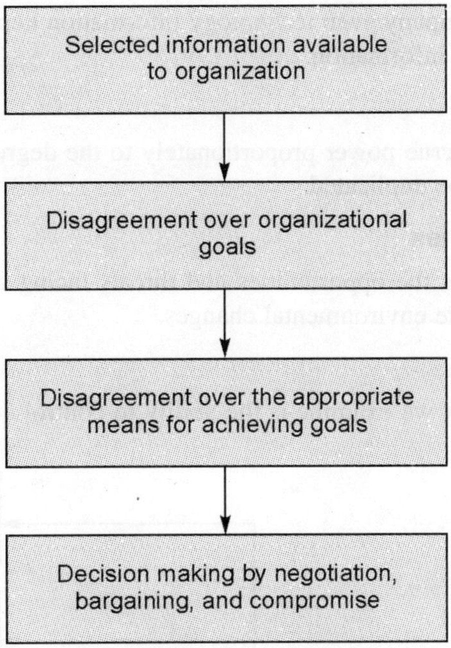

Figure 16.2: Political View of Decision Making

Figure 16.2 indicates the political view of decision-making. Goals and objectives are set through compromise, bargaining and negotiation. Politics refers to the activities through which different individuals or groups in the organization try to influence the strategic management process to further their own interest.

POWER

Power is defined as "the ability of one individual, function, or division to cause another individual, function, or division to do something that it would not otherwise have done". Power is different from authority, which stems from holding a formal position in the hierarchy.

SOURCES OF POWER

Major sources of power are identified below:

Ability to Cope with Uncertainty

It can be reduced for another function of organization.

Centrality

Powers also derives from the centrality of a division or function. Centrality refers to the extent to which a division or function is at the center of resource transfer among divisions.

Control Over Information

Control over information is the basic need for power. Division manager control over information when they are operated, its ultimate effective formulation and implementation of organizational goals. Therefore, information is the asset of company even technology information kept control by division manager. It is the better way control over information.

Non-substitutability

A function or division can accrue power proportionately to the degree to which its activities are non substitutable – that it cannot be duplicated.

Control over Contingencies

The nature of contingencies is the opportunities and threats facing a company from the competitive environment will change as the environmental changes.

Control over Resources

The final source of power that we examine is the ability to control and allocate scarce resources.

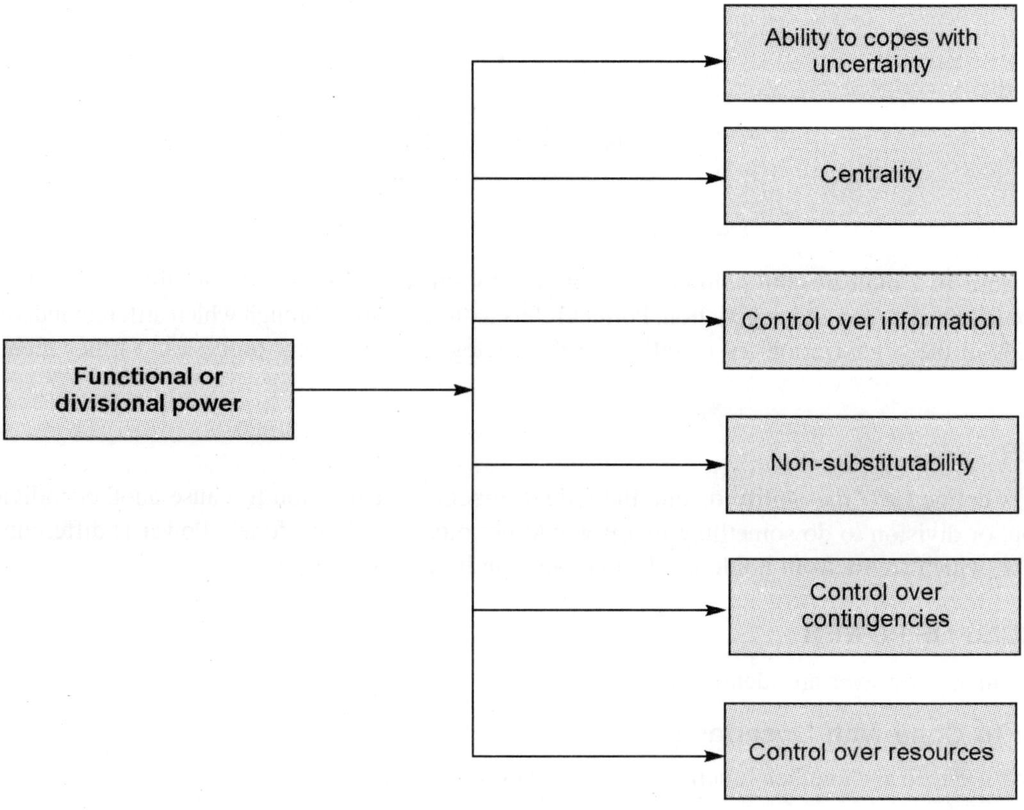

Figure 16.3: Source of Power

Effects of Power and Politics on Strategic Change

Politics and power can strongly influence a company's choice of strategy and structure. Company has to maintain organizational structure and is responsible for the various divisions, functions and managers and need to change in the remote environment. Companies have to face power problems within the organizational structure. Therefore, changes of the environmental trends of the organization. When environment changes, companies are not responding faster. In this circumstance excessive politicizing and power struggles to reduce a company's flexibility. It cause inertia and erode competitive advantage.

Managing Organizational Politics

Organization can manage its politics; company has arrangement of power balance among the various functions of the organization. In big organization, a staff play major role to balancing of power. In the case of sole trading concern, partnership strong chief executive can manage and balance the power of their firms.

ORGANIZATIONAL CONFLICT

Politics can influence by one parties goals and decision making of the organization to further its own interest. Although, the attempt of one group has to failure or and other success their goals. Its results the conflict within the organization. Conflict can be defined as situation that arises when the goal directed behavior of one organizational group blocks and goal-directed behavior of another. In this chapter, we attempt to examine the following

- Conflict is good or bad
- Sources of conflict
- The organizational conflict

Conflict is Good or Bad

The effect on conflict either good or bad on organization structure performance is continually debated. In past conflict is always bad. Therefore, it leads to lower organizational performance. According to this opinion, conflict arises because managers have not implemented strategy correctly and have not designed the appropriate structure that would make functions to achieve objectives, without doubt. Bad implementation cause conflict due to staff and line conflict within organization. If strategic managers carefully and interested to manage and prevent conflict, it is the best option for organization to accomplishment of goals for efficient allocation of resource and proper decision-making is essential.

Sources of Conflict

Figure 16.5 indicates the sources of organizational conflict. There are three sources of organizational conflict. They are listed below:

- Differentiation in the organization
- Task relationships in management and workforce
- Scarcity of resources in organization

Differentiation in the Organization

Differentiation in the organization divides authority and risk responsibilities of the company. The process of splitting organizational functions and hierarchy levels may produce conflict.

This kind of conflict has created two main causes are as follows:

- Differences in subunit orientation
- Status in consistencies

Differences in Subunit Orientation

Difference leads to the emergence of different functions of company. Each groups have develop a unique orientation toward the organization special priorities and efficiency naturally different. Therefore, the difference occurs in subunit orientation in the company.

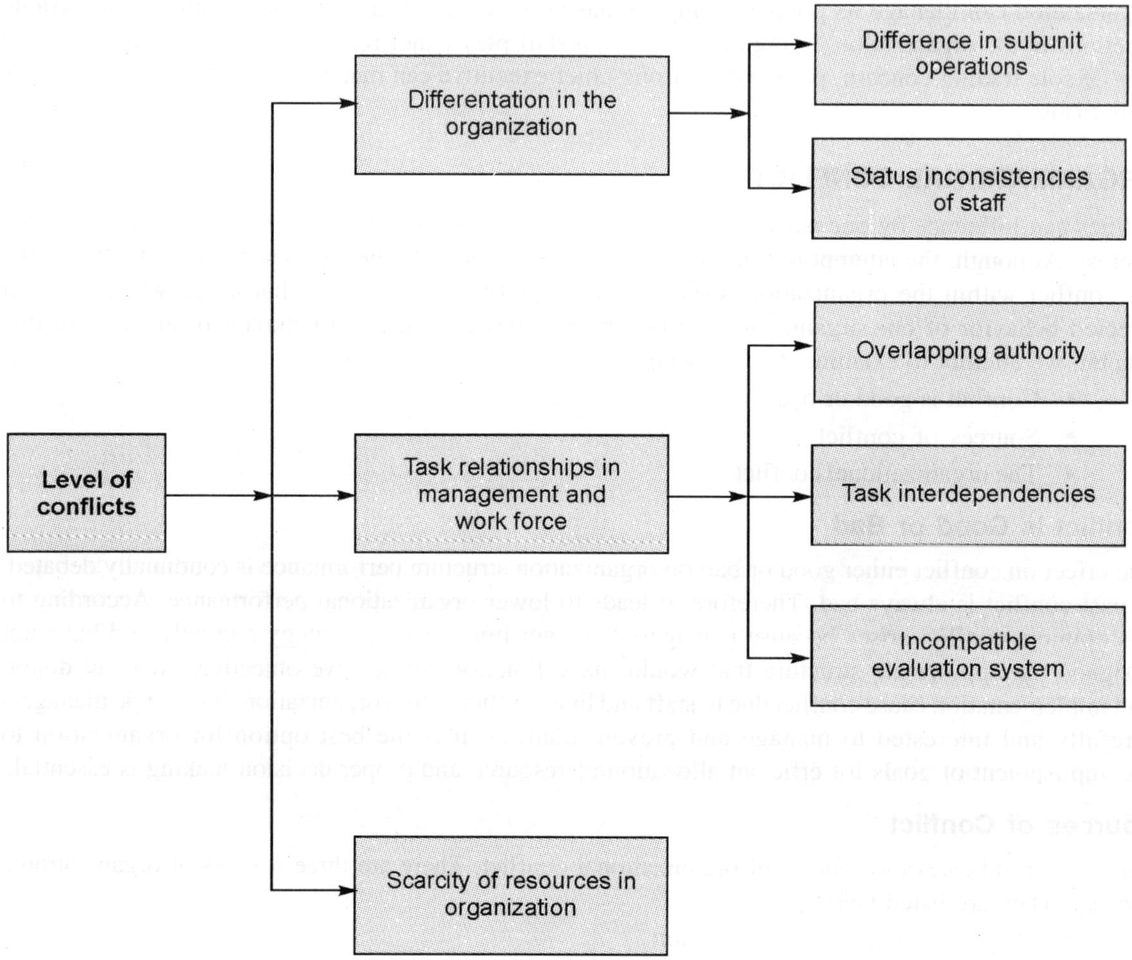

Figure 16.4: Sources of Organizational Conflict

Status Inconsistencies of Staff

Organization consists of staff organization and line organization. Line organization is the policy maker and staff organization members execute it. However, differences occur on the basis of status inconsistencies in formulating, implementing and monitoring strategies. This is the second cause to create conflict of the organization.

Task Relationships of Division

Task relationships may generate conflict among functions and divisions in overlapping authority, task interferences and incompatible evaluation system.

Overlapping Authority of Employee

If two different functions claim authority and responsibility for the same task, soon conflict may develop in an organization. This happens when an organization is growing and functional relationships are not yet fully worked out.

Task Interdependencies of Workforce

To develop, create or produce goods and services of the organization. The work of one function flows horizontally to the next so that each function can build on the contribution of the others. If one function does not do its job well, then others function nest line is seriously hampered in its work, and this too, generate conflicts.

Incomputable Evaluation System

A company has to design its evaluation and reward system does not interfere with task relationships among functions and divisions inequitable systems stirr-up conflict.

Scarcity of Resources

Competition over scarce resources also generates conflict. This kind of conflict occurs among divisions and between divisions and corporate management over the allocation of capital.

PROCESS OF THE ORGANIZATIONAL CONFLICT MODEL

Process of the organizational conflict model has developed by Lou R.Pondy. It shows how the conflict process operates within organization. Several steps created the organizational conflict mode from the point view of strategic conflict. It is an important process to understand occurs of conflicts in the organizations.

Figure 16.5 represents the stages in the conflict process. They are discussed as below:

Latent Conflict

Latent conflict is frequently activated by changes in an organizations strategy or structure that affect the relationship among functions or divisions.

Perceived Conflict

Perceived conflict is the second stage in the conflict process. Perceived conflict means that managers become aware of the clashes after a change in strategy and structure. Managers discover the actions of another function or group obstructing the operations of their group.

Felt conflict

Felt conflict is an important process of their organizational conflict. A manager is to start to react to the situations in the organization and from the perceived stage. They go quickly to the felt conflict stage. Here managers start to personalize the conflict.

Manifest Conflict

Manifest conflict stage is also one of the vital processes of the organizational conflict. The conflict comes into open among the departments and each group strives to thwart the goals of the other. Groups compete to protect their own interests and block the interests of the other groups. Manifest conflict can take many forms. The most important is opened aggression among top managers as they start to blame other functions for causing the problem. Other forms of manifest conflict are transfer pricing battles and knowledge hoarding. Defamatory information about other divisions is also likely to be circulated at this stage in the conflict process.

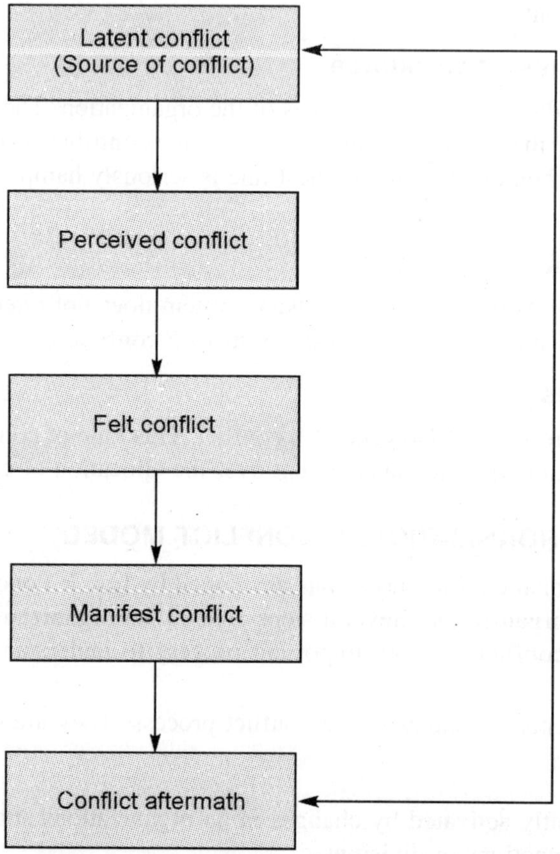

Figure 16.5: Stages in the Conflict Process

Conflict Aftermath

Conflict aftermath is the last stage of conflict of the organization. Company can change a strategies led to conflict over transfer prices. The conflict aftermath in each company was different because in one company, conflict was resolved successfully but in the other, it was not.

MANAGING CONFLICT STRATEGICALLY

Good strategic planning early can prevent many of the problems that occur latter. In addition, it can facilitate the process of change. Managers intervention is possible only between the felt and the manifest stage. It is at midpoint that managers may have the best chance of resolving the problem.

CONFLICT RESOLUTION STRATEGIES

Managers can adopt a number of different conflict resolution strategies. They are mentioned below:

- Using authority

- Changing task relationship
- Changing controls

Using Authority

Chief executive officer or manager is using their authority to resolve the conflict among the divisions of the organization. They are act as mediation and try to open up the situations so that the parties in conflict can find their own solution.

Changing Task Relationships

Chief executive or manager aims to change interdependence among functions of the organization. However, which in this way conflict is removed. Strategic managers can reduce the degree of dependence among the parties in high tech companies and its managers can use a matrix structure to provide the integration necessary to resolve conflict.

Changing Conflicts

Conflict also is managed by altering the organization control and evaluation system. For example, reward system that has achieved the targets.

IMPLEMENTING STRATEGIC CHANGE: STEPS IN THE CHANGING PROCESS

The management of strategic change involves serious steps that managers must follow if the change process is to be succeeding. The major important steps are listed below:

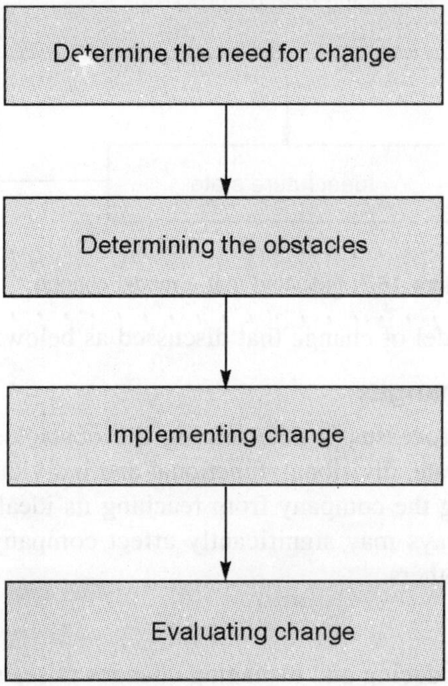

Figure 16.6: Stages in the Change Process.

Figure 16.6 indicates the stages in the change process:

- Determining the need for change
- Determining the obstacles to change
- Implementing change
- Evaluating change

Determining the need for change

According to Sunbeam's turnaround suggests, the first step in the change process involves determining the need for change, analyzing the organization current position and determining the ideal future state that strategic managers would like it to attain, we conduct swot analysis, first we examine strengths and weakness. Once identified strength, weakness then determine the change of the management.

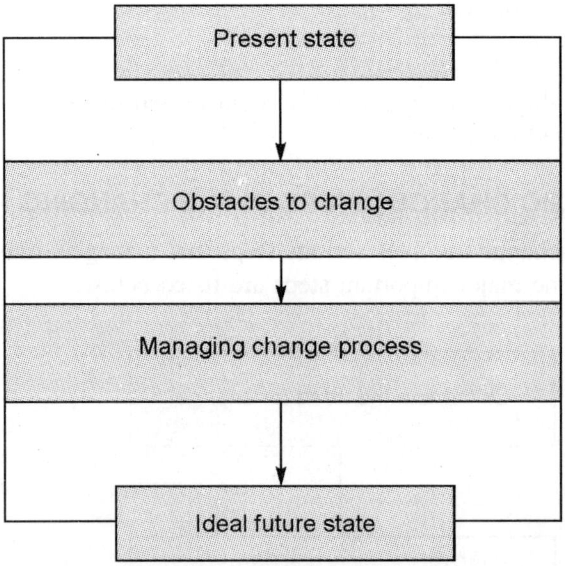

Figure 16.7: Indicated that a model change

Figure 16.7 indicates the model of change that discussed as below:

Determining Obstacles to Changes

The second step in the change processes is determining the obstacles to change. Strategist must analyses the factors such as corporate, divisional, functional and individual. These factors are causing organization inertia and preventing the company from reaching its ideal future state at the corporate level strategy seemingly trivial ways may significantly affect company's behavior some corporate culture are easier to change than others.

Implementing Change

Implementing change stage is introducing and managing changes raises several questions generally, a company can take two main approaches to change. They are listed below:

- Top-down change
- Bottom-up change

In the case of top-down change approach, CEO implementing change in the organization. Bottom up change approach, in the case low Level management response to top level made changes in the organizational decision-making.

Evaluating Change

This is the last step in the changes process. It is to evaluate the effects of the changes in strategy and structure on organization performance. It is more difficult however, to assess the effects of changes in structure on company performance.

QUESTIONS FOR DISCUSSIONS

1. Briefly, discuss the organizational politics and power.
2. Define organizational conflict. Briefly, describe the different steps involved in a process of the organizational conflict.
3. How to implementing strategic change? Describe the steps in change.

REFERENCES

1. Charles W.L. Hill / Gareth R. Jones, *Strategic Management Theory an Integrated Approach*, All India Publishers and Distributors Regd. 2001.
2. A.A.Thomson and A.J. Strickland, *Strategic Management Concepts and Cases*, Tata McGraw –Hill Publishing Company Limited, New Delhi, 2003.
3. John, A. Pearce II, Richard B. Robinson, JR. *Strategic Management Strategy Formulation and Implementation*. A.I.T.B.S. Publishers & Distributors (Regd), New Delhi, 2002.
4. Stephen P. Robbins, *Organisational Behaviour*, Prentice–Hall of India, New Delhi, 1997. pp. 267.
5. Robert A. Paton and James McCalman, *Change Management–A Guide to Effective Implementation*, 2000, Response Books, pp. 2.
6. W.L.Franch and C.H. Bell J. *Organisation Development: Behavioural Science Interventions for Organisation Improvement*, Engle Wood Cliffs, New Jersey, Prentice–Hall, 1990.
7. Edgar F. Huse, *Organisation Development and Change*, West publishing, 1975.
8. Miles, R.E., and C.C. Snow, *Organisational Strategy, Structure, and Process*. NewYork, McGraw Hill, 1975.
9. Gadbraith, Jay R., and Daniel A. Nathanson, *Strategy implementation, the role of Structure and Process*, 2nd ed. St. Paul. minn, West publishing, 1978.
10. Hrepeniak, Lawrence G., and William F. Joyce, *Implementaing Strategy*, Newyork: Macmillan, 1984.

Chapter – 17

Tailoring Strategy Analysis

CONTENTS

- Introduction
- Strategies for competing in emerging industries of the future
- Strategies for competing in turbulent, high velocity markets
- Strategies for competing in mature industries
- Strategies for firms in stagnant or declining industries
- Strategies for competing in fragmented industries
- Strategies for weak and crisis-ridden business

LEARNING OBJECTIVES

This chapter aims to provide the following information:

- Companies competing in emerging industries of the future.
- Companies competing in turbulent, high-velocity markets.
- Companies competing in mature, slow-growth industries.
- Companies competing in stagnant or declining industries.
- Companies competing in fragmented industries.
- Companies pursuing rapid growth.
- Companies in industry leadership positions.
- Companies in runner-up positions.
- Companies in competitively weak positions or played by crisis conditions.

INTRODUCTION

"This best strategy for a given firm is ultimately a unique construction reflecting its particular

– Michael E Porter

This chapter looks at the tailoring strategy to fit specific company and industry situations:

- Companies competing in emerging industries of the future.
- Companies competing in turbulent, high-velocity markets.
- Companies competing in mature, slow-growth industries.
- Companies competing in stagnant or declining industries.
- Companies competing in fragmented industries.
- Companies pursuing rapid growth.
- Companies in industry leadership positions.
- Companies in runner-up positions.
- Companies in competitively weak positions or played by crisis conditions.

STRATEGIES FOR COMPETING IN EMERGING INDUSTRIES OF THE FUTURE

An emerging industry is one in the early formative stage of the company. Emerging company's features like perfect technologies, adding human resource, acquiring on constructing facilities, gearing up operating facilities, and trying to broaden distribution and marketing channels and gain buyer acceptance. Emerging industries are facing an important product design problems and technological problems that remained to be worked out.

Competing in emerging industries managers are presented with some unique strategy for making and facing challenges. They are listed below:

- The market is new and unproven track record, this time strategic managers may be speculation and many opinions about how it will function, how fast it will grow and how big it will get.
- Many of the competition in emerging industries, strategist should know the new technological development in product design and production of products and service.
- Strategic manager will study of the external environment factors like competitors, technology, market, demand, and socio cultural activities, political and legal environment.
- Strong companies in terms of resource which are successfully in competition in emerging industries. If low companies in terms of resource which have entry barriers tend to be relatively low.
- Strong companies allowing significant cost and price reductions of outputs and for this purpose strategy manager adapt generic strategy.
- An emerging industry all buyers are first time users. Therefore, the marketing task is to induce initial purchase and to overcome customers concerns about product features, performance reliability and conflicting claims of rural firms.
- Potential buyers always expect to improve quality products and service.
- Companies some time have trouble securing ample suppliers of raw materials and components. Therefore, strategic manager always depend on numerous suppliers of raw materials and components.
- Under capitalized companies have been finding themselves short of funds to support needed R&D and get through several lean years, until product catches on, and up merging with

competitors or being acquired by financially-strong outsiders looking to invest in a growth market.

The two critical strategic issues confronting firms in an emerging industry are as follows:

- How to finance initial operations until sales and revenues take off.
- What market segments and competitive advantage to go after in trying to secure a front-runner-position.

Successful in an Emerging Industry

Strategic success in an emerging industry calls for bold entrepreneurship and a willingness to pioneer and take risks and take quick response to decisions for development of products and service. It will be identified risks and opportunitistic strategy making. Dealing with all the risks and opportunities of an emerging industry is one of the most challenging business strategy problems to be successful companies usually having to pursue one or more to the following strategic avenues.

- Try to win the early race for industry leadership with risk taking entrepreneurship and a bold with creative strategy.
- Push to perfect the technology, to improve product quality and to develop additional attractive performance features of products and service.
- If any technological uncertainty arises a company adopt quickly a dominant technology that emerges in the market.
- Form strategic alliances with key suppliers to gain access to specialized skills, technological capabilities and critical materials or components.
- Acquire or form alliances with companies that have related or complementary technological expertise to out compete rivals on the basis of technological superiority.
- Try to capture any first mover advantages associated with early commitments to promising technologies, allying with the most capable suppliers, expanding product selection, improving, styling, planned to be capturing market share and getting well positioned in new distribution channels.
- Make it easy and cheap for first time buyers to try the industry as first generation product.

The early leaders in an emerging industry cannot afford to relax and rest on their laurels. They must drive foreword to strengthen their resource capabilities and effective utilization of resource for strong position towards to attract new customers and successfull survival in the market.

Problems in an Emerging Industry

Exhibit 17.1: Problems in an Emerging Industry

- Emerging industries failure to manage and expansion of their business activities.
- Emerging industries failure to defend against competitors trying to horn in on their success.
- Emerging industries failure to build a competitive position extending beyond their initial product or market.

STRATEGIES FOR COMPETING IN TURBULENT HIGH-VELOCITY MARKETS

High-velocity change is the striking feature of cotemporary business. The central strategy making challenge in a turbulent market environment is managing change. Competing in turbulent high velocity industries managers are presented with some unique strategy for making and facing challenges. They are listed below:

- It can be reacting to change
- It can be anticipating change
- It can be leading change

It Can be Reacting to Change

Turbulent high velocity markets can be reacting to change in the following circumstance:

- Adjust to new government policies like monetary and legal etc.
- Introduce better products in response to new offering of rivals in the market.
- Quick respond to unexpected change buyer needs and preference in the market.
- Strategist reacts and responds urgently wherever problems are generated as needed.
- Turbulent market strategy should defend and protect the company's position.
- The reacting to change is defensive postures.

It can be Anticipating Change

Companies looking ahead what is likely to analyze, what is likely to occur and then preparing and positioning for that future. Turbulent high velocity markets can be anticipating change in the following circumstance:

- It conducts research to know the buyer behavior, buyer needs, and buyer expectations to get insight into how the market will evolve and then reacting to change.
- Anticipating change is still fundamentally defensive in reacting to change forces outside the enterprise are in the driver's seat.
- It can open up new opportunities, therefore, is a better way to manage change than just pure reaction.
- It analysis the prospects for market globalization.
- It monitors new technological developments closely to product future path.
- It reacting to anticipating change is defensive postures
- It adapts strategy for the following purpose
    - Strong distribution channels
    - Plan for expected future changes.
    - Add /adopt resources and competitive capabilities.
    - Improve product line.

It Can be Leading Change

Companies are initiating the first to market with an important new product to market ahead of rivals, and having products whose features and attributes shape customer preferences and expectations. It means proactively seeking to shape the rules of the game; leading change is an offensive posture. Turbulent high velocity markets can be leading change in the following circumstances:

- Seek to set industry standards in the turbulent high-velocity markets.
- To adapt pioneer new and better technologies.
- To introduce innovative products that open new markets and spur the creation of whole industries.
- Industry leaders are proactive agents of change and analyzers, therefore, these change helps to improve and expansion of business activities very rapidly.
- To invest aggressively in research and investment edge of translating technological advances into innovative new products is necessity for industries where technology is the primary driver of change.
- To develop and maintain the organizational capability quickly to the moves of rivals and surprising new developments, shifting resources, internally adapting existing competencies and capabilities, creating new competencies and capabilities.
- To rely on strategic partnership with outside suppliers and with companies making tie in products. For this purpose, Companies build their competitive position not just by strengthening their own internal resources base but also by partnering with those suppliers making state of the arts paths and by collaborating closely with both the developers of related technologies and makers of tie in products.
- To initiate fresh actions every few months, not just when a competitive response is needed. For this purpose a company can be proactive by making time paced moves – introducing a new or improved product every four months, rather than when moves - introducing -new or improved product every four months, rather than when the market tapers afford a rival introduces a next generation model.
- To keep the company's products and service fresh and exciting enough to change taking place. For this purpose, companies in depth expertise, speed, quickly adapt changes, innovativeness, opportunism, and resources flexibility is critical for organizational capabilities.
- It adapts strategy for the following purpose.
- Force rivals to follow in the turbulent market.
- Seize the offensive change in the market.
- It set changes in industry place.
- It Influence the rules of the game in the market and industry.

STRATEGIES FOR COMPETING IN MATURE INDUSTRIES

A maturing industry is one type industry which is moving from rapid growth to significantly slower growth. An industry is said to be mature when nearly all-potential buyers are already users of the industry's products and services. Industry maturity can be forestalled by the emergence of new technological advances factors, product innovations factors, and marketing driving factor like demand for products and service, combination of place, promotion, price and product. The market maturity usually produces fundamental changes in the competitive environment of the industry. Special strategies for competing in mature industries are listed below:

- To slow growth in buyer demand generates more head-to-head competition in market. For this purpose, mature industry plan to price-cutting of products and service, increased advertising and other aggressive tactics to gain market share.
- To buyers more sophisticated, often driving a harder bargain on repeat purchases. Therefore,

buyers are able to evaluate different brands and can use their knowledge to negotiate a better deal with sellers.

- Seller offers the products and service to buyer. Therefore, buyer prefers to buy quality and the best combination of price and service offered by the seller.
- A maturing industry is moving from rapid growth to significantly slower growth in terms of slow down its capacity expansion and slow down industry growth in market. It spends too much price for advertising for promoting products and service, hence it adversely affect company future.
- A maturing industry is very difficult to create new product feature which based on innovation and difficulty to find further user of the products and service in the market.
- A maturing industry growth in domestic market and start to seek out sales opportunities in foreign market. This stage, international competition increased due to cost leader and market leader.
- A maturing industry increases competition; it induces number of mergers and acquisitions among former competitors. The weaker companies out of the industry and market.
- Inefficiency firms and firms with weak competitive strategies can achieve respectable results in a fast-growing industry with booming sales; it is only possible to adapt to cost leader, market leader, generic strategy, and new technology there by mergers and acquisition to develop competitive market.

Strategic Moves in Maturing Industries

New competitive character of industry maturity begins to hit full force; any of several strategic moves can strengthen an industry's competitive position. They are listed below:

- Pruning marginal products and models
- More emphasis on value-chain innovation
- A stronger focus on cost reduction
- Increasing sales to present customers
- Purchasing rival firms at bargain prices
- Expanding internationally
- Building new or more flexible capabilities

Characteristic of Maturing Industries

Important characters of strategic moves in maturing industries are listed below:

Pruning Marginal Products and Models

It refers to a wide selection models, features and product options. Pruning and product models sometimes have competitive value during the growth stage. It introduces new many product versions works against achieving growth and increased the manufacturing cost. The main advantage of pruning marginal products are opened the door for cost savings and permits more concentration on items whose margins are highest and where firms have a competitive advantage.

More Emphasis Chain Innovation

It refers to new innovation which adopt by industry. Innovation adopted industry provides better products and service at lower costs even quality and introducing new versions to market. Manufacturers can mechanize innovation in terms of high-cost activities, re-design production lines to improve labor efficiency and build flexibility into the assembly process. Therefore, it customized product versions can be easily produced and increase use of advanced technology. Suppliers, distributors and collaborators use internet technology and e-commerce techniques to streamline various value chain activities and implement cost saving innovations in organisation..

Strong Focus on Cost Reduction

Company can take strong options like supplier supply of raw material at competitive price, implementing tighter supply chain management practices in business, cutting low value activities out of the value chain, developing more economical product designs, re-engineering its technology, adapt advanced e-commerce process technology for internal and external purpose, and make more economical distribution arrangements for products and service.

Increasing Sales to Present Customers

In mature industries market, companies can take more responsibility to expand sales to existing customers. Mature companies provide complementary items and ancillary service like sales after service, and finding more ways for customer to use their company products in the market. These are ways suitable for mature industries thereby planned to increase sales to present customers.

Purchasing Rival Firms at Bargain Prices

In mature industries market, mature companies can acquire the facilities and the assets of the struggling rival firms in the market at quite bargain prices. Purchasing rival firms at bargain prices can help to create a low-cost position if they also present opportunities for greater operating efficiency. Further more, it helps to mature industries to acquire strong customer base of rival firms, it is an opportunity for expansion of market and greater economies of scales of product and service.

Expanding Internationally

Mature industries are planned to expand their business activities into global market. It happened because of two reasons:

- Mature industries strongly in resource like market, finance, human resource, distribution channels, alliance, mergers and advanced technology.
- Mature industries are strong in domestic market. They are expanding internationally for this purpose use domestic firm's skill reputation and products are ready to transferable to foreign market.

Building New or More Capabilities that is Flexible

The mature market can often be combated by strengthens by the company's resource base and competitive capabilities. It is adding new competencies or capabilities that depending existing competence to make them harder to initiate or striving to make core competitive capabilities and even more adaptable to changing customer requirements and expectations.

Strategic Failure in Maturing Industries

Strategic failure in maturing industries due to the following reasons:

- Mature industries failure to provide quality product at low cost.

- It compromises between low cost and reduces the quality of outputs.
- It fails due to ill-defined strategy like market identity, no competitive advantage, an average image in the market and little prospect of becoming an industry leader.
- It slows to adapt existing competencies and capabilities to defend against stiffening competitive pressures.
- It is protecting short-term profitability than a building or maintaining long-term competitive position.
- It is waiting too long to respond to price cutting by rivals.
- Over expanding of business become slow growth.
- Over expanding an advertising and sales promotion efforts is a losing effort to combat the growth slow down.
- It fails to pursue cost reduction of products and service as compared to rivals.

STRATEGIES FOR FIRMS IN STAGNANT OR DECLINING INDUSTRIES

Three competitive approaches are requiring achieving competitive advantage in stagnant or declining industries. Three competitive approaches are listed below:

- Focusing on growing market segments within the industry
- Differentiating on the basis of better quality and frequent product innovation
- Becoming a lower-cost producer.

Focusing on Growing Market Segments Within the Industry

Focusing on growing market segments within the industry is the first competitive approaches of strategies for firms in stagnant or declining industries. Stagnant or declining markets are composed of numerous segments or niches, frequently, one or more of these segments are growing rapidly, despite stagnation in the industry as a whole. An astute competitor who zeroes in on fast-growing segments in industries and does a first rate job of meeting the needs of buyers which comprising these segments can often escape stagnating sales and profits and even gain decided competitive advantage in industry.

Differentiating on the Basis of Better Quality and Frequent Product Innovation

Differentiating on the basis of better quality and frequent product innovation is the second competitive approach of strategies for firms in stagnant or declining industries. It either enhanced quality or innovation can rejuvenate demand by creating important new growth segments or inducing buyers to trade up in industry. Successful product innovation opens an avenue for competing besides meeting or beating rival prices in industry. Differentiation based on successful innovation has the additional advantage. It is being difficult and expensive to declining industries for rival firms to imitate.

Becoming a Lower-Cost Producer

Becoming a lower cost producer is the third approach of strategies for firms in stagnant or declining industries. Companies in stagnant industries can improve profit margins and return on investment by pursuing innovative cost reduction year after year. Potential costs saving actions are as follows:

- Cutting marginally-beneficial activities out of the value chain in industry.
- Outsourcing functions and activist that can perform more cheaply by outsiders in business.

- Redesigning internal business process to exploits cost reducing through using e-commerce technologies.
- Consolidating underutilized production facilities.
- Adding more distribution channels to ensure the unit volume needed for low-cost production in factory.
- Closing low volume, high cost retail outlets.
- Pruning marginal products from the firm is offering.

The stagnating or declining companies are making the most common strategic mistakes are as follows:

- Getting trapped in profitless war of attrition in industry.
- Diverting too much cash out of the business too quickly in industry.
- Being overly optimistic about the industry's future and spending too much on improvements in anticipation that things will get better into industry.

STRATEGIES FOR COMPETING IN FRAGMENT INDUSTRIES

The major competitive feature of a fragmented industry is the absence of market leaders with king sized market shares; widespread buyer recognition of products and service and widespread market distribution channels etc. Several reasons can be counted for an industry to be fragmented. They are as follows:

- Market demand is so extensive and so diverse. In fragment industries, large numbers of firms can easily context trying to accommodate the range and variety of buyer's preferences and requirements and to cover all the needed geographic locations.
- Low-entry barriers allow small firms to enter quickly and cheaply to market.
- Absences of sale economies have permitted small companies to compete on an equal cost footing with larger firms in market.
- Buyers require relatively small quantities of customized products. Therefore demand for any particular product version is small and sales volumes are not adequate to support producing, distributing or marketing on a scale that yields advantages to a large firm.
- The market for the industry product or service is becoming more global, putting fragment companies in more and more countries in the same competitive market arena.
- The technologies embodied in the industry's value chain are exploding into so many just new areas and along so many different paths in companies competing in fragment industries. This specialization is essential just to keep abreast in any one area of experience.
- The industry is young and crowded with aspiring contenders in market, with no firm having yet developed in terms of resource base, competitive capabilities and market recognition to command a significant market share.

Some fragmented industries overtime as growth slows and the market matures. The stiffer competition that accompanies slower growth. It produces a shake out of weak inefficient firms and a greater concentration of larger, more visible sellers. Others remain stuck in a fragmented state due to existing firms lack the resources in business.

Competitive rivalry in fragmented industries can vary from moderately-strong to fierce in fragment industries. Low barriers tend to make entry to new competitors on ongoing threat. Competition from substitutes may or may not be a major factor. The relatively small size of companies in fragmented industries puts them in a relatively weak position to bargain with powerful suppliers and buyers for products and services, although sometimes they can become members of a cooperative formed for the purpose of using their combined leverage to negotiate better sales and purchase terms in market.

Suitable Competitive Strategy Option in a Fragmented Industry

Suitable competitive strategy options in a fragmented industry are as below:

- Constructing and operating "formula" facilities
- Becoming a low-cost operator
- Specializing by product line
- Specializing by customers type
- Focusing on a limited geographic area

Constructing and Operating "formula" Facilities

Constructing and operating formula facilities refers to strategic approach is frequently employed in health club and retailing business operating at multiple locations. It involves constructing standardized outlets in favorable locations at minimum cost and then operating them super efficiency.

Becoming a Low-Cost Operator

Becoming a low-cost operator refers to prices competition, is intense and profit margin are under constant pressure. Companies can stress – no frills operations featuring like low overhead, high productivity, low-cost labor, lean capital budgets and dedicated pursuit of total operating efficiency. Successful low-cost producers in a fragmented industry can play significantly the price discounting game and still earn profits above the industry average.

Specializing by Product Life

Specializing by product life cycle refers to Fragmented industries products include a wide range of styles or services of products and service. Suitable competitive strategy suggests to Fragmented industries to focus one product or service category that can be very effective.

Specializing by Customer Types

Specializing by customer types refers to a firm can stake out a market niche in a fragmented industry by catering to their customers who are interested in low prices, unique product attributes, customized features-care-free service etc.

Focusing on a Limited Geographic Area

Focusing on a limited geographic area refers to firms in a fragmented industry which cannot win a big share of the total industry wide sales. It can still try to dominate local or regional geographic areas. Concentrating company efforts on a limited territory can produce greater operating efficiently. Speed delivery and customer's service, promote strong brand awareness, and permit saturation advertising supermarkets, banks, convenience stores, and sporting goods relatives successfully-operated multiple locations within a limited geographic area.

STRATEGIES FOR WEAK AND CRISIS-RIDDEN BUSINESS

The strategic options for a competitively weak and crisis-ridden business companies include waging modest offensive to improve its position, how to defend its present position, how to turnaround of business crisis being acquiring by other company or employing an end-game strategy in domestic and global market.

Turnaround Strategies for Business Crisis

Turnaround strategies are prerequiste to business crisis companies when a business worth rescuing goes into crisis: the main objective is to arrest and reverse the sources of competitive and financial weakness as quickly as possible. Management's first task is to formulating a suitable turnaround strategy. The turnaround strategy is based on the following questions:

- Is it an unexpected down-turn sales brought on by a weak economy?
- Is it an ill chosen competitive strategy?
- Is poor execution of an alternative workable strategy?
- Are high operating costs?
- Is important resource deficiencies?
- Is overload of debt?
- Can the business be saved, or is the situation hopeless?

These questions help the strategist for understanding what is wrong with the business and how serious. Therefore, strategist should know the different strategic problems in the business. Strategic problems are essential because different diagnosis lead to different turnaround strategies.

Important business troubles are listed below:

- Overestimating the potential sales growth of the business units.
- Ignoring the profit-depressing effects of the business.
- Rivalry competition in domestic and global market.
- Outdated technology.
- Old plant and equipment.
- Heavy fixed costs because of inability to use plant capacity.
- Lack of financial resource.
- Ignoring research and development, its impact on innovations of new products and services.
- Marketing problems etc.

These are important problems of the business strategist to be optimistic about the ability to penetrate new markets, making frequent changes in strategy, and being over powered by more successful rivals.

Curing these kinds of problems and achieving a successful business turnaround that can be involved any of the following actions:

- Selling-off assets to raise cash to save the remaining part of the business.
- Revising the existing strategy
- Lunching efforts to boost
- Using a combination of these efforts

Selling-off Assets

Selling-off assets is achieving a successful business turnaround strategy. It refers to asset reduction strategy, is essential when cash flow is a critical consideration and when the most practical ways to generate cash in the following circumstances:

- Through sale of some of firm's asset like plant and equipment, land, patents, inventories, or profitable subsidiaries.
- Through retrenchment like pruning of marginal products from the product line, closing or selling older plants, reducing the workforce, withdrawing from outlet markets, cutting back customer service and sometimes crisis-ridden companies sell-off assets not so much to unload losing operations and to stem cash drains as to raise funds to save and strengthen remaining business activities in company.

Strategy Revision

Strategy revision is achieving one of the successful business turnaround strategies. When work performance is caused by bad strategy, the task of strategy overhaul can proceed along any of the several paths as follows:

- Shifting to new competitive approach to rebuild the firm's market position.
- Overhauling internal options and functional area strategies to better support the same overall business strategy.
- Merging with another firm in the industry and forging a new strategy. It is keyed to all newly merged firm's strengths.
- Retrenching into a reduced core of products and customers. It is closely matched to the firm strategies.

These are the most appealing path demands on prevailing industry conditions, the firm's particular strengths and weakness. Its competitive situation analysis of the industry, major competitors and the firm's own competitive positions and its skills and resources are a prerequisite for turnaround action.

Boosting Revenues

Boosting revenues is also achieving one of the successful business turnaround strategies. Firm sets primary task to increase sales volume, this is only boosting revenues and aims to generate huge income from the business operation. There are a number of revenue building options are as follows:

- Price cuts
- Increased promotions
- A bigger sales force
- Added customer services
- And quickly achieved product improvement

Firm attempts to increase revenues and sales volume necessary in following circumstances:

- When there is little or no room in the operating budget to cut expenses and still break even point of the product.
- When the key restoring profitability is increased utilization of existing capacity, if buyer demand isn't especially price sensitive due to differentiating features the quickest way to boost short-term revenues. It may raise prices rather than opt for volume building price cuts.

Cutting Cost

Cutting cost is the third option for achieving a successful business turnaround strategy. Cost reducing turnaround strategies work best in the following circumstance:

- When an ailing firm's value chain and cost structure are flexible enough to permit radical surgery in business.
- When the firms costs are important bloated and there are many places where savings can be quickly achieved.
- When the firm is relativity close to its spread even point accompanying a general belt-tightening can be an increased emphasis on paring administrative overheads.
- Estimation of non-essential and low value added activates in the firms value chain.
- Modernization of existing plant and equipment to gain greater productivity.
- Delay of nonessential capital expenditures and debt restructuring to reduce interest costs and stretch out repayments.

Combination Efforts

Combination turnaround strategies are usually essential in grim situations that require fast action on abroad front. Likewise, combination frequently comes into play when new mergers are brought in and given in a free hand to make whatever changes they see fit.

Liquidation–the Strategy of Last Resort– Liquidation Strategy is Important

Sometimes a business crisis is too far gone to salvage or is not worth salvaging given the resources it will take and its profit prospects. Closing a crisis-ridden business down and liquidating its assets at the best and wisest strategy alternative wise sold in the market. Liquidation is most unpleasant and painful due to the hardships of job eliminations and the effect of business closings in local communities. Therefore, in hopeless situations, an early liquidation effort usually serves owner-stock holder interests better than an inevitable bankruptcy.

End-Game Strategies

End-game strategy steers a middle course between pressuring the status quo and existing as soon as possible.

An end-game strategy is a reasonable strategic option for a weak business in the following circumstances:

- When the industry's long-time prospects are unattractive.
- When rejuvenating the business would be too costly or at best marginally profitable.
- When the firm's market share is becomingly costly to maintain or defend.
- When reduced levels of competitive effort will not trigger an immediate or rapid falloff in sales.
- When the enterprise can re-deploy the freed resources in higher opportunity areas.
- When the business is not a crucial or core component of a diversified company's overall lineup business.
- When the business does not contribute other desired features to a company's business portfolio.

QUESTIONS FOR DISCUSSIONS

1. Discuss the companies competing in emerging industries of the future.
    - Discuss the companies competing in turbulent, high-velocity markets.
    - Discuss the companies competing in mature, slow-growth industries.
    - Discuss the companies competing in stagnant or declining industries.
    - Discuss the companies competing in fragmented industries.
    - Discuss the companies pursuing rapid growth.
    - Discuss the companies in industry leadership positions.
    - Discuss the companies in runner-up positions.
    - Discuss the companies in competitively weak positions or played by crisis conditions.

REFERENCES

1. Charles W.L. Hill/Gareth R.Jones, *Strategic Management Theory an Integrated Approach*, All India Publishers and Distributors Regd. 2001.
2. A.A.Thomson and A.J. Strickland, *Strategic Management Concepts and Cases*, Tata McGraw –Hill Publishing Company Limited, New Delhi, 2003.
3. John, A. Pearce II, Richard B. Robinson, JR., *Strategic Management Strategy Formulation and Implementation*. A.I.T.B.S. Publishers & Distributors (Regd), New Delhi, 2002.
4. Afuah, Allan, *Strategies to Turn Adversity into Profits*. Sloon Management Review 40, no.2 (Winter 1999), pp 99-109.
5. Beinhocker, Eric D., *Robust Adaptive Strategies*. Sloon Management Review 40, no. 3 (Spring 1999), pp 95.
6. Campbell, Andrew, Michael Goold, and Marcus Alexander., *Corporate Strategy: The Quest Parenting Advantage*. Harvard Business Review 73, no.2 (March–April 1995).
7. Collis, David j., and Cynthia A. Montgomery., *Creating Corporate Strategy*. Harvard Business Review 76, no.3 (May–June 1998), pp 70-83.
8. Eisenhardt, Kathleen M., and Shona L. Brown., *Patching : Restitching Business Portfolios in Dynamic Markets*. Harvard Business Review 77. no.3 (May- June) pp 72-82.
9. Haspeslagh, Phillippe C., and David B. Jamison., *Managing Acquistions: Creating Value through Corporate Renewal*. Newyork: Free Press, 1991.
10. Day, George S., *Strategies for Surviving a Shakeout*. Harvard Business Review 75, no.2. (March–April), pp 92–102.
11. Feldman, Lawrence P., and Albert L. Page., *Harvesting : The Misunderstood Market Exit Strategy*. Journal of Business Strategy 5, no.4 (Spring 1985), pp 79-85.
12. Finkin, Eugene F., *Company Turnaround*. Journal of Business Strategy 5, no.4 (Spring 1985).
13. Gordon Geoffrey L, Roger J. Calantrone, and C. Anthony di Benedetto., *Mature Markets and Revitalization Strategies : An American Fable*. Business Horizons (May–June1991) pp 39-50.

14. William K. Hall, *Survival Srtegies in a Hostile Environment.* Harvard Business Review 58, no 5 (September–October 1980).
15. Frederick M. Zimmerman, *The Furn Arround Experience: Real World Lessons in Revisaling Corporations*, McGraw Hill, Newyork 1991.
16. Kotler, *Marketing Management* 23: Michael E. Porter, Competitive Advantage Freepress, Newyork, 1985.
17. Eric D. Beislocker. *Roburt Adapt Strategics*. Sloan Management Review 40, no 3 (Spring 1999).
18. R. G. Hamermesh and S.O. Silks, *How to Compete in Stagnant Industries*, Harvard business Review 57, no 5 (Setember-October 1979).
19. Shona L. Brown and Kathleen M. Eisenhardt, Competing on the Edge: Strategy as Structured Chaus, Harward Business School Press, 1998.
20. Michael E. Porter, *Competitive Strategy*, Freepress, Newyork 1980.

Chapter – 18

Corporate Culture and Leadership

CONTENTS

LEARNING OBJECTIVES

In this chapter, we shall explore

- Corporate culture
- Leadership.

INTRODUCTION

"Weak leadership can wreck the soundest strategy; forceful execution of even a poor plan can often bring victory" – Sun zi

"An organization's capacity to execute its strategy depends on its "hard" infrastructure – Its organizational structure and systems–and on its "soft" infrastructure, its culture and norms" – Amar Bhide

"The biggest levers you've got to change a company are strategy, structure, and culture. If I could pick two, I'd pick strategy" – Wayne Leonard, CEO, Entergy

In this chapter, we shall explore corporate culture and leadership.

CONCEPT OF CORPORATE CULTURE

A concept of corporate culture refers to the following factors:

- A company's values
- Beliefs
- Business principles
- Traditions
- Ways of operating
- Internal environment of the company
- Assumptions
- Norms
- Rules and regulations
- Policies and procedure of the corporate

CORPORATE CULTURE

Exhibit 18.1: Satyam'Corporate Culture and Philosophy

Core Purpose

"To leverage information, knowledge and technology to enhance human endeavor." Satyam develops and deploys intelligent applications in technology for diverse situations meeting varying requirements. Satyam helps businesses and organizations push the limits of excellence, and helps optimize their strengths. Satyam's core values are expressed in the way teams are built and the manner in which they operate and achieve results. These values have been identified based on internal strengths of the organization. They are the guiding parameters for all organization-wide initiatives.

Belief in People

Satyam believes its true strength lies in the potential of its Associates. Associates work in an atmosphere of trust and confidence. Every individual Associate is a leader. This leadership is expressed in the way tasks are assigned and taken up, the freedom with which work styles are negotiated and high standards of quality set independently by each and every Associate. A high degree of operational freedom helps Associates exercise their creativity and expertise in approaching tasks and achieving Customer Delight.

(Contd...)

Entrepreneurship

At Satyam, it's idea that drive people. A variety of programs help associates create tangible value, constantly encouraging associates to convert ideas into market value, in the true spirit of entrepreneurship.

Customer Orientation

As a customer-centric enterprise, we are very sharply focused on delivering not only what the customer demands but also providing them with the weapons to compete with. In other words we deliver business competitiveness. All this eventually leads to Customer Intimacy.

Pursuit of Excellence

Achieving excellence in anything we do is a part of our corporate DNA. It is not just lip service. Rather a process-driven strategy that allows us to benchmark everything against the global best and then surpass it, so that we set the benchmark for others to follow. In the process we are always a couple of steps ahead of our nearest competitor. Satyam adheres to stringent quality processes that meet and exceed international standards that are continuously monitored.

Corporate Social Responsibility

As a larger expression of its mission and core values, Satyam is actively involved in a variety of public service projects in education, environment and public health. Working through Alambana, an umbrella organization that brings together committed Satyam associates and their spouses, the Company contributes to social causes and organizes initiatives for social change, primarily in the areas of education, environment and healthcare.

Source: Satyam

Corporate culture is the set of important assumptions. Every company has its own culture followed by all the members of the company. Corporate culture is similar to an individual's personality, principles, concept and trade practice ethical opinion actions within the company or organization.

Basic Elements of Corporate Culture

Organization culture is the set of important assumptions sufficiently central to the life of the organization or company. Basic elements of corporate culture are as listed below:

- Basic assumptions and beliefs
- Cultural artifacts
- Values
- Norms

Basic Assumptions and Beliefs

Basic assumptions and beliefs are important to the corporate world. In addition to know, how it actually works, basic assumptions and beliefs derive from personal experience and are reinforced by it in the company. Corporate staff is relying to some degree on the judgment and expertise of others based on the basic assumptions and beliefs. They trust or can identify to help them and to decide what to believe or what not to believe. It underpins the various aspects of organizational activity and represents the core ideology of the business. Some examples of basic assumptions and beliefs underlying organizational culture:

- Market-oriented communication system
- Customer orientation
- Employee participation, open communication and security
- Entrepreneurism, self discipline and control

Cultural Artifacts

Cultural artifacts are the visible manifestation of culture. It reflects in the physical and social environment of the organization like its structure systems, subsystems, symbols and plaques etc., an important cultural artifacts are public documents, media reports and stories about the organization, its rituals, ceremonies, rules, procedures and observable behavior of its members. Therefore, these cultural artifacts form a system of support and maintenance for the set of prevailing beliefs.

Values

Values refer to conception of what members of an organization regard as desirable. They are the deep-rooted feelings about ideas and physiology, desires and preferences, emotions and beliefs that influence the members' reaction and responses to any situation. Corporate culture involves shared values, social ideals, or normative beliefs about proper behavior in various situations. Organizational values are reflected in terms of beliefs, emotions, desires, preferences and behaviors of the members of the organization. It stated reasons therefore, in neutral value, orientation emotions are not expressed freely. However, organizations are having affective value generation and encourage free expressions among the people and the groups. In specific value orientation interactions between people, are direct, purposeful, precise, and transparent and authority relationship are confined to work situation. Organizations are espousing diffuse value that encourage maintaining relationships among the organizational people outside the organization also.

Norms

Norms are the paradigms, the informal rules of the game telling employees what they are supposed to be saying, believing, and doing and what is right and what is wrong. For example, as per the IBM norms, employees should attentively listen to their demands. Norms are generally passed on to new employees by word of mouth and enforced by the social approval or disapproval of one's behavior in terms of its congruence or in congruence with prevalent norms.

CONTENTS OF CORPORATE CULTURE

Corporate culture contents that ultimately derive from three major sources are as follows:

- It influence to the business environment in general and the industry in particular.
- Founders, leaders, directors and corporate employees bring a systematic pattern of assumptions with them when they join the corporate world. These assumptions are dynamic in terms of personal experience, regional, ethnic, religious, occupational and professional communities from which they came.
- Reality and experience of human resource of the corporate world to make and use the solution and coping with the basic problems of corporate culture world.

STRENGTHS OF CORPORATE CULTURE

The strength of a culture has influenced the intensity by which organization members comply with it as they go about their day-to-day activities. The specific feature of culture that determine the basic strengths of corporate culture are as follows:

- Strong-culture companies
- Weak-culture companies
- Unhealthy culture
- Adaptive culture
- Thickness culture
- Extent of sharing culture
- Clarity of ordering culture

Strong-Culture Companies

A strong-culture is a valuable asset when it matches strategy and dreaded liability when it does not. Strong-culture companies refer to company conduct its business according to clear and explicit set of principles and values. Strong-culture is the strength and one of the features of the culture. Therefore, strong-culture companies typically have creeds or values statements and executives regularly stress the importance of using these values and principles as the basis for decisions and actions taken throughout the organization. There are three important factors contribute to the development of strong-culture factors. They are as listed below:

- A founder or strong leader who establishes values, principles and practice that are consistent and sensible insight of customer needs, competitive conditions and strategic requirements of the business.
- A sincere, long-standing company's commitment to operating the business according to these established traditions, thereby creating an internal environment which supports decision-making and strategies based on the cultural norms in strong culture companies.
- Generic concern for the well-being of the organization's three biggest constituencies like customers, employees and shareholders. Continuity of leadership, small group rise, stable group membership, geographic concentration and considerable organizational success all contribute to the emergence and sustainability of a strong culture.

Weak-Culture Companies

Weak-culture companies refer to company's culture, there is little cohesion and glue across organization units – top executives don't repeatedly expose any business philosophy or exhibit commitment to particular values or extoll uses of particular operating practices. Due to dearth of common values and ingrained business approaches. Organization members typically have no deeply-felt senses of corporate identity. In weak culture, there are no traditions, beliefs, values, common bonds or behavioral norms. It provides little or no strategy implementation assistance in the management. It can use as levers to mobilize commitment to executing the choosen strategy.

Unhealthy Cultures

Unhealthy culture refers to companies they are adopted number of unhealthy cultural characteristics which can undermine a company's business performance. Unhealthy culture characteristics are as follows:

- A political internal environment allows and influencing managers to operate autonomous 'fieldoms' and resist needed change.
- The second unhealthy cultural trait is that one can plague companies suddenly confronted with fast-changing business conditions, is hostility to change and to people who champion new ways of doing things in routine in business.
- Unhealthy characteristic is promoting managers who are good at staying within their budgets, exerting close supervisory control over their units handling administrative detail as opposed to managers who understand vision, strategies and culture building and who are good leaders, motivators and decision makers in company.
- The last trait of unhealthy culture is a version to looking outside the company for superior practices and approaches for personal gain..

Adaptive Culture

Adaptive culture is a valuable competitive asset. Sometimes it is a necessity for organization; in fast changing environments for instance, today's *dot com* companies are classic example of adaptive culture.

In adaptive cultures, members share of confidence that the organization can deal with whatever threats and opportunities come down the pike: they are receptive to risk taking, experimentation, innovation, and changing strategies and proactive whenever necessary to satisfy the legitimate interests of stakeholders, customers employees, shareowners, suppliers and the communities where the company operates.

Thickness Culture

Thick cultures have many, thin culture has few cultures with many layers of implement shared beliefs and values generally have a stronger influence behavior.

Extent of Sharing Culture

Some of important assumptions are more widely shared than others. Few are completely shared in the sense that every member of the organization has internalized them. Culture with more widely shared beliefs and value has a more pervasive impact because they guide more people.

Clearity of Ordering Culture

Some organizational cultures, the shared beliefs and values are clearly ordered. Cultures whose shared assumptions are clearly ordered have a more pronounced effect on behavior –because members of the organization are sure of which values should prevail incase of conflicting interests.

DECIPHERING A CULTURE

Reading a culture is an interpretive subjective activity. One cannot decipher a culture simply by relying on what people say about it, other evidence, both historical and current, must be taken into account to infer the culture.

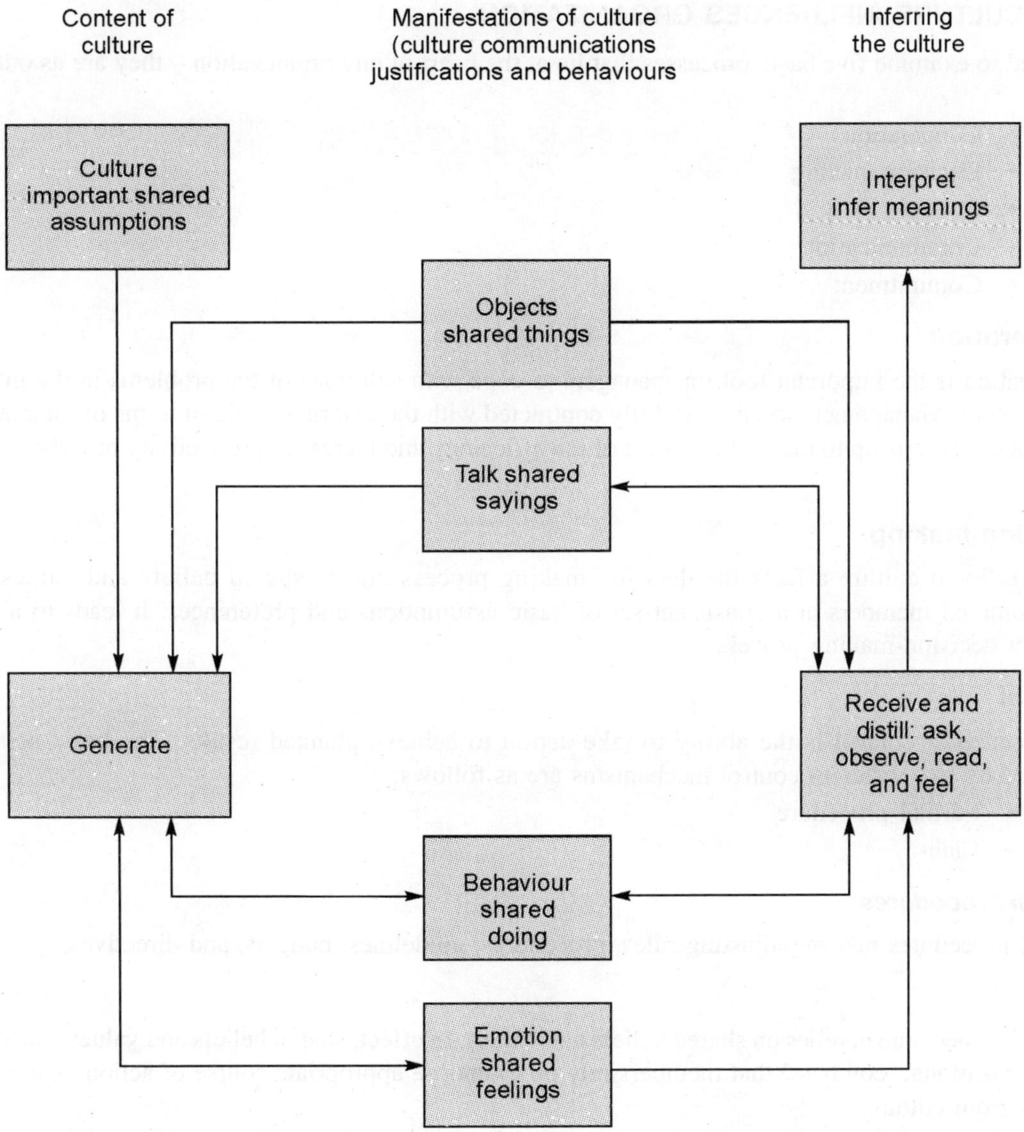

Figure 18.1: Frame Work for Deciphering Culture

Source: Vijay Sathe, Culture and Related Corporate Realities(Homewood,Ill.:Richard D.Irwin,1985)

Figure 18.1 indicates the frame work for deciphering culture. It presented systematic method to help decipher or infer an organization culture. Each important shared assumption creating an organizations culture may be inferred from one or more shared things, shared sayings and feelings, the important point is to distill from these various cultural manifestations a much more concise set of important shared beliefs and values.

HOW CULTURE INFLUENCES ORGANIZATION

We need to examine five basic processes that lie at the heart of any organization – they are as outlined below:

- Cooperation
- Decision making
- Control
- Communication
- Commitment

Cooperation

Cooperation is the important tool for managers to cope with solutions of the problems in the internal environment. Management to take carefully contracted with the external world in terms of maintaining very good relationship to the improvement of the efficiency and increased productivity of the corporate culture.

Decision-making

Organizational culture affects the decision-making process due to shared beliefs and values give organizational members at a consistent set of basic assumptions and preferences. It leads to a more efficient decision-making process.

Control

The essence of control is the ability to take action to achieve planned results. The basic action is provided by two different control mechanisms are as follows:

- Formal procedure
- Clans

Formal Procedures

Formal procedures rely on adjusting rules, procedures, guidelines, budgets, and directives.

Clans

The clan's mechanism relies on shared beliefs and values. In effect, shared beliefs and values constitutes on organizational 'compass' that members rely on to choose appropriate course of action clan control derives from culture.

A strong culture facilitates the control process by enhancing clan control. Clan control is highly efficient, although, efficiency and effectiveness should not be confused.

Communication

Communication should be clear and clear to understand by one person to another *i.e.*, communication. Corporate culture reduces these dangers of miscommunication into ways are as follows:

- There is no need to communicate in matters for which shared assumptions already exist.
- Shared assumptions provide guidelines and clues to help interpret messages that are received.

Therefore, a strong culture encourages efficient and effective communication. Communication is the lifeblood of organizations.

Commitment

A person feels committed to an organization when he or she identifies with it and experiences some emotional attachment to it. A variety of incentives like as salary, prestige, and personal sense of worth. Strong culture encourages efficient and effective commitments.

BUILDING ETHICS INTO CULTURE

An ethical corporate culture has a positive impact on a company's long-term strategic success; an unethical culture can undermine it. Values and ethical standards must not only be explicitly stated but must also be ingrained into the corporate culture. Implementing the values and code of ethics entails the following actions:

- The incorporation of the statement of values and the code of ethics into employee training and educational programmes.
- To explicitly giving attention to values and ethics in recruiting and hiring to screen-out applicants who don't exhibit compatible character traits.
- To communication of the values and ethics code to all employees and explaining compliance procedures.
- To management involvement and oversight from CEO down to first-line supervisors.
- To word of mouth indoctrination.
- To strong endorsements by the CEO.

STRATEGIC LEADERSHIP

Strategic manager has to play significant different leadership role as listed below:

- Visionary
- Chief entrepreneurial and strategist
- Chief administrator and strategy implementer
- Culture builder
- Resource acquirer and allocator
- Capabilities builder
- Process integrator
- Coach crisis solver
- Task master
- Spokesperson
- Negotiator
- Motivator
- Arbitrator
- Consensus builder
- Policy maker
- Policy enforcer
- Mentor
- And head cheer leader

Sometimes, it is useful to be authoritarian and hardnosed; sometimes it is best to be a perceptive listener and a compromising decision maker, sometimes strong participative, collegial approach works best; and sometimes being a coach and adviser is the proper role.

Strategic leader act as many occasions call for a highly-visible role and extensive time commitments. While others entailed a brief ceremonial performance with the details delegated to subordinates.

Strategic managers have five leadership roles to play in pushing for good strategy execution as follows:

- He has to closely monitor progress of the top management and study the overall changes in organization, for this purpose he has to learn what obstacles lies in the path of good execution.
- To promote a culture and esprit de corps that mobilizes and energizes organizational members to execute strategy in a competent fashion and perform at high level.
- To keep the organization responsive to changing conditions alert for new opportunities, bubbling with innovative ideas, and ahead of rivals in developing competitively valuable competencies and capabilities.
- To exercise ethics leadership and insisting that the company conduct its affair like a model corporate citizen.
- To push corrective actions to improve strategy execution and overall strategic performance.

Two leadership issues are of fundamental importance:

- The role of the chief executive officers (CEO)
- The assignment of key managers

ROLE OF THE CEO

Exhibit 18.2: Dhirubhai H. Ambani

Founder Chairman, Reliance Industries Limited, India
December 28, 1932 - July 6, 2002

Major Group Companies: Reliance Industries Limited, India's largest private sector company.

Description of Group's Business: The Reliance Group founded by Dhirubhai H. Ambani (1932-2002) is India's largest business house with total revenues of over Rs 99,000 crore (US$ 22.6 billion), cash profit of Rs 12,500 crore (US$ 2.8 billion), net profit of Rs 6,200 crore (US$ 1.4 billion) and exports of Rs 15,900 crore (US$ 3.6 billion).

The Group's activities span exploration and production (E&P) of oil and gas, refining and marketing, petrochemicals (polyester, polymers, and intermediates), textiles, financial services and insurance, power, telecom and infocom initiatives. The Group exports its products to more than 100 countries the world over. Reliance emerged as India's Most Admired Business House, for the third successive year in a TNS Mode survey for 2003.

Reliance Group revenue is equivalent to about 3.5% of India's GDP. The Group contributes nearly 10% of the country's indirect tax revenues and over 6% of India's exports. Reliance is trusted by an investor family of over 3.1 million - India's largest.

Birthplace: Chorwad, village in Saurashtra (Gujarat), India

Father's Name: Hirachand Govardhandas Ambani

Mother's Name: Jamunaben Hirachand Ambani

(Contd...)

Career: At the age of 17 went to Aden (now part of Yemen) and worked for A. Besse & Co. Ltd., the sole selling distributor of Shell products.

In the year 1958 returned to Mumbai and started his first company, Reliance Commercial Corporation, a commodity trading and export house.

In the year 1966, as a first step in Reliance's highly successful strategy of backward integration, he started the textile mill in Naroda, Ahmedabad.

In the year 1975, a technical team from the World Bank certified that the Reliance textile plant was "excellent by developed country standards."

In the year 1977, the company went public.

Credited with a number of financial innovations in the Indian capital markets. Today, the Reliance Group has one of the largest family of shareholders in the world. With an investment of over Rs 36,000 crore (US$ 9 billion) in petroleum refining, petrochemicals, power generation, telecommunication services and a port terminal in a three-year time frame, has steered the Reliance Group to its current status as India's leading textiles-petroleum-petrochemicals-power-telecom player.

Achievements: Voted India's 'Top Businessman' in the 'Best of India' poll conducted by Zee News, August 2003.

Petrotech Society conferred posthumously the 'Lifetime Achievement Award' for his outstanding contribution to Downstream Petroleum Industry in India, January 2003.

Rated as one of 'India's Most Admired CEOs' for the fourth consecutive year in the *Business Barons* - Taylor Nelson Sofres - Mode Survey, July 2002.

Conferred the 'Lifetime Achievement Award' by India HRD Congress, February 2002.

Conferred 'The Economic Times Award for Corporate Excellence for Lifetime Achievement', August 2001.

Felicitated by the Municipal Corporation of Greater Mumbai with a citation at a civic reception, December 2000.

Conferred the 'Man of the Century' award by Chemtech Foundation and Chemical Engineering World in recognition of his outstanding contribution to the growth and development of the chemical industry in India, November 2000.

Conferred the 'Indian Entrepreneur of the 20th Century' award by FICCI (Federation of Indian Chambers of Commerce and Industries), for his meticulous scripting of one of the most remarkable stories of business endeavour of the 20th century, March 2000.

Thrice (in the years 2000, 1998 and 1996) nominated as one of the 'Power 50 - the most powerful people in Asia' by *Asiaweek* magazine.

Voted as the most admired Indian of the millennium in the field of Business & Economics in 'Legends - A Celebration of Excellence' poll audited by Ernst & Young for Zee Network, January 2000.

Voted as 'Creator of Wealth' of the Century in *The Times of India* poll, January 2000.

(Contd...)

Chosen as one of the three 'makers of equity' by India Today in their special millennium issue entitled '100 People Who Shaped India in the 20th Century', January 2000.

Chosen by the Indian Merchants' Chamber as "An Outstanding Visionary of the 20th Century" in recognition of his unique achievements and contribution in the development of industry and capital markets in India, December 1999.

Voted as 'Indian Businessman of the Century' in *Business Barons* Global Multimedia Poll, December 1999.

Amongst 'The Power 50 - India's 50 most powerful decision-makers in Politics, Business & Finance', *Business Barons,* August 1999.

Declared 'Most Admired Indian Business Leader' by *The Times of India,* Indiatimes.com poll, July 1999.

The only Indian industrialist in 'Business Hall of Fame' in *Asiaweek,* October 1998.

Awarded the Dean's Medal by The Wharton School, University of Pennsylvania, for setting an outstanding example of leadership, June 1998.

Chosen as 'Star of Asia' by *Business Week,* USA, June 1998.

Leading business magazine *Business Barons* placed him in its list of 'India's 25 Most Influential Business and Financial Leaders', June 1998.

Awarded the Companion Membership of the Textile Institute, UK, an award which is limited to 50 living members who have "substantially advanced the general interests of the industries based on fibres", 1994.

Chosen 'Businessman of the Year 1993', *Business India,* January 1994.

Family: Wife: Kokilaben. Four children: two sons, Mukesh, who is Chairman & Managing Director and Anil, Vice-Chairman & Managing Director of Reliance Industries and two daughters, Dipti Salgaocar who lives in Goa and Nina Kothari, who resides in Chennai. Reliance gets an award for Corporate Social Responsibility–naïve population, low cost for technical services, and use of English as the primary business and medical language is ideal for completing trials rapidly and cost efficiently.

"RCRS expects to leverage the India advantage with its value proposition to deliver world-class clinical research services to global pharmaceutical, biotechnology, medical device and nutraceutical organisations", said Mr. K.V. Subramaniam, Sr. Executive Vice President, Reliance Industries Limited.

Source: Reliance Industries Limited

The chief executive officer is the catalyst in strategic management. CEO is most closely identified with and ultimately accountable for a strategy's success. In most corporate world, particularly larger ones, CEOs spend into 80 percent of their time developing and guiding strategy.

The nature of the CEO role is both a symbolic and substantive in strategy implementation as follow:

- The CEO is a symbol of the new strategy. CEO actions and the perceived seriousness of his other commitment to a choosen strategy, particularly if the strategy represents a major change, except a significant influence on the intensity of subordinate managers commitment to implementation.

- The organization mission, vision, strategy and key long term objectives are strongly influenced by the personal goals and values of its CEO. To the extent that the CEO invests time and personal values for choosen strategy. He or she represents an important source for clarification, guidance and adjustment during implementation.
- Major changes in strategy are often quality followed by a change in CEO. Successful strategy implementations directly linked to the unique characteristics, orientations and actions of the CEO.

Exhibit 18.3: Key Consideration In Managerial Assignments To Implement Strategy

A new strategy subject issue	Advantages	Disadvantages
• Using the Existing executives to implement	• Already know key people, Practice and conditions. • Personal qualities better known and understand by associates. • Have established relationships with peers, subordinates, suppliers, etc. • Symbolizes organizational commitment to individual careers.	• Less adaptable to major strategic changes because of knowledge, attitudes and values. • Past commitments may hamper hard decisions required in executing a new strategy. • Less ability to become inspired and credibly convey the need for change.
• Bringing Outsiders to implement a new strategy	• Outsiders may already believe inland have "lived" the new strategy. • Outsider is unencumbered by internal commitments to people. • Outsiders come to the new assignment with heightened commitment and enthusiasm. • Bringing in an outsider can spend powerful signals throughout the organization that change is expected.	• Often costly, both in terms of compensation and learning to work together time. • Candidates suitable in all respects (Exact experience) may not be available leading to compromise choices. • Uncertainty in selecting the right person. • The "morale" costs when an outsider takes a job several insiders wanted. • "What to do with poorly free" problem.

Source: Adapted from Boris Yavitz and William H. Newman, Strategy in action (New York: Free Press, 1982) and Paul J. Stonich, Implementing Strategy (Cambridge, Mass: Ballingr, 1982) chap.4.

FOUR MANAGERIAL ASSIGNMENT SITUATIONS

Four managerial assignment situations are

- Selective blend
- Turnover
- Stability
- Reorientations

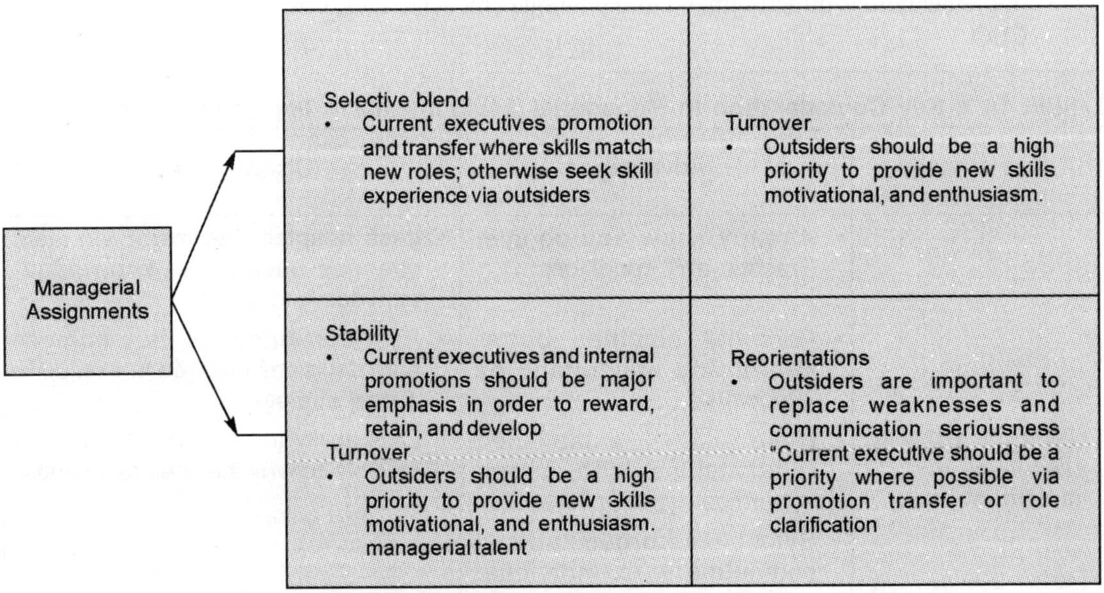

Figure 18.2: Four Managerial Assignments

Figure 18.2 indicates the four managerial assignment situations like selective blend, turnover, stability and reorientation. These four managerial assignments are bringing changes which are required to implement the new strategy in organisation.

QUESTIONS FOR DISCUSSIONS

1. Discuss the corporate culture.
2. Discuss the elements of the corporate culture.
3. Discuss the CEO role.
4. Discuss the four managerial assignment situations.
5. What is Strategic Leadership?
6. Briefly explain the culture influence in organisation.
7. What is adaptive culture?
8. What is thickness culture?
9. What is deciphering a culture?

10. What is unhealthy cultures?
11. What is weak-culture companies?
12. What is strong culture companies?
13. Discuss the four managerial assignment situations.

REFERENCES

1. Charles W.L. Hill/Gareth R. Jones, *Strategic Management Theory an Integrated Approach*, All India Publishers and Distributors Regd. 2001.
2. A.A.Thomson and A.J. Strickland, *Strategic Management Concepts and Cases*, Tata McGraw –Hill Publishing Company Limited, New Delhi, 2003.
3. John, A. Pearce II, Richard B. Robinson, JR., *Strategic Management Strategy Formulation and Implementation*. A.I.T.B.S. Publishers & Distributors (Regd), New Delhi, 2002.
4. Warren Wilhelin, *Changing Corporate Culture - or Corporate Behaviour? How to Change Your Company*, Academy of Management Executive, Nov. 1992, pp 72.
5. Edgar H. Schein, *Organisational Culture and Leadership*, Jossey-Bass, San Francisco, 1985, pp 9.
6. P. Flanagan, *The ABCs of Changing Corporate culture, Management Review*, American Management Association, July, 1995, pp 57-61.
7. *Corporate Culture and Performance*, Free Press, New York, 1992, pp 7.
8. Kotter and Meskett, *Corporate Culture and Performance*, pp 5.
9. Edgar H. Schein, *Organisational Culture and Leadership*, op, cit, 223-243.
10. Scholz, Christian. *Corporate Culture and Strategy - The Problem of Strategic Fit*. Long Range Planning 20 (Auguest), pp 78-87.
11. Kotter, John P., and James L. Heskett. *Corporate Culture and Performance*. NewYork; Free Press,1992.
12. Boris Yavitz and William H. Newman, *Strategy in Action*, Free Press, Newyork, 1982.
13. C.W. Hofer, E.A. Murray, Jr.R., R. Charan, and R. A. Pitts, *Strategic Management* (St. Paut, minn: West publishing, 1984).
14. Vijay Sathe, *Culture and Corporate Realities* (Homewood, III. Rechard D. Irwin, 1985).
15. Deal, Terrence E., and Allan A. Kennedy. *Corporate Cultures, Reading Mass*: Addision–Wesley publishing, 1982.
16. Hairiz Weihrich and Harold Koonlz, *Management– A Glopbal Perspective*, McGraw–Hill International Editions, 1994.
17. Warren Wilhelin, *Changing Corporate Culture– or Corporate Behaviour? How to Change Your Company*. Academy of management executive, No, 1992. p. 72.
18. Edgar H. Schein, *Organisational Culture and Leadership*, Josscy–Bass, San Francisco, 1985.
19. Stanely M. Davis, *Managing Corporate Culture*, M. A. Cambridge, Bellenger, 1984.
20. Frank Petrock, *Corporate Cultures Enhances Profils*, H.R. Magazine 35, November 1990, pp. 64-66.

21. Rechard Pascale, *Fitting New Employees into the Company Cultures*, Fortune, May 18, 1984, pp 28-43.
22. Terrance E. Deal and Allen A. Kennedy, *Corporate Cultures* (Reading. MA, Addison– Wesley, 1982).
23. John P. Kolter and James L. Herkett, *Corporate Culture and Performance* (Newyork, Freepress, 1992).
24. Goleman. Daniel, *What makes a leader*. Harvard Business Review 76, no 6, (November–December 1998), pp. 92-102.
25. Kolter, John P. *What Leaders Realy Do*. Harvard Business Review 68, no. 3 (May-June 1990), pp. 103-111.
26. Scholz, Christian, *Corporate Culture and Strategy– The problem of Strategic Fit* long range planning 20 (August 1987).

Chapter – 19

Designing Organization Structure

CONTENTS

- Introduction
- What is organizational design?
- Types of organizational structure
- Vertical differentiation
- Horizontal differentiation
- Simple structure
- Functional structure
- Divisional organizational structure
- Strategic business units
- Matrix organizational structure
- Product team structure
- Geographic structure
- Integration and integrating mechanisms
- Types and forms of integrating mechanisms

LEARNING OBJECTIVES

In this chapter, we shall examine the organizational structure available to strategic managers to coordinate and motivate employees that result in increased productivity and efficiency of the organization. This chapter has to present structural alternatives, their advantages and disadvantages.

INTRODUCTION

In this chapter, we shall examine the organizational structure available to strategic managers to coordinate and motivate employees that result in increased productivity and efficiency of the organization. This chapter has to present structural alternatives, their advantages and disadvantages.

What is Structure?

Structure is the basic and simple concept: it is the division of task for efficiency and clarity of purpose in organization. It is coordination between the interdependent functional parts of the organization to ensure organizational effectiveness. Organization structure balances to the need for specialization with the need for integration. It is providing for decentralizing and centralizing that consistent with the organizational and control needs of the strategy.

Exhibit 19.1: Organizational Structure of Satyam industry

Satyam: A customer-centric organization

Satyam's organizational structure is inspired by a unique concept–the **Network of Circles**. Each Circle offers a specific set of business offerings based on its competency profile. The result is an internal culture where new ideas are nurtured and acted upon and new competencies developed. This way Satyam continuously provides services right across the IT value chain. At the center of the Network of Circles is the customer, whose business requirements are the driving force. Accordingly, the Circles are categorized as:

- Verticals Business Units (Based on the customer's line of business)
- Horizontal Competency Units (Based on competency requirements)
- Regional Business Units (Based on the regions the unit operates)

Source: Satyam Website

WHAT IS ORGANIZATIONAL DESIGN?

Designing an organization's structure is the task of management who have the responsibility of designing, implementing and achieving the organization's mission. This is accomplished by dividing the work of the organization and then coordinating the various responsibilities. It defines how the organization's goals will be reached and how work will be done. This is a complex task, to assemble or alter a system. Designing an organization's framework involves issues like complexity, formalization, centralization and determines what level of each will be required. It considers advance technology and environment to determine the appropriate structure to achieve organizational strategy.

TYPES OF ORGANIZATIONAL STRUCTURE

- Vertical differentiation
- Horizontal differentiation
- Integration and integrating mechanisms

VERTICAL DIFFERENTIATION

Vertical differentiation is an important element of an organizational structure. It is to specify the reporting relationships that link people, tasks and functions at all levels of a company or organization. It means that management chooses the appropriate number of hierarchical levels and the correct span of control for implementing a company's strategy effectively. The organizational hierarchy establish to span of control *i.e.*, authority flows the top to bottom. The basic choice is a flat structure or tall structure.

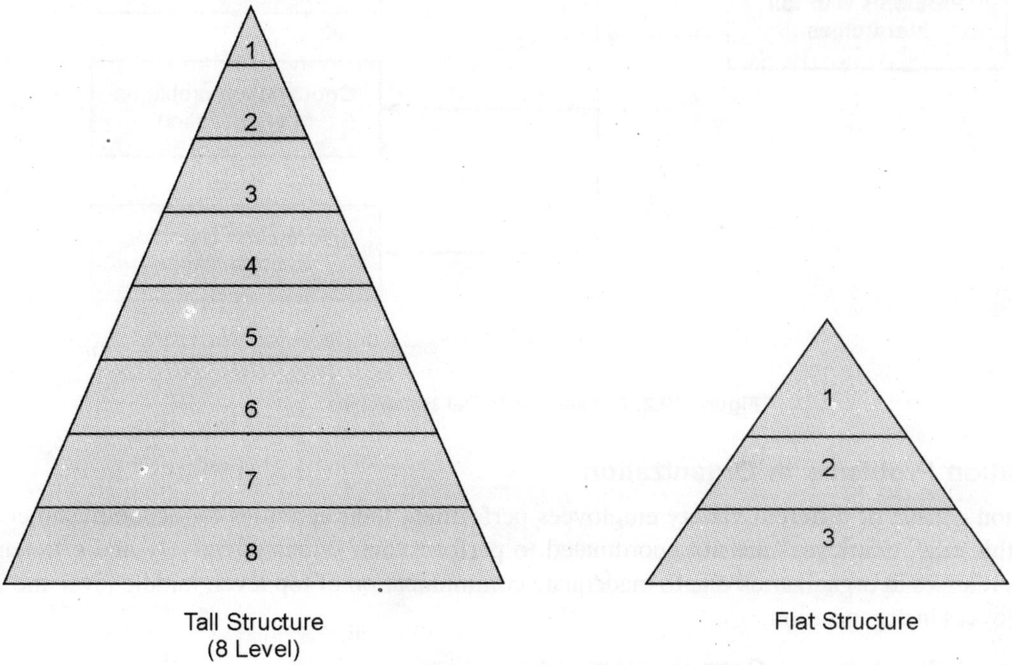

Figure 19.1

This chart indicate that the tall structure have many hierachical levels relative to size. Flat structures have few levels relative to size.

Problems with Tall Hierarchies

Figure 19.2 highlights the tall hierarchies' problems in organization. Tall hierarchies' problems are as listed below:

- Coordination problems in organization
- Motivational problems in organization
- Information problems in organization
- Number of middle managers in organization

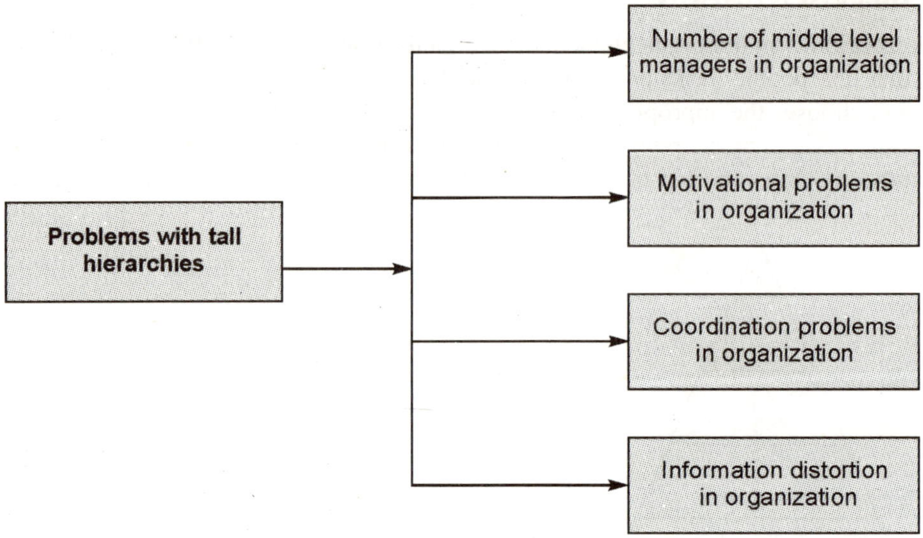

Figure 19.2: Problems with Tall Hierarchies

Coordination Problems in Organization

Organization consist of different variety employees performing their activities for accomplishment of goals. In this case, employees are not coordinated to perform their duties effectively and efficiently. Therefore, it arises in organization due to inadequate communication of top level, middle level and low level employees in organization.

Motivational Problems in Organization

Organizational hierarchy is essential to the need for motivational aspects to motivate employees who perform their duties in organization. Praises, recognition and additional improvement of facilities and perk to employees are the motives for employees in organization. Sometimes, top management motivates their employees in terms of punishment. It is also one of the major problems of the organizational structure.

Information Problems

Management hierarchy wants new information from the customers, bankers, shareholders, debt holder, financial institution, and internal human resource of the organization. It has delay to provide to adequate information. Thus, it is one of the problems of the hierarchy structure.

Number of Middle Management

Organization appoints more middle-level managers to manage and control the organization. Therefore, it is expensive for organization. This factor also is one of the unhealthy factors of the organizational structure.

Vertical differentiation further classified into two broad categories. They are as follows:

- Centralization
- Decentralization

Centralization

Authority is centralized when managers at the top levels of the organizational hierarchy retain the authority to make the most important decisions. Now-a-days, the centralization of organization structure is not important to formulation, implementation and monitor and controlling of the objectives of an organization.

Decentralization

When the authority is decentralized, it is delegated to divisions, functional departments and managers at lower levels in the organization. Some important strategic factors are relating with the formulation, implementation and monitor and controlling the major objectives of an organization.

- Strategic managers delegate operational decision making responsibility to middle managers. Therefore, it reduces information overload to strategic managers in organization. In addition, strategic managers can spend more time on strategic decision-making process in organization for formulation, implementation and controlling the mission and vision of the organization.
- Managers of the organization become responsible for adapting the organization policy to suit local conditions, their motivation, and accountability to increase efficiency and productivity.

HORIZONTAL DIFFERENTIATION

Horizontal differentiation organization structure as follows:

- Simple structure
- Functional structure
- Divisional structure
- Strategic business unit
- Matrix structure
- Product team structure
- Geographic structure

SIMPLE STRUCTURE

Simple structure is suitable to small business enterprises. All strategic and operating decisions are centralized in hands of owner-cum-manager. This structure maximizes control by owners-cum-manager. Simple structures encourage employee involvement in more than activity.

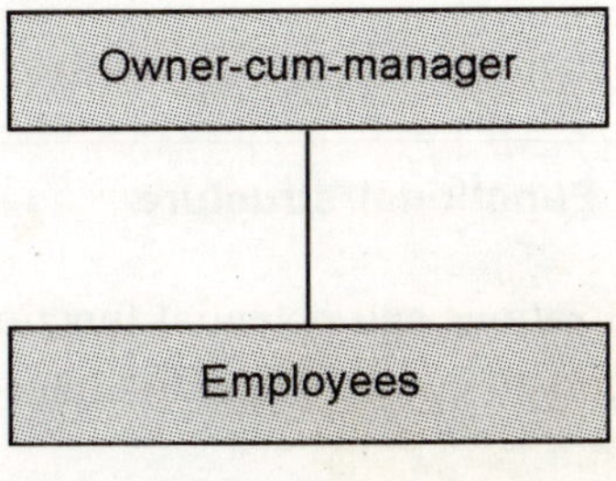

Figure 19.3: Simple Structure

Merits

Exhibit 19.2: Merits of simple structure

- It facilitate to control all the business activities.
- To make rapid decision making and ability to change with market signals.
- It is simple and informal motivational control systems.

Disadvantages

Exhibit 19.3: Disadvantages of Simple Structure

- It is very demanding on the owner cum manager.
- It increasigly inadequates as volume expands.
- It does not facilitate development of future managers.
- It tends to focus owner-cum-manager on day-to-day matters and not on future strategy.

FUNCTIONAL STRUCTURE

Functional structure consists of several functions as follows:

- Finance/accounting
- Research and development
- Human resource
- Marketing
- Production
- Engineering
- Sales and marketing

Advantages

Exhibit 19.4: Advantages of Functional Structure

- To efficiency through specialization.
- To improve development of functional expertise.
- To differentiate and delegate day-to-day operating decisions.

Disadvantages

Exhibit 19.5: Disadvantages of Functional structure

- It promotes narrow specializations and potential functional rivalry or conflict.
- It creates difficulty in functional coordination and inter-functional decision-making.
- It creates staff-line conflict.
- It limits internal development of general managers.

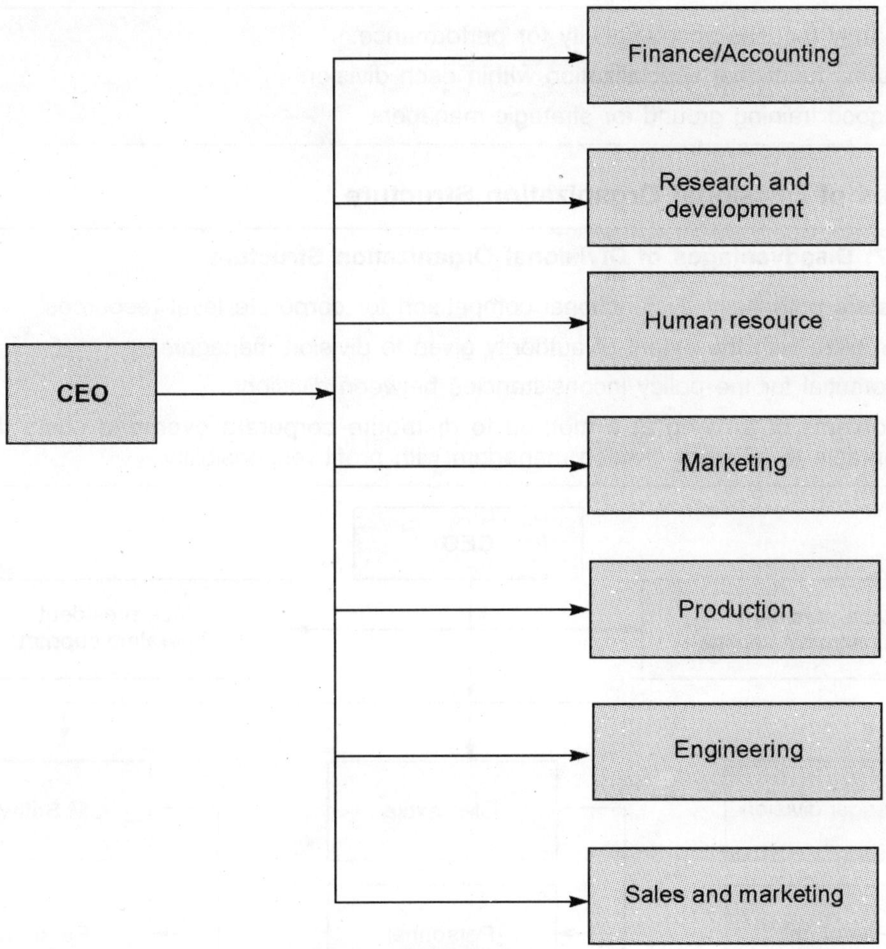

Figure 19.4: Functional Structure

DIVISIONAL ORGANIZATIONAL STRUCTURE

An organization programme diversifies its product/service line. It covers broad geographic areas and utilized unrelated market channels, or begins to serve distinctly different customer groups and a divisional structure is needed for organization.

Advantages

Exhibit 19.6: Advantages of Divisional Structure

- It focuses on coordination and necessary authority down to the appropriate level for rapid response.
- It frees chief executive officer for broader strategic decision-making.
- It places strategy development and implementation in closer proximity to the divisions unique environment.

(Contd...)

- It sharply focuses accountability for performance.
- It retains functional specialization within each division.
- It is good training ground for strategic managers.

Disadvantages of Divisional Organization Structure

Exhibit 19.7: Disadvantages of Divisional Organization Structure

- It fosters potentially dysfunctional competition for corporate level resources.
- To problem with the extent of authority given to division managers.
- To potential for the policy inconsistencies between divisions.
- It problems of arriving at a method to distribute corporate overhead costs that is acceptable to different division managers with profit responsibility.

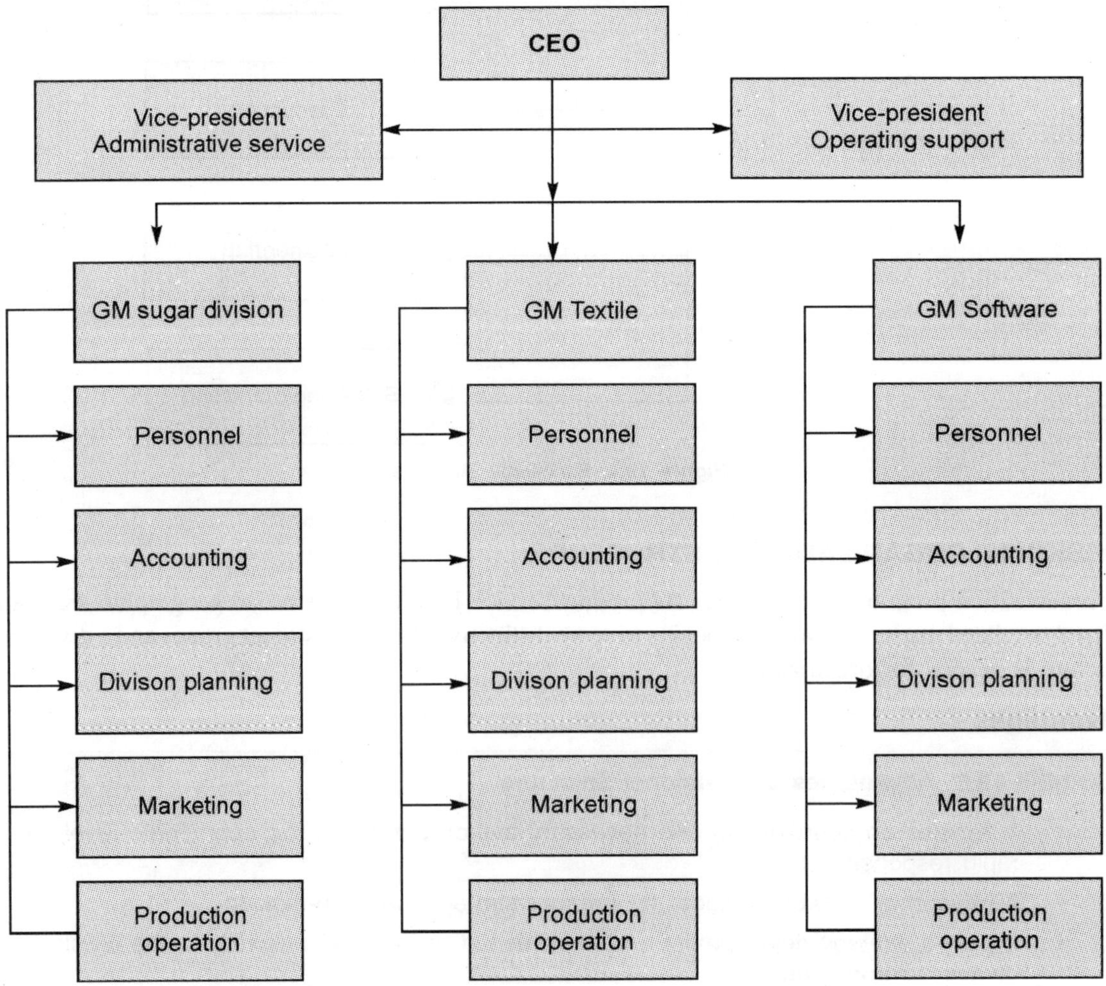

Figure 19.5: Divisional Organizational Structure President

STRATEGIC BUSINESS UNITS

Some organizations encounter difficulty in controlling their divisional operations as the diversity, size, and number of these units continues to increase. And corporate management may encounter difficulty in evaluating and controlling its numerous, often multi industry divisions. Under these conditions, it may become necessary to add another layer of management to improve strategy implementation, promotion synergy, and gain greater control over the diverse business interests. It can be achieved by grouping various divisions' in terms of common strategic elements. These groups commonly called Strategic Business Units (SBUs)

Advantages of SBUs Organizational Structure

Exhibit 19.8: Advantages of SBUs Organizational Structure

- It improves coordination between divisions with similar strategic concerns and product /market environment.
- It tightens the strategic management and control of large, diverse business enterprises.
- It facilitates distinct and in-depth business planning at the corporate and business levels.
- It channels accountability to distinct business unit.

Disadvantages of Strategic Business Unit Organizational Structure

Exhibit 19.9: Disadvantages of Strategic Business Unit Organizational Structure

- It places another layer of management between the divisions and corporate management.
- Its dysfunctional competition for corporate resource may increase.
- The role of the group, vice-president can be difficult to define.
- It is difficult in defining the degree of autonomy for the group, vice-presidents and division managers.

MATRIX ORGANIZATIONAL STRUCTURE

The matrix organization provides dual channels of authority, performance responsibility, evaluation and control. It is essential; subordinates are assigned to both a basic functional area and a project or product manager. The matrix form is included to combine the advantages of functional specialization and product/project specialization.

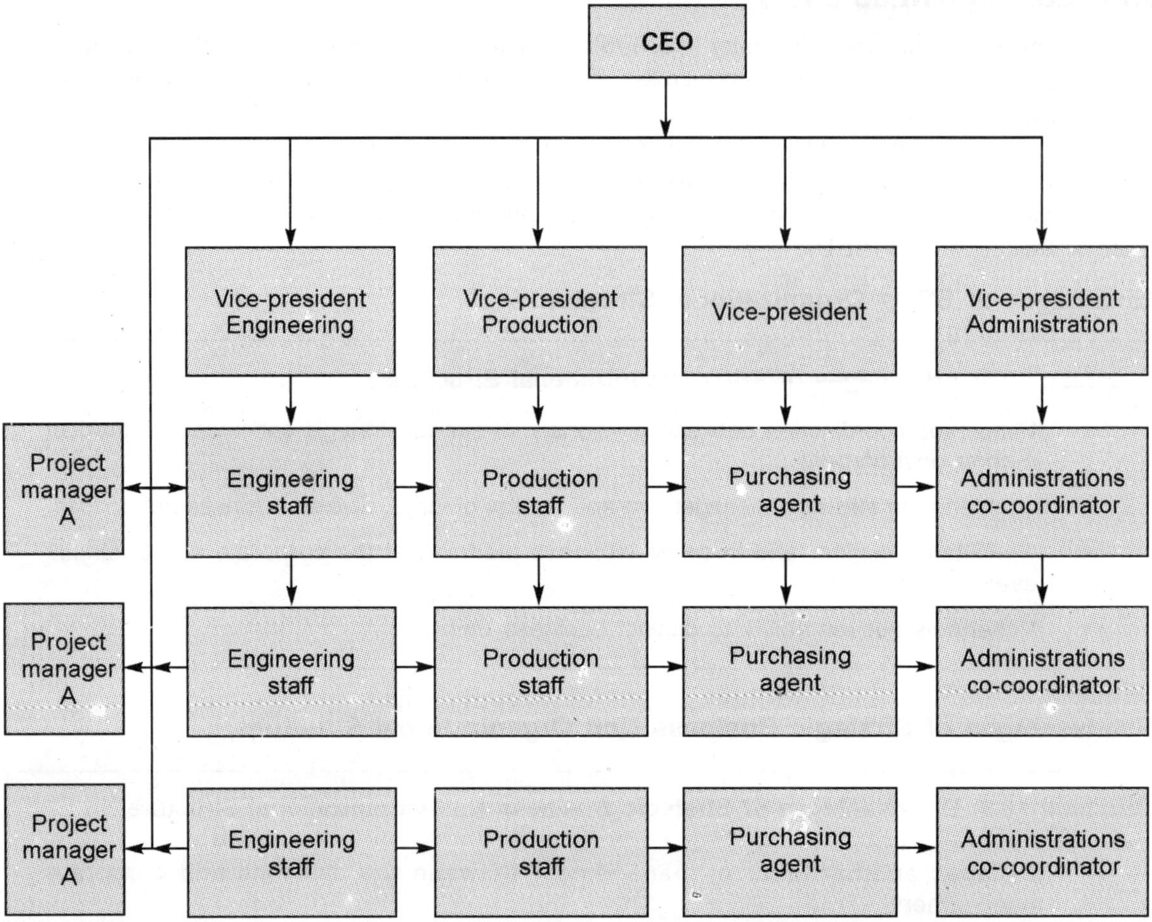

Figure 19.6: Matrix Organizational Structure

Advantages of Matrix Organizational Structure

Exhibit 19.10: Advantages of Matrix Organizational Structure

- It accommodates a wide variety of project-oriented business activity.
- It provides good training ground for strategies managers.
- It maximizes efficient use of functional managers.
- It fosters creativity and multiple sources of diversity.
- It is broader middle management exposure to strategic issues for the business.

Disadvantages of Matrix Organizational Structure

Exhibit 19.11: Disadvantages of Matrix Organizational Structure

- It acts as accountability can create confusion and contradictory policies.
- Necessities tremendous horizontal and vertical coordination.

PRODUCT TEAM STRUCTURE

Product team structure is a major structural innovation in recent years. It has similar advantages to a matrix structure but is much easier and for less costly to operate because of the way people are organized into permanent cross-functional teams.

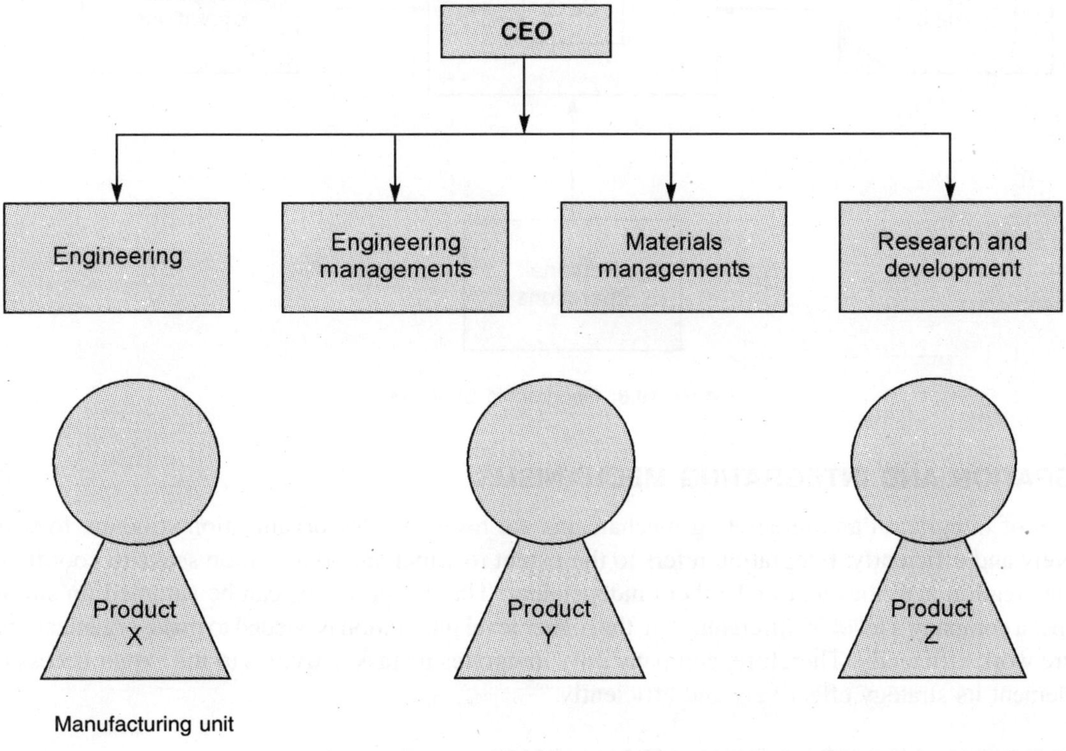

Figure 19.7: Product Team Structure

GEOGRAPHIC STRUCTURE

Company operates as a geographic structure; geographic regions become the basis for the grouping of organizational activities. For instance, a company may divide its manufacturing operations and establish manufacturing plants in different regions of the country. Service organizations like store chains or banks may organize their sales marketing activities on a regional, rather than national level to get closer to their customer.

Geographic structure provides more control than a functional structure because there are several regional hierarchies carrying out the work previously performed by a single-centralized hierarchy.

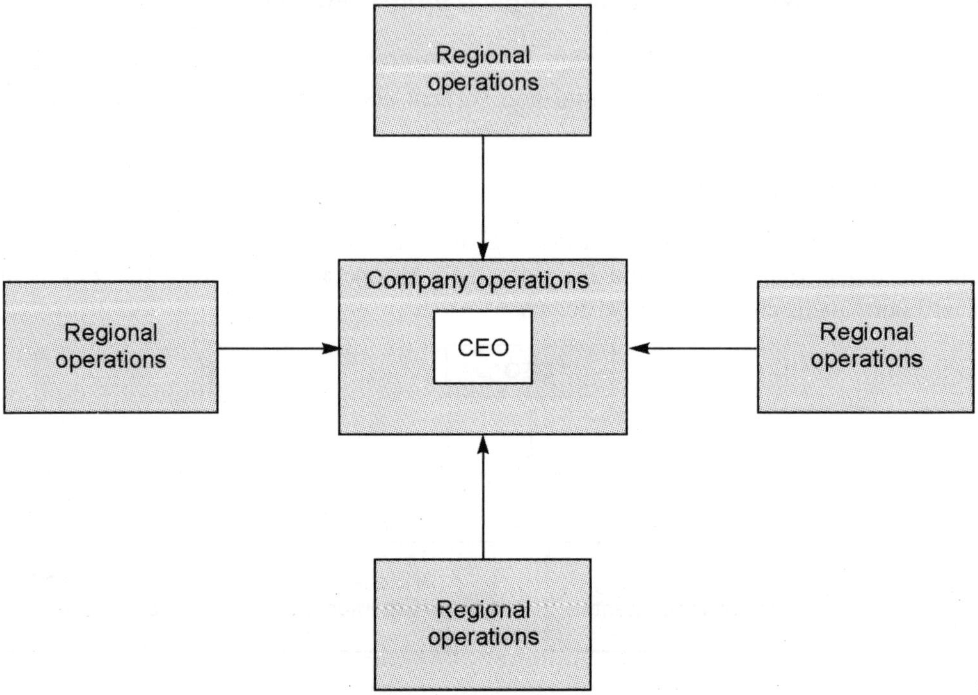

Figure 19.8: Geographic Structure

INTEGRATION AND INTEGRATING MECHANISMS

The level of integration and integrating mechanisms are necessary for organization structure to work effectively and efficiently. Integration refers to the extent to which an organization seeks to coordinate its value creation activities and make them independent. The design issues can be summed up simply the higher a company's level of differentiation, the higher level integration is needed to make organizational structure work efficiently. Therefore, company only integrates its task activities to the extent necessary to implement its strategy effectively and efficiently.

TYPES/FORMS OF INTEGRATING MECHANISMS

Forms/types of integrating mechanisms of company can be used to increase its level of integration. Types/forms of integrating mechanisms are listed below:

- Direct contact
- Liaison roles
- Task forces
- Teams
- Integrating roles
- Integrating departments
- Matrix

Direct Contact

Chief executive officer has directly contacted among managers from different divisions or functional department can work together to solve mutual problems. Different functions managers have tend to equal authority for accomplishment of goals and objectives of the organization with cooperation and motivation.

Interdepartmental Liaison Roles

A company has improved its efficiency through interdepartmental liaison roles among managers in the organization. When volume of contact is increased two or more departments, its result is improved cooperation and coordination. Therefore, functional managers are contacting among managers of organization, weekly, monthly. It builds up healthy relationships among employees of the company.

Temporary Task Forces

Task force involves the planning and solutions of the difficult and complex problems. It arises from different functional departments of the company. Task force is a just like committee to solution of problems of the organization. Task force is temporary, therefore, once the problem is solved, members of the task force should return to their normal roles in their departments or are assigned to other task forces. Task force members also perform many of their normal duties while serving on the task force.

Permanent Teams

Task force solves the problems effectively and efficiently, an organization must establish permanent integrating mechanisms like as a permanent team. Example – product development committee.

Integrating Roles

Integrating roles means, a functional/divisions managers job is a full time. Who is normally a senior manager with a great deal of experience in the joint needs of the two departments? The job is to coordinate the decision process among departments/divisions so that the synergetic gains from cooperation can be obtained.

Integrating Department

The permanent integrating department is established at corporate headquarters. This department consists mainly of strategic planners and may indeed be called the *strategic planning department*. Corporate head quarter's staffs in a divisional structure can also be viewed as an integrating department from the divisional perspective.

Matrix Structure

Lastly, differentiation is high and the company must be able to respond quickly to the environment, a matrix structure becomes the appropriate integrating device.

Institutionalizing the Strategy

Three organizational elements provide the fundamental and long term for institutionalizing the company' strategy as follows:

- Structure
- Leadership
- Culture

QUESTIONS FOR DISCUSSIONS

1. Discuss the types of organization structure.
2. Explain the vertical differentiation.
3. Describe the horizontal differentiation.
4. What is simple structure?
5. What are the advantages and disadvantages of simple structure?
6. Briefly explain the functional structure.
7. Describe the advantages and disadvantages of functional structure.
8. What is divisional structure?
9. Discuss the advantages and disadvantages functional structure.
10. What is strategic business units.
11. What are the advantages and disadvantages of strategic business units.
12. What is matrix organization structure.
13. Discuss the advantages and disadvantages of matrix organization structure.
14. Explain the product team structure.
15. Discuss the advantages and disadvantages of product team structure.
16. What is geographic structure.
17. Explain the advantages and disadvantages of geographic structure.
18. What is integration and integrating mechanisms?
19. Describe the types of integrating mechanisms.

REFERENCES

1. Henry Mintzburg, *The Structuring of Organisation: A Synthesis of Research*, Prentice- Hall, Englewood Cliffs, N.J. 1975, Chpts.1 and 2.
2. J.T. Cannon, *Business Strategy and Structure and Policy*, Harcourt Brace and World, Inc, New York,1988.
3. A.D. Chandlor,Jr., *Strategy and Structue : Chapters in the History of the American Industrial Enterprise*, MIT Press, Cambridge,1962.
4. R.E. Miles and C.C. Snow, *Organisation Strategy, Structure and Process*, McGraw-Hill, New York, pp 179.
5. Jonathan Weeks, *Planning for Physical Distribution; Long Range Planning,* Auguest, 1977,pp 78.
6. Charles W.L.Hill / Gareth R. Jones, *Strategic Management Theory an Integrated Approach*, All India Publishers and Distributors Regd. 2001.
7. A.A.Thomson and A.J. Strickland, *Strategic Management Concepts and Cases*, Tata McGraw –Hill Publishing Company Limited, New Delhi, 2003.
8. John, A. Pearce II, Richard B. Robinson, JR. *Strategic Management Strategy Formulation and Implementation.* A.I.T.B.S. Publishers & Distributors (Regd), New Delhi, 2002.

9. Henry Mintsburg, *The Structuring of Organization: A Sunthesis of Research*, Prentice-Hall, englewood cliffs, N.J, 1975.
10. J.T. Cannon, *Business Strategy and Policy*, Harcourt Brace and World, Inc., Newyork, 1998.
11. R.E. Miler and L.C. Snow, *Organisation Structure and Process*, McGraw-Hill, Newyork, 1978.
12. William K. Hall, *SBVs: Hot, New Topics in the Management of Diversification*, Business Horizons, February 1978, pp. 19.
13. Robert H. Waterman, Jr., T.J. Peters, *Structure is not Organisation*. Business Horizona, June 1980, p. 20.
14. Peters, Thomas J., *Beyond the Matrix Organization*. Business Horizons, October 1979, pp. 15-27.

Chapter – 20

Strategic Control System

CONTENTS

- Introduction
- Strategic control systems
- Characteristics of strategic control systems
- Steps/process in designing an effective control system in organization
- Levels of control
- Types of strategic control
- Operational control systems
- Types of strategic budgets
- Strategic reward systems

LEARNING OBJECTIVES

In this chapter, we shall outline the establishing strategic controls, let us discuss the strategic control systems and process and the different types of strategic control. Next, we shall examine the main operational control system

INTRODUCTION

In this chapter, we shall outline the establishing strategic controls, let us discuss the strategic control systems and process and the different types of strategic control. Next, we shall examine the main operational control system; monitoring performance and evaluating deviations, strategic control systems allow top managers to monitor and evaluate the performance of divisions, functions, and employees and to take corrective action to improve their performance. Strategic control is the process of establishing the appropriate types of control system at the corporate, business and functional levels in a company which allow the strategic managers for guiding and evaluating the strategy in the organization.

Control strategy can be characterized as a form of 'steering control' ordinarily, a significant time span occurs between initial implementation of a strategy and achievement of its intended results. During that time, numerous projects are undertaken, investments are made, and actions are undertaken to implement the new strategy. In addition, during that time, both the environmental situation and firm's internal situation are developing and evolving. Strategic control is necessary to steer the firm through these events. They must provide the basis for correcting the actions and directions of the firm in implementing its strategy to development and changes in its environment and internal situation take place.

STRATEGIC CONTROL SYSTEMS

Strategic control systems are vital aspect of implementing strategy of an organization. The primary function of strategic control systems is to provide information for management. Information needs to control its strategy and structure. Strategic control systems are the formal target setting, monitoring, and evaluation and feedback systems. It provides information to management about the organization's strategy and structure. Both are meeting strategic performance and mission and vision of an organization.

CHARACTERISTICS OF STRATEGIC CONTROL SYSTEMS

Exhibit 20.1: Characteristics of Strategic Control Systems

- It should provide accurate information and is giving a true picture of organizational performance.
- It should be flexible enough to allow managers to respond as necessary to unexpected events in organization.
- It should supply information to managers in a timely sense.

STEPS/PROCESS IN DESIGNING AN EFFECTIVE CONTROL SYSTEM IN ORGANIZATION

Figure 20.1 highlights the steps or process in designing in effective control system in organization. There are four stages involved for designing an effective control system of an organization. They are as follows:

- Establish standards and targets
- Create measuring and monitoring system
- Compare actual performance against the established targets
- Evaluate result and take action if necessary

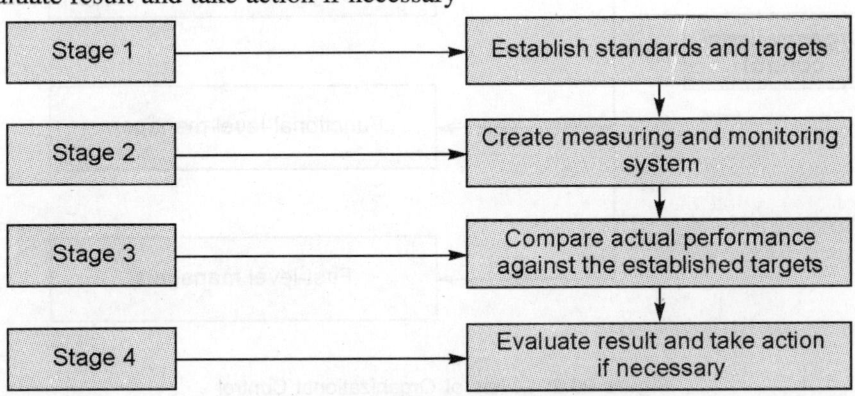

Figure 20.1: Steps or Process in Designing an Effective Control System in Organization

Establish Standards and Targets

Establish standard and targets is the first stage in designing an effective control system. Company managers select standard targets to evaluate its performance. Standard targets are major objectives and goals of the company. It is accomplished and monitored by managers of company or organization.

Create Measuring and Monitoring Systems

This is the second stage of the establishing strategic control systems. Company has established procedures for assessing work goals at all levels in the organization. Either work goal achieved or not achieved. Organization task is the difficult task to measure and monitor task force of an organization.

Compare Actual Performance Against the Established Targets

Strategic management is to select the best decision out of the set of decisions. Therefore, strategist should estimate future targets on the basis past and present performance the organization. Therefore, in this stage, comparison is essentially needed to the past, present and future performance of the organization.

Evaluate Result and Take Action if Necessary

Evaluate result and take action if necessary is the last stage of the evaluating, monitoring and guiding to the strategy to the CEO, managers and finally response from the low-level employees of the organization. Top managers spent huge time for policy making and monitoring to overall project of the organization. Strategy always leads to achievement even with difficult external environment. This goal is to continually enhance an organization's competitive advantage.

LEVELS OF CONTROL

Organization performance is measured at four levels.

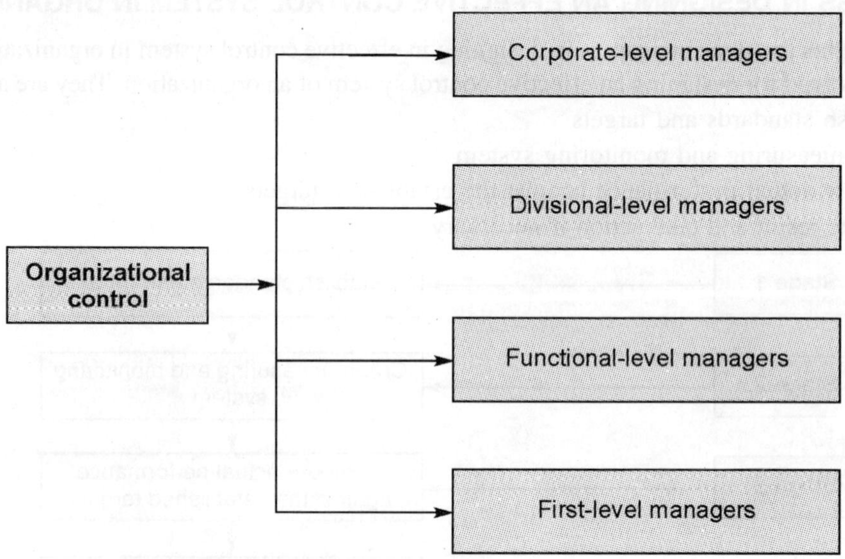

Figure 20.2: Levels of Organizational Control

Figure 20.2 indicates the level of organizational control. There are four levels are involved to control organizational structure. They are as follows:

- Corporate-level managers
- Divisional-level managers
- Functional-level managers
- First-level managers

Managers at the corporate level are most concerned with overall and abstract measures of organizational performance like profit, return on investment or total labor force turnover. The main aim is to choose performance standards. It measure overall corporate performance. Similarly, managers at the other levels are most concerned with developing a set of standards to evaluate business or functional level performance. These measures should be closely tied with possible task force activities and accomplishment of the corporate objectives.

TYPES OF STRATEGIC CONTROL

There are six types of strategic control. They are as listed below:

- Premise control
- Implementation control
- Strategic surveillance
- Special alert control
- Market control
- Output control

Premise Control

Strategy is based on assumed or predicted conditions. These predictions or assumptions are planning premises. Company's strategy can be designed around these predicted conditions. Premise control can be designed to check systematically and continuously. Whether premises set during the planning and implementation process are still valid or not valid. If a vital premise is no longer valid, therefore, then the strategy may have to be changed and premise can be recognized and revised for the better changes and acceptable.

Premises are primarily concerned with two factors listed below:

- Environmental factors
- Industry factors

Environmental Factors

A company has little or no controllable over environmental factors. But these factors exercise considerable influence over the success of the strategy. Environmental factors like inflation, technology, interest rates, regulation, demography and social changes etc. These factors are influenced to strategy formulating, implementation and control and monitoring of premises.

Industry Factors

Industry factors like competitors, suppliers, substitutes and barriers to entry. These are a few examples to affect the performance of industry. Industry factor differ from one industry to another industry. A company should be aware of the factors that influence to success for particular industry.

Some premises are major and some are minor. Premises are often made about numerous environmental and industry variables, therefore, to attempt to track every premise must be selected and on the basis of variables likely to change and would have a major impact on the company and its strategy.

The key premises should be identified during the planning process. The premises should be recorded and responsibly for monitoring, then should be assigned to the persons of the departments who are qualified sources of information.

Implementation Control

The implementation control phase is an important phase of strategic management. It locates in the series of steps, programmmes, investments and moves undertaken over a period to implement strategy. In this stage, special programmes are undertaken by company to implement and control for accomplishment of objectives. A company function areas initiate several strategies that relating to managers convert broad strategic plans into concrete actions and results for specific units and individuals for implementing strategy.

Implementation control can be designed to assess whether the overall strategy should be changed in light of unfolding events and results associated with incremental steps and actions. There are two basic factors involved for implementation control. They are listed below:

- Monitoring strategic thrusts/projects
- Milestone reviews

Monitoring Strategic Thrusts/projects

It involves implementation of strategies in companies that undertaking several new strategic projects or thrusts. These projects or thrusts provide a source of information to manager. Strategic manager can obtain the information from the feedback. It helps to determine either the overall strategy can be progressed as planned or it needs to be adjusted to change.

There are two important approaches useful in enacting implementation control. It focuses on monitoring strategic projects. They are as listed below:

- The planning process of projects or thrusts
- Monitoring strategic projects or thrusts

Milestone Reviews

Managers are attempted to identify critical milestone in organization, it will occur over the time period. Strategy can be implemented in a critical milestone like major resource allocations. In each critical case, review and full-scale reassessment of the strategy and advisability of continuing or refocusing the direction of the organization or company.

Strategic Surveillance

Strategic surveillance can be designed to monitor a broad range of events inside and outside the company or organization. They are likely to threaten the course of the company's or organization's strategy. It should be encouraged in the form of monitoring a source of information.

Special Alert Control

Another type of strategic controls is a special alert control. A special alert control can be needed to thoroughly and often rapidly reconsider the company's or organization basic strategy. It is based on a sudden and unexpected event.

Market Control

It is an important objective of output control. It is helpful to strategist to analyse and monitor the marketing performance of organization. Market control focuses on the performance of one company compare as to another company in terms of stock-market price and return on investment. These things help to appraise financial performance of the company or organization.

Output Control

This is the last type of control system design of the company or organization. Output control concentration on output like divisional goals, functional goals, individual goals which are monitored, evaluated and guided by the strategic managers. Strategic manager aims to establish projects with execution of different types of control systems for measuring and improving efficiency of the organizational strategic objectives.

OPERATIONAL CONTROL SYSTEMS

Strategic control concerns with "steering" with company's future direction. Strategic control can be useful to top management in monitoring and steering the basic strategic direction of the company. Therefore, operating managers also need appropriate control methods at all levels for strategy formulation and implementation and control operational system of an organization or company. The primary aim of the operating level can be allocated and use of the company's resources.

Operational control systems can guide, monitor and evaluate progress in current objectives of the company. Effective operational control systems must take into four steps. They are as below:

- Set standards of performance
- Measure actual performance
- Identify deviations from standards
- Initiate corrective action or adjustment

Types of Operational Control Systems

There are three types of operational control systems. They are listed below:

- Budgeting systems
- Scheduling
- Key-success factors

Budgeting Systems

Budgeting systems provide to efficient resource allocation among the divisions /functions of the company. A budget involves to simply resource allocation plan, helps managers for coordination operations and facilitates managerial control.

Types of Strategic Budgets

There are three type of Strategic budget listed below:

- Revenue budgets
- Capital budgets
- Expenditure budgets

Revenue Budgets

Companies prepare revenue budget to monitor their sources of revenue /income of the organization. The revenue budget provides important information for the daily management of financial resources and key feedback as to whether the strategy is working. A revenue budget is particularly important as a tool for control of strategy implementation. It provides an early warning system about the effectiveness of the company's strategy.

Capital Budgets

Capital budgets look for specific expenditures for plant, equipment, machinery, inventories and other capital items are needed during the budget period. Organization always looks for strong sales. It can lead to a strong growth of the organization. Capital is required for diversification/retrenchment of its current operations to generate additional resources. It carefully plans the acquisition and expenditure of funds for effective control. A company has additional to prepare another two budgets as mentioned below:

- Cash budget: It forecasts receipt and expenditure of the organization.
- Balance sheet: It forecasts the status of assets, liabilities and net worth at the end of the budget period.

Expenditure Budgets

Expenditure budget aims to record all expenditure belonging to division/function of the organization. Expenditure budgets introduction is necessary to company to control and implementation of strategy in various operating units of the company. It can set standards to assess expenditure of the all divisions/ functions of the organization. It can provide an effective communication link between top management and operating managers. It provides another warning system which alerts management to problems in the implementation of the company's strategy.

Scheduling

Scheduling is the key factor in the success of the strategy. It is simply a planning tool for allocating the use of a time-constrained resource or arranging the sequence of interdependent activities. Scheduling offers a mechanism with which to plan for, monitor and control these dependencies.

Key-Success Factor

Key factors are very important to implementation of the project. Successful key factors are listed below:

- Improved productivity
- High employee morale
- Improved product/service quality
- Growth in market share
- Completion of new facilities

Monitoring Performance and Evaluating

Organization carefully watches all goals, objectives discharged by employees of the organization. A successful measure is a monitoring all activities of divisions/functions. It can be the best way reduce to the errors and mistakes and bring very good productivity. Then we shall accomplish the objectives of the organization. Control can be needed on all activities of the company.

STRATEGIC REWARD SYSTEM

Strategic reward system is also important to implement, control and monitor the activities of the organization. Top-level executives want strategic reward in terms of

- Praise
- Recognition
- Morale support

While in the case of middle-level and low level-management employees want strategic reward in terms of:

- Piecework plans
- Commission systems
- Bonus plans
- Profit-sharing systems
- Employee stock option systems

These benefits when given to employees control and monitor the organizational activities.

QUESTIONS FOR DISCUSSIONS

1. Discuss the strategic control.
2. Discuss the process of strategic control system.
3. Discuss the different types of strategic control.

REFERENCES

1. Charles W.L.Hill/Gareth R. Jones, *Strategic Management Theory an Integrated Approach*, All India Publishers and Distributors Regd. 2001.
2. A.A. Thomson and A.J. Strickland, *Strategic Management Concepts and Cases*, Tata McGraw –Hill Publishing Company Limited, New Delhi, 2003.
3. John, A. Pearce II, Richard B. Robinson, JR. *Strategic Management Strategy Formulation and Implementation*. A.I.T.B.S. Publishers & Distributors (Regd), New Delhi, 2002.
4. Philip R. Cateora and John M. Hess, *International Marketing*.
5. Bales, Carter. *Strategic Control: The President's Paradox*. Business Horizons, August 1977, pp 17-28.
6. Camillus, J.C. *Six Approaches to Preventive Management Control*. Financial Executive, December 1980, pp 28-31.
7. Christopher, W. *Achievment Reporting–Controlling Performance against Objectives*. Long Range Planning, October 1977, pp 14-24.
8. Horovits, J.N. *Strategic Control: A New Task for Top Management*. Long-Range Planning, June 1979, pp 2-7.
9. Merchant, Kenneth A. *The Control Function of Management*. Sloan Management Review 23. no 4 (1982), pp 43 –55.

10. Newman, W.H. *Constructive Control: Design and Use of Control Systems*. Englelann Cliffs.
11. B. Yavitz and W.H. Wewman, *Strategy in Action* (Newyork, Freepress, 1982).
12. Peter Lorange, *Corporate Planning* (Englewood cliffs, N.J, Prentice Hall, 1980).
13. Bales, Carter, *Strategic Control: The president's paradox*. Business Horizons, August 1977, pp. 17-28.
14. Merchant, Kenneth A, *The Control Function of Management*, Sloan Management Review 23, no 4 (1982), pp. 43-55.

Chapter – 21

Matching Structure and Control Analysis

CONTENTS

- Introduction
- Matching structure and control analysis at the functional level
- Matching structure and control at the business level
- Designing a global structure
- Multidomestic strategy and structure
- International strategy and structure
- Global organizational structure
- Matching structure and control at the corporate level

LEARNING OBJECTIVES

This chapter discusses how strategic choices to match different forms of structure and control to strategy. First, we shall discuss how functional level strategy influences the choice of structure and control for implementing the strategy. Secondly, let us examine how company's choice of generic business level strategy. Third, we shall focus on the implementation of a global strategy and discuss how to match different global strategies with different global structure. Fourth, we shall take up the special problems that different kinds of corporate level strategy pose for strategic managers in designing a structure.

INTRODUCTION

This chapter discusses how strategic choices to match different forms of structure and control to strategy. First, we shall discuss how functional-level strategy influences the choice of structure and control for implementing the strategy. Secondly, let us examine how company's choice of generic business level strategy. Third, we shall focus on the implementation of a global strategy and discuss how to match different global strategies with different global structure. Fourth, we shall take up the special problems that different kinds of corporate level strategy pose for strategic managers in designing a structure.

MATCHING STRUCTURE AND CONTROL ANALYSIS AT THE FUNCTIONAL LEVEL

Matching structure and control analysis strategy at the functional level are as below:

- Manufacturing functions/divisions
- Research and development functions/divisions
- Marketing division/functions
- Human resource division
- Accounting and finance division
- Customer welfare division
- Production departments

These are the matching structure of the functional level. Functional level strategies are discussed in the earlier chapter. Therefore, there is no need to discuss again these aspects in this chapter.

MATCHING STRUCTURE AND CONTROL AT THE BUSINESS LEVEL

Matching structure and control at the business level are as below:

- Generic business level strategies
- Cost leadership strategy and structure
- Differentiation strategy and structure
- Implementing a combined differentiation and cost-leadership strategy
- Focus strategy and structure

These are the matching structure of the business level. Business level strategies are detailed to discuss in the earlier chapter. Therefore, there is no need to discuss this topic in this chapter.

DESIGNING A GLOBAL STRUCTURE

Global structure is consisting of the following areas:

- Multidomestic strategy and structure
- International strategy and structure
- Global strategy and structure
- Transnational strategy and structure

MULTIDOMESTIC STRATEGY AND STRUCTURE

A company pursues a multidomestic strategy; it generally operates business with a global area structure.

Figure 21.1 highlights the multidomestic area structure. A company duplicates all values like value creation activities and establishes a foreign decision in every country or world in which it operates. Authority can be decentralized to managers in each foreign division and they devise the appropriate strategy for responding to the needs of the local environment. Corporate head quarter is much farther away from the scene of operations. It makes sense to decentralize, control and grant decision authority to managers in foreign operations. Managers at global headquarters use market and output controls as listed:

- Rate of return
- Growth in market share
- Operation costs evaluate the performance of foreign divisions.

On the basis of these comparison in global level and they can make global capital allocation decisions and global transfer of new technical knowledge.

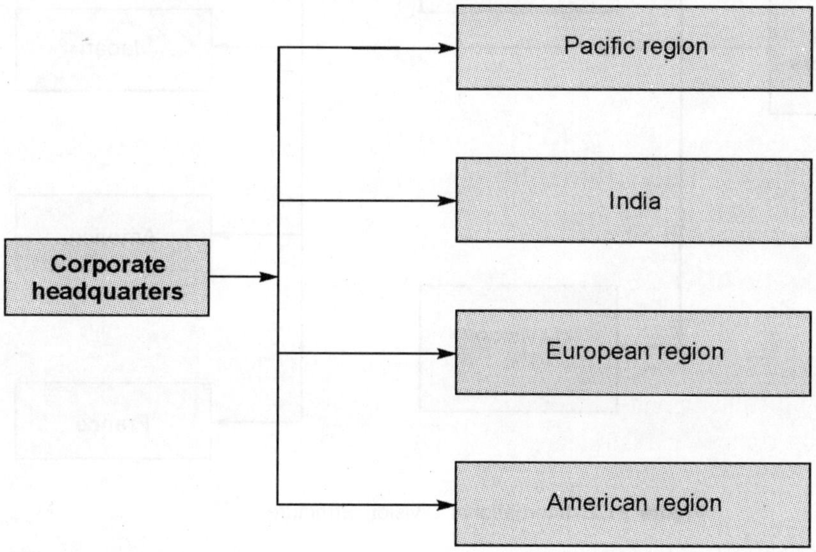

Figure 21.1: Global Area Structure

INTERNATIONAL STRATEGY AND STRUCTURE

A company has adopted international strategy to enter into international market for global expansion. Normally, the company shifts to this strategy when it begins selling its domestically-made products in foreign markets.

Figure 21.2 indicates the international division structure. A company has managed as a separate divisional business in International operations. International company has provided the authority and responsibility to managers for coordinating domestic product divisions and foreign market. The international division also controls the foreign subordinate, market the products and decides how much authority to delegate to foreign management.

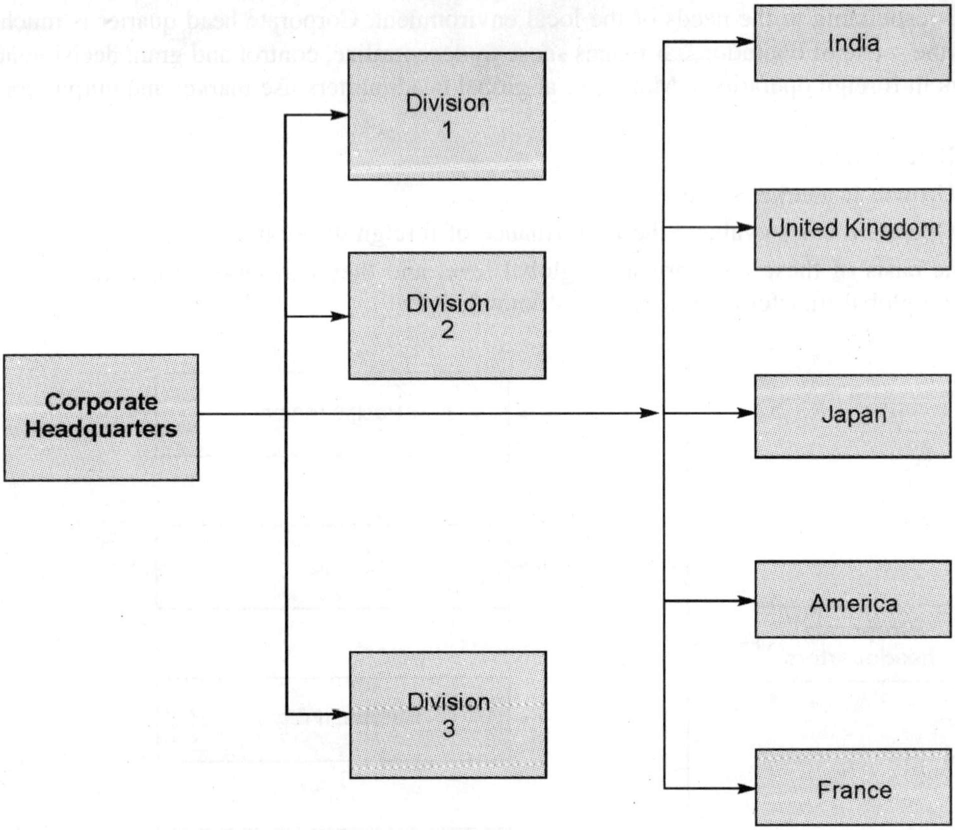

Figure 21.2: International Division Structure

GLOBAL ORGANIZATIONAL STRUCTURE

Growing of international business operations and increasing of business competitive environment. Its results in global organizational structure. It further classified into five categories. They are as follows:

- Global products structure
- Global area structure
- Global functional structure
- Global customer structure
- Hybrid/mixed structure

Global Products Structure

Figure 21.3 highlights the global product structure. The worldwide product structure is based upon major product groups. Global product structure responsibilities are involved for all functions for marketing a specific product group or class throughout the world. It can be delegated to a group within each product division. Therefore, there is a corporate staff at the headquarters to provide wide expertise and provide some degree of assistance to each product division; the product divisions have a good deal of autonomy with their own functional staff.

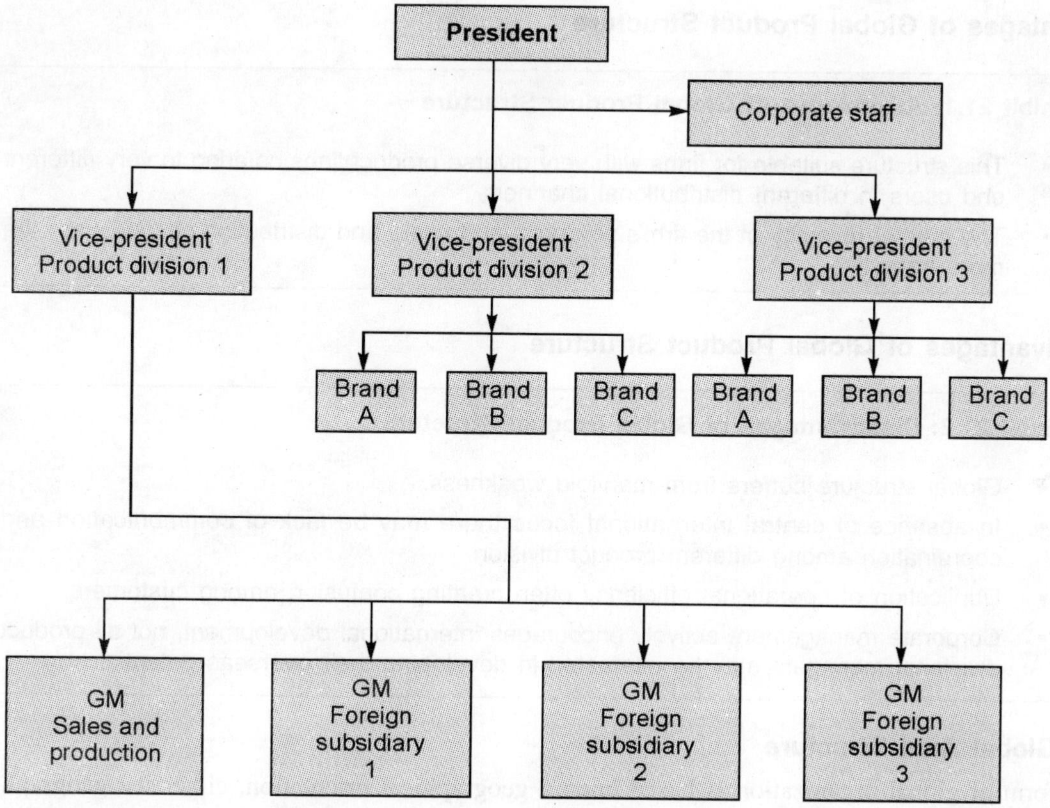

Figure 21.3: Global Product Structure

Company's international activities like product-oriented structure are allocated among the various product divisions. Therefore, the significance of the overseas operations varies substantially. Some of the firm's products may be more amenable to export or import markets than others or the management of some division may simply have more international experience than do managers in other divisions.

The global product structure has the advantage of focusing upon and optimizing the firm's production strengths. The managers of different product divisions have developed a great deal of knowledge that relates to the following:

- Products
- Competitors
- Production facilities
- Market
- Customer characteristics

They develop familiarity with the environmental constraints of products and how best to position these products in various markets for variety of users. The product managers can also develop a worldwide perspective regarding sales and marketing for their groups.

Advantages of Global Product Structure

Exhibit 21.1: Advantages of Global Product Structure

- This structure suitable for firms with very diverse product lines catering to very different end users in different distributional channels.
- The greater diversity of the firm's products, end users and distribution channels are the more attractive.

Disadvantages of Global Product Structure

Exhibit 21.2: Disadvantages of Global Product Structure

- Global structure suffers from manifold weakness.
- In absence of central international focus there may be lack of communication and coordination among different product division.
- Duplication of operational efficiency often creating confusion among customers.
- Corporate management actively encourages international development, not all product divisional managers may be interested in developing their overseas potential.

The Global Area Structure

This form of global organization is based upon a geographical orientation, either the geographical location of customers or of the company's productive facility. Figure 21.4 indicates the global area structure. The firm is organized on the basis of geographical areas of its international markets. The configuration of the geographical structure depends on the markets in which a multinational corporation operates but typical divisions occur according to major market area like India, North America, Europe, Middle East, and South America. Under the global area structure, all of the firm's activities relating to any products or service that is bought, sold or produced within a region, are under the control of the regional group head who reports directly to the president of the firm.

Advantages of the Global Area Structure

Exhibit 21.3: Advantages of the Global Area Structure

- This form of organization follows the marketing concept in as much as individual areas and markets are given concentrated attention.
- Geographical-oriented corporate structure, a multinational firm can place greater emphasis on the specific needs, market characteristics and market requirements of the individual market areas. The firm can pay concentrated attention to satisfy local demands and thereby improve its market share.

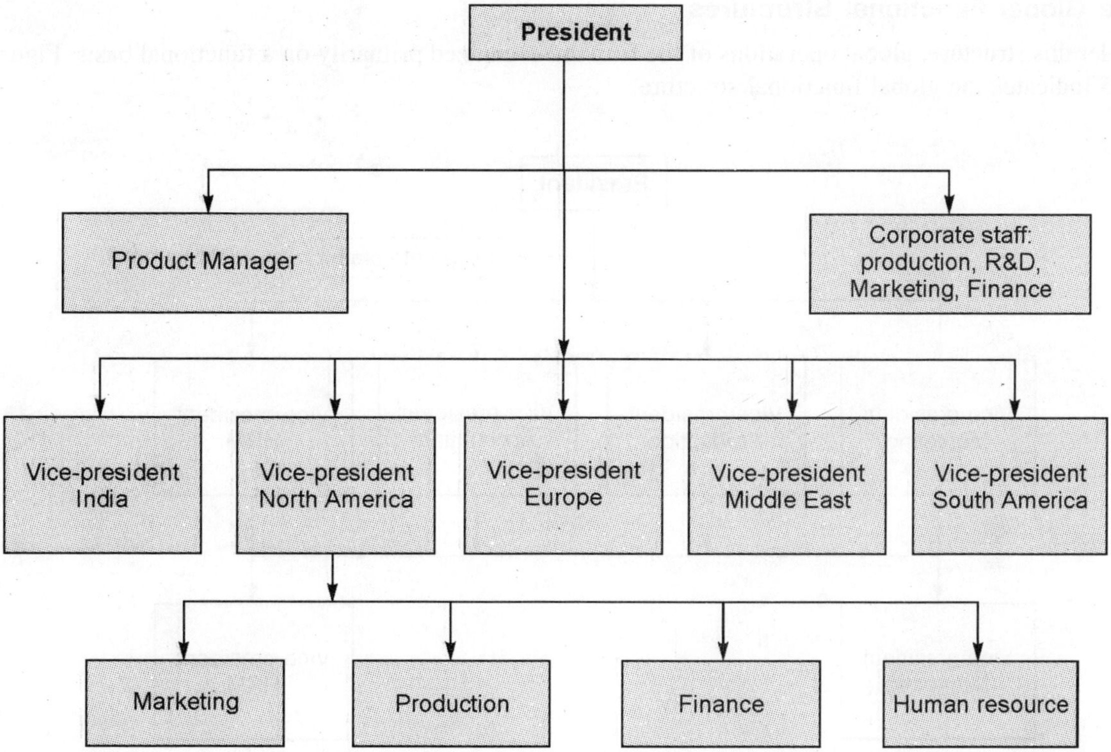

Figure 21.4: The Global Area Structure

Exhibit 21.4: Disadvantages of the Global Area Structure

- The major weakness of this form of global organization is that by emphasizing regional operations, it fails to facilitate the development of the coordination of functional or product-line activity worldwide.
- The firm misses the opportunity of economies of scale introduction or in raw materials sourcing.
- It fails to learn regional operation of the organization factors like as production, development, and marketing on a global basis.
- Another draw back to this type of structure is that it requires the allocation of considerable resources to establish regional headquarter headed by area managers· There are certain problems involved in this form of structure. It involves duplication of specialists in the different divisions, since such services are not centralized in the geographically structured company.
- The geographical orientation tends to give the managers in such group a geographical rather than a company-wide perspective.

The Global Functional Structures

Under this structure, global operations of the firm are organized primarily on a functional basis. Figure 21.5 indicates the global functional structure.

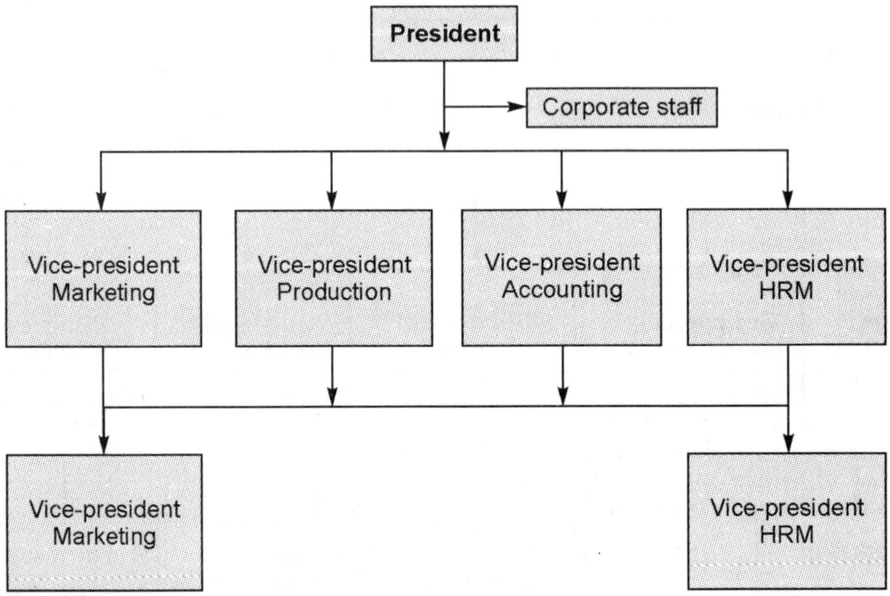

Figure 21.5: The Global Functional Structure

Advantages of Global Functional Structures

Exhibit 21.5: Advantages of Global functional structures

- This structure has the economies of scale gained within each functional area.
- Duplication of expert service is kept to a minimum with consequent savings in manpower.
- Functional form of organizational structure finds favor with multinational firms having narrow range of products and homogenous markets around the world.

Disadvantages of Global Functional Structures

Exhibit 21.6: Disadvantages of Global functional structures

- Problem of coordination between functions or divisions of the company.
- Lack of flexibility for a firm attempting to market number of products in a number of markets.
- Managers in this form of organization develop a too narrow perspective in emphasizing their own functions rather than the overall welfare of the company.

The Global Customer Structures

Sometimes firms may organize its global operations according to the customer goods. Figure 21.6 indicates the global customer structures. The global customer structures as listed below:

- Individuals
- Business
- Governments
- Corporate staff

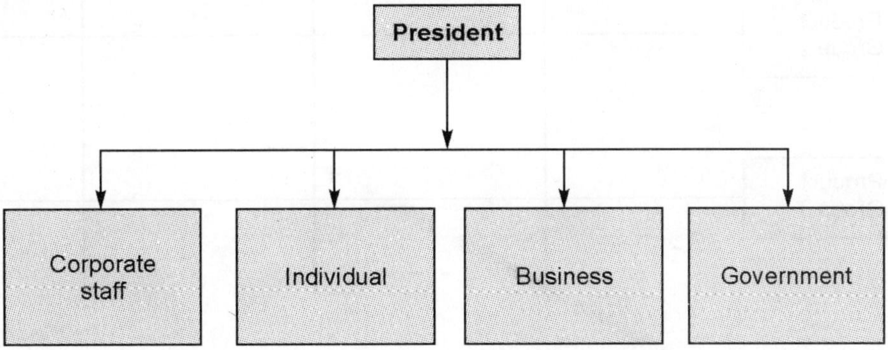

Figure 21.6: Global Customer Structure

This form of structure obviously places greatest stress upon the customer and can be provided the most specialized and personalized service. Therefore, however, it also tends to require duplication of skills in each group and a separation between such specialists in each group. However, corporate staff can reduce some of these disadvantages but can never totally overcome them.

Global Matrix Structure

This structure makes it very difficult for the different product groups to trade information and knowledge and obtain the benefits of corporation. Sometimes the potential gains from sharing product, marketing and research development knowledge between products groups are very high.

Matrix structures work help companies to develop strong international organizational culture to facilitate communication and coordination among managers.

MATCHING STRUCTURE AND CONTROL AT THE CORPORATE LEVEL

Matching structure and control at the corporate level are as below:

- Related diversification
- Unrelated diversification
- Vertical integration
- Mergers
- Internal new ventures

We shall refer to earlier chapter.

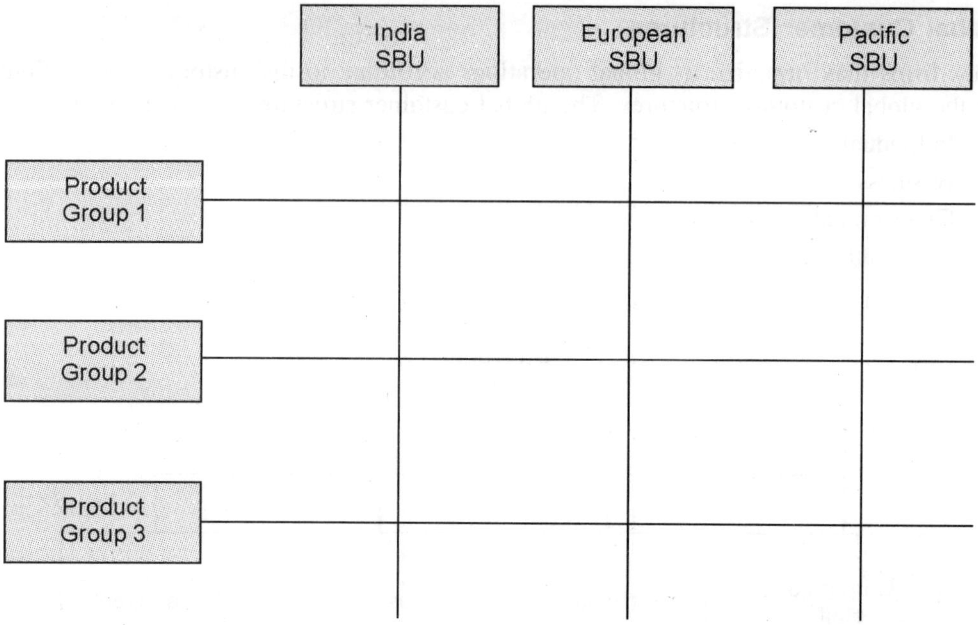

Figure 21.7: Global Matrix Structure

QUESTIONS FOR DISCUSSIONS

1. Briefly explain the matching structure and control analysis at the functional level.
2. What is business level matching structure?
3. What is global structure?
4. Explain the multi-domestic strategy and structure.
5. Describe the international strategy and structure.
6. Briefly explain the turn-around strategy and structure.
7. Explain the matching structure control at corporate level.

REFERENCES

1. Henry Mintzberg, *The Structuring of Organisation: A Synthesis of Research*, Prentice –Hall, Englewood Cliffs, N.J. 1975, chap.1 and 2.
2. J.T. Cannon, *Business Strategy and Policy*, Harcourt Brace and World, Inc, New York, 1988.
3. A.D. Chandlor, Jr., *Strategy and Structure : Chapters in the History of the American Industrial Enterprise*, MIT Press, Cambridge,1962.

4. R.E. Miles and C.C. Snow, *Organisation Strategy, Structure and Process*, McGraw-Hill, New York,1978
5. Hanos J. Krifen, *Formulating Corporate Objectives and Strategies*, Long Range Planning, June 1977, pp. 64.
6. Charles W.L.Hill/Gareth R.Jones, *Strategic Management Theory an Integrated Approach*, All India Publishers and Distributors Regd. 2001.
7. A.A.Thomson and A.J. Strickland, *Strategic Management Concepts and Cases*, Tata McGraw –Hill Publishing Company Limited, New Delhi, 2003.
8. John, A. Pearce II, Richard B. Robinson, JR. *Strategic Management Strategy Formulation and Implementation*. A.I.T.B.S. Publishers & Distributors (Regd), New Delhi, 2002.
9. Chkravarthy, Balaji S., and Howard V. Perlmulter, *Strategic Planning for a Global Business*, Columbia Journal of World Business, Summer 1985, pp. 3-10.
10. Fay Weather J., and Kapoor, *Strategy and Negotiation for the International Corporation*, Cambradge, Mass: Ballinagar, 1976.
11. Levitt, Theodore. *The Globalisation of Markets*, Harvard Business Review, September-October 1982.
12. Miler, R.E., and C.C. Snow, *Organisational Strategy, Structure, and Process*, Newyork: McGraw-Hill, 1978.
13. Peters, Thomas J., *Beyond the Matrix Organisation*, Business Horizons, October 1979, pp, 15-27.
14. Henry Mintzburg, *The Structure of Organisation: A Synthesis of Research*, Prentice-Hall, Englewood Cliffs, N.J. 1975.

Index

304/16/2/09